From the sa
Published by Create

- Astrology for a better life (t

- Horary astrology (a ne

- The art of forecasting wit

Titles in French only

L'astrologie au quotidien (éditions Grancher - Paris 2002)

Published by CreateSpace & Amazon

- La pratique du voyage astral assistée par l'astrologie

- Vesta et Chiron en astrologie

- Les Révolutions Solaires

- Cours complet d'astrologie pratique
(Les bases essentielles de l'astrologie)
Available in four separate books or compiled in one publication

- Les transits planétaires en astrologie prévisionnelle

- Le voyage astral (assisté par l'astrologie)

- Destin, Karma et réincarnation
(Manuel d'astrologie karmique)

- Le Chemin (novel)

Published by Editions Pardès (France)
- B.A BA d'astrologie médicale
- B.A BA d'astrologie karmique
- Le Couple idéal en astrologie
- Chiron et Vesta (dans l'analyse astrologique)

Roland Legrand
Your Karma revealed by astrology

Introduction

DESTINY, KARMA and REINCARNATION

Beyond social trends that create active yearnings among those who are predisposed to think alike; beyond our deep needs to search for an absolute truth that we strive to idealise to make it more valuable and meaningful; beyond the meaning we give to life to motivate our actions and bear the consequences, lies "karma", a true cosmic record of the debts we have accumulated during past incarnations, and that our mission in this present existence is to settle once and for all. Quite a program! ...

No one can deny the existence of destiny which is nothing more than the progression of life over time. From birth until death, we think we understand what is happening, but we are far from certain of the spiritual reason behind our presence on Earth for such a short while compared to the age of the planet and to the universe around.

Thought dominates life as if it depended only on brain activity to support itself, while neuroscientists debate and challenge such a theory.

Consciousness is dominated by a thought process that forces it to retreat in favour of a philosophical approach that takes on various forms on the social, familial, intellectual, or spiritual level.

Interest is the great disruptor in our society of progress, production and consumption which tends to run out of steam in favour of a return to basics that some see as the only possible way out towards happiness or, at least, peace of mind. We have more and more difficulty in conceiving "free act" because we are manipulated by forces which we believe to use wisely while they undermine our potential and our talent while seeming to favour them ...

The notion of "karmic debt" on which "reincarnation philosophy" is based should not be viewed in a pejorative way by making you feel guilty about what has been done during past existences. However, assuming the possibility of being reborn in another body after death implies an awareness of the consequences of ONE4S Chiron life, at all levels.

The "boomerang effect" is an extraordinarily subtle phenomenon that should be examined with the greatest care. Often thought of as a "backlash", it can also have very pleasant repercussions, depending on whether it is an "invoice" or a "credit note" recorded by fate. Although problems or existential satisfactions are not systematically related to karma, they play a very important role in the "liberation" or "loading" of it. In other words, the events have various origins and reasons for being. Either they come from spiritual debts that need to be repaid, or they serve indirectly to settle such debts without any apparent concrete link being established, allowing their origin or even their raison d'être to be recognised.

Whatever the motivation or the "cosmic reason" for an event to occur, if responsibilities are bravely dealt with and the obstacle is overcome, the results or the rewards are always better than if this same event is experienced as an unfair burden. It results in an improvement of the quality of life by increasing inner strength and energy reserves necessary to access the next stage in a future incarnation. And so on until a certain form of interior harmony and wisdom is reached.

However, the progression of life, when viewed in this way, requires constant personal effort and constant vigilance. Approving the meaning of the above paragraphs does not imply putting them into practice. You have to have good reasons to do it and as it is always easier to criticise your neighbour than to judge yourself, the vagaries of life will have to be particularly disruptive for a sustained personal effort to be made.

Fate has many surprises in store for us! Who has not been disturbed, even shocked, by dramatic revelation about a loved one whose private life and unapparent behaviour stunned family and friends? Such event unfortunately occasionally makes news headlines ...

What are the underlying reasons for alcoholism or drug addiction, for example? There are many. They are explained and treated by therapies that rely on life experiences and deep motivations. These make it possible to decode important messages aimed at solving the problem by chain reactions. They lead to the awareness of the realities and of the absolute need to take care of oneself, for one's own wellbeing but also (and above all!) for others, who suffer more concretely and acutely of the affected person's condition.

When the notion of "karmic debt" is put forward to explain someone's misfortunes, we commonly forget their role in dealing with our own karma. Perhaps, populations martyred by war, famine or epidemics serve to purify their karma and that of those who live at ease in privileged countries when they care enough for these people to help them courageously. Many in our Western societies have understood this. They have joined in humanitarian missions, volunteering, and helping the unfortunate in many ways. They do it in such an intense and complete manner that they sometimes become examples of goodness, altruism, and wisdom, revered by all for their exemplary actions ...

Karma is therefore a load of responsibilities that every human being must assume. When a problem is let for someone else to solve it, the karma of the "helped" becomes the karma of the "helper". A link is created that must be clearly evaluated to produce the best results. If the action is carried out automatically, without special interest or without care, the results are sometimes deplorable, and failure becomes one more reason to complain and cultivate a negative approach to life.

How to evaluate and understand the role of karma? Different approaches are possible. Buddhism offers access to karmic information through meditation and constant observation of the self to explore its most unrevealed aspects.

Hypnosis or self-hypnosis can help open up to past lives and awareness of possible spiritual debts to repay. The fact of "seeing" what our past life was like, even in a state of modified consciousness, can, however, produce troubling effects. Caution in any practice of this type, and confidence in the hypnotist are essential to avoid emotional or psychological traumas that would only increase the karmic load rather than lighten it ...

Astrology offers an approach of great value because it relies on astronomical data that reduces guilt feelings or remorse. It would certainly be, in combination with self-hypnosis, a great way to discover what happened in the previous life and, most importantly, to explain and understand the present incarnation.

Astrology also provides various ways and tools to use for positive evolution and the settlement of past debts. It shows our potential to deal with karmic loads rather than denies them. Astrology does not judge, it explains, and offers valuable tools for personal and spiritual evolution. It shows the spiritual reason for hardship and plays down the conflicts with an environment where loved ones are involved and sometimes responsible for the karmic connotation of challenging situations and relationships.

"Mother of all sciences," astrology leads the way to success through determining the most appropriate "therapy". Associated with holistic medicine, psychology, meditation, hypnosis, or any other chosen approach, it gives excellent results.

If the present incarnation is not satisfactory, admitting that it comes from a "questionable" management of our past life should motivate to react in the right way to allow for substantial improvement and certainly a better "future incarnation". Astrology helps identify our limits and reinforces a more accurate view of the self to favour inner progress and wellbeing.

When the barriers of disbelief have fallen and we can accept the existence of cosmic forces; when the elements in a birth chart causing recurring challenges are explained and linked to the placements and movements of the planets; when we understand how to act and react based on astrological data, we are better equipped to accept adversity with renewed energy and determination to defeat opposing forces and overcome spiritual obstacles ...

Young children are close to their karma, especially during the very first years of life. That is why everything that happens is so important for their personal development. An illness, a family problem, an accident, or any other "trauma" fits directly into the logic of evolution that they must follow from the moment of conception until the end of their life.

Fortunately, not all children face significant trauma. All children have different karmic backgrounds. Some have similar life paths which bring them together. They become brothers, sisters, cousins, husband, wife, close friends, or worst enemies.

Karma is not our sole responsibility. It is also that of those around with whom we are in significant contact. Whether it be a schoolteacher whose influence on education and vocation can be profound; whether it be a parent with their determining effect on the future of the child; whether it be a close friend who reveals potential or talent; or whether it be a combination of circumstances that generates a major event, karma holds the key and the answers to existential questions of any kind.

But how to recognise and accept such karmic load? How to analyse a natal chart to shed light on our life path and the trials that await on our earthly journey? And how to determine the tools needed to make the best out of our karma?

That is what I invite you to discover in this book, understanding symbolic data that we have to adapt case by case so that, akin to astro-psychological analysis, karmic reading does not suffer from any rigidity or determinism, and unnecessary guilt.

Nothing is fateful if we acquire the means to manage our life with strong will and determination. Those who succeed know it well; hard work, consistency and a determination are the major assets to reach the higher summits and realise the most improbable dreams.

Whatever your level of initiation in astrology, the next lessons will be useful to unveil your inner truth, to improve your life and that of those around you. Whether it is on an intimate, family, social, professional, philosophical, or spiritual level, what you will learn from this book should hopefully contribute to the success and wellbeing you envision.

Before reading this book any further, please note that it is not about finding out WHO you were in your previous life, but more importantly HOW and WHY you experienced what you will discover. The social background, the period and whatever was of major importance to you will be revealed. More remarkably, you will discover the reasons behind whom you are today, as well as the reasons that motivate your relationships with family members, friends, and social acquaintances. Finally, on the basis of my personal journey and daily practice of astrology spanning several decades, I offer you a calculation technique meant to determine your most probable previous date of birth!

Let us embark for a voyage into the fourth dimension with KARMIC ASTROLOGY!

Roland Legrand - A Better Life Astrology School - © 2022

Foreword

The fictive points

Before we begin lesson 1, here is a quick introduction to the fictive points.

What is a "fictive point"?

A fictive point is an area around the birth chart marked by the energy from an invisible and materially non-existent element. Thus, the intersections of the orbit of the Moon with the ecliptic determine the positions of the Lunar Nodes. Likewise, the accumulation of energy resulting from the solar and lunar magnetic fields determines the position of the Dark Moon (Lilith). Finally, the addition of the difference between the positions of the Moon and the Sun to that of the Ascendant determines the third fictive point considered in this book, the Part of Fortune.

The Black Moon or Lilith.

Its position is calculated according to the orbit of the Moon and its force field relative to that of the Sun with respect to the Earth. This is called the "empty focus" of the Moon, a fictive point which is also the subject of controversy.

Astronomers do not all agree on its position. That is why we find two positions in the ephemerides and sometimes three! The "true" position, the "mean" position, and the "rectified" position. We sometimes notice a difference of more than 25° between them for the same given day! My experience has led me to use the average or "mean" position. It gives good results in my readings.

The Part of Fortune

In a birth chart, the Part of Fortune (PART OF FORTUNE) is determined according to the positions of the Ascendant, the Sun, and the Moon. Here is the formula:

Position of the ASC + the distance Sun / Moon = Part of Fortune.

Here is an example:

In a chart, the Sun is at 10° in Taurus, and the Moon at 4° in Virgo. They are separated by 114°. If the Ascendant is at 22° in Virgo, adding 114° puts the PART OF FORTUNE at 16° in Capricorn.

The Lunar Nodes

They are defined by the intersection points of the ecliptic and the orbit of the Moon. These two points are called respectively "North Node" and South Node ".
There are two positions listed in the ephemeris. The "true" position and the "mean" position. Note that the "true" position does not imply that it is the right one ... Astrologers generally use the "mean" position.

The difference between these two positions varies from a few seconds to a few degrees of arc around the zodiac. This only becomes a problem in the case of a conjunction with a House cusp or when the Lunar Nodes change signs according to their "mean" or "true" position.

Constant Retrogradation

The Lunar Nodes move clockwise around the zodiac circle, making a complete revolution in eighteen years. The "true" Lunar Nodes, however, move back and forth from retrogradation to direct motion. They are never very far from the "mean" Lunar Nodes.

The South Node

Represents what in your previous life influenced you the most. That is why in this present life you instinctively develop strong needs, behaviour, or relationships motivated by those unconscious reminiscences. Your present-life mission is to detach yourself from such instilled habits in order to take on new responsibilities in relation to your spiritual path of evolution.

The North Node

It represents the direction to take and what we must do to get rid of the innate tendencies represented by the South Node. The North Node represents the direction we must take during the present lifetime to free ourselves from a degree of dependency in the areas represented by the House where it is found, and the sign and House where its "regent" is found.

Example

South Node in House X (MC)- North Node in House IV (FC or NADIR).

(South node in House X): The previous life was mainly motivated by social success and what pros and cons it implied, with a strong influence on the general attitude in human relations and in dealings with society, but most probably to the detriment of family life.

(North node in House IV): You need to refrain from the desire for social success and orient your life more towards family realisation and the conception of a solid home, contrary to what was achieved in your previous life.

Note that the realisation of the North Node is easier said than done. It poses various problems that can make for complicated circumstances and situations. The life of the person whose chart was taken as an example is quite representative. Various marriages, two children from different fathers, one of the children killed very young in a car accident during a "family" holiday; a bohemian end of life, away from the madding crowd, unsure of the direction to take while the original aspirations were for most of her life resolutely oriented to mix with the upper class in society ...

The latter years of her life could be spent reflecting or meditating on these points, but I think it will be otherwise because humans have this disappointing tendency to find convincing reasons and excuses to stay safe in their "uncomfortable comfort zone"...

The Lunar Nodes in your chart

Consult your birth chart and take note of the positions of the Lunar Nodes. The list of aphorisms contained in the additional section called "The Lunar Nodes in Houses" provides a basic approach to these positions. Take note of them and keep them aside. You will need them later to complement the interpretation of your chart from a karmic point of view.

Let us now investigate the meaning of the Lunar Nodes and of the other fictive points, beginning with the first lesson of this course.

Lesson 1

Link to the video of Lesson 1 (The Lunar Nodes)
https://youtu.be/823kKumiCSk
Copy/paste it in your Internet browser

The Lunar Nodes

You already know a little about them, but in this lesson, you will find more useful information to complement the analysis of these important fictive points.

As seen earlier, there are two Lunar Nodes, the South Node, and the North Node. The drawing on the following page shows how they are created. On this drawing, see the orbit of the earth with the earth turning around the Sun. Look at the orbit of the Moon around the earth. It's not a perfect circle. It is quite elliptic. The points where the Moon's orbit crosses the orbit of the Earth are called "**North and South Lunar Nodes**".

If that is important to know on an astronomical point of view, it doesn't tell us what they mean in astrology, how the influence of the South and North Lunar Nodes operates. That's a very important concept to consider, especially in 'karmic astrology".

However, and once again on an astronomical point of view, ***there are Lunar Nodes and Lunar Nodes.*** Why? Because there are two different approaches to the calculations leading to determine the positions of the Lunar Nodes. Consequently, as seen in the introduction to this book, there is what is called the "**mean**" Lunar Nodes and the "**exact**" or "**true**" Lunar Nodes. The true nodes move back and forth, whereas the mean Lunar Nodes always move backward. They retrograde.

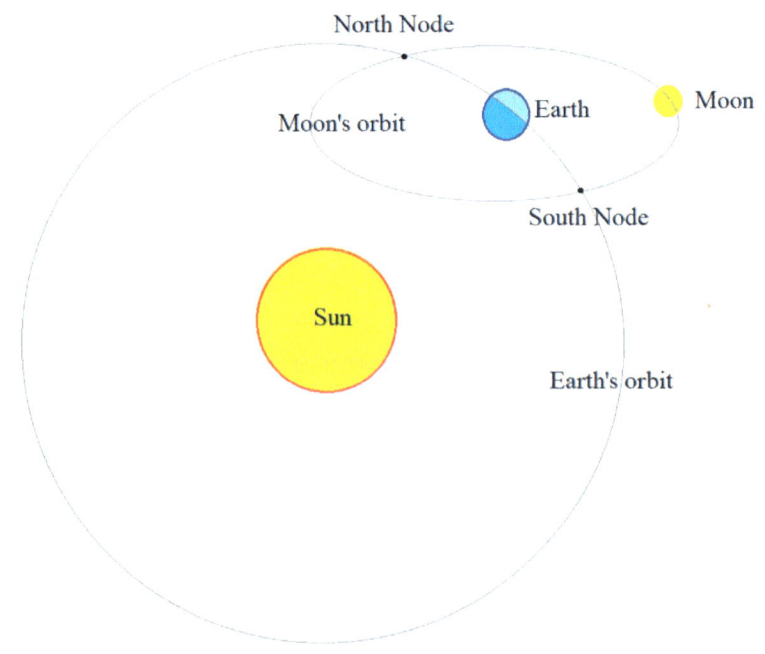

In this lesson, we will find out what the Lunar Nodes mean and how you can find them in the "**ephemeris**", a book in which all the positions of the planets and other elements are listed day by day for a great number of years.

Let's have a look at the page of the ephemeris where we find the mean and true positions of the Lunar Nodes for a person born on the 29th of May 1917. On the line corresponding to that date, you see first, the day's number, then the TS (Sidereal Time or cosmic time) of the day at midnight GMT, then the Sun, the Moon, Mercury, Venus, Mars, Jupiter, Saturn, Uranus, Neptune, Pluto, and then you see the "true" Lunar Node at 11° retrograde in Capricorn, and next, the mean Lunar Node at 12°32' in the same sign. The difference is minimal; only one degree. Although it is not a drastic difference, if you prefer to use the true Lunar Nodes, it's your choice, you can do that. I personally use the mean position and that is the one I will be teaching you about in this lesson.

MAY 1917 **00:00 UT**

Day	Sid.t	☉	☽	☿	♀	♂	♃	♄	♅	♆	♇	☊	☊	⚸	⚷	Day
T 1	14 33 24	10♉ 2'40	29♌21	28♉32	11♉15	27♈ 3	16♉14	24♋48	23♒24	2♌11	2♋42	12°R59	14♑ 1	19♌21	28♓18	T 1
W 2	14 37 21	11° 0'51	11♍18	28°54	12°29	27°48	16°28	24°52	23°25	2°11	2°43	12♑55	13°58	19°28	28°21	W 2
T 3	14 41 17	11°59'01	23°25	29°11	13°43	28°33	16°42	24°56	23°26	2°12	2°44	12°48	13°55	19°35	28°24	T 3
F 4	14 45 14	12°57'09	5♎46	29°23	14°57	29°18	16°57	25° 0	23°28	2°12	2°45	12°40	13°51	19°41	28°27	F 4
S 5	14 49 10	13°55'15	18°23	29°29	16°11	0♉ 3	17°11	25° 4	23°29	2°13	2°46	12°30	13°48	19°48	28°30	S 5
S 6	14 53 7	14°53'19	1♏17	29°R29	17°25	0°48	17°25	25° 8	23°30	2°14	2°47	12°20	13°45	19°55	28°32	S 6
M 7	14 57 3	15°51'22	14°27	29°25	18°39	1°33	17°39	25°12	23°31	2°15	2°48	12°10	13°42	20° 1	28°35	M 7
T 8	15 1 0	16°49'23	27°54	29°16	19°53	2°18	17°54	25°17	23°32	2°16	2°49	12° 2	13°39	20° 8	28°38	T 8
W 9	15 4 56	17°47'22	11♐33	29° 2	21° 7	3° 3	18° 8	25°21	23°33	2°16	2°51	11°56	13°36	20°15	28°40	W 9
T 10	15 8 53	18°45'20	25°22	28°44	22°21	3°48	18°22	25°25	23°34	2°17	2°52	11°53	13°32	20°21	28°43	T 10
F 11	15 12 50	19°43'17	9♑19	28°22	23°35	4°33	18°36	25°30	23°35	2°18	2°53	11°D52	13°29	20°28	28°45	F 11
S 12	15 16 46	20°41'12	23°22	27°57	24°49	5°17	18°51	25°35	23°36	2°19	2°54	11°52	13°26	20°35	28°48	S 12
S 13	15 20 43	21°39'06	7♒29	27°29	26° 3	6° 2	19° 5	25°39	23°37	2°20	2°55	11°53	13°23	20°41	28°50	S 13
M14	15 24 39	22°36'59	21°38	26°58	27°16	6°47	19°19	25°44	23°37	2°21	2°56	11°R54	13°20	20°48	28°53	M14
T 15	15 28 36	23°34'50	5♓48	26°25	28°30	7°31	19°33	25°49	23°38	2°22	2°57	11°53	13°16	20°55	28°55	T 15
W16	15 32 32	24°32'41	19°57	25°50	29°44	8°16	19°48	25°54	23°39	2°23	2°59	11°51	13°13	21° 1	28°58	W16
T 17	15 36 29	25°30'30	4♈ 4	25°15	0♊58	9° 0	20° 2	25°59	23°39	2°24	3° 0	11°46	13°10	21° 8	29° 0	T 17
F 18	15 40 25	26°28'18	18° 5	24°40	2°12	9°45	20°16	26° 4	23°40	2°25	3° 1	11°40	13° 7	21°15	29° 2	F 18
S 19	15 44 22	27°26'05	1♉56	24° 6	3°26	10°29	20°30	26° 9	23°41	2°26	3° 2	11°33	13° 4	21°21	29° 4	S 19
S 20	15 48 19	28°23'50	15°35	23°32	4°39	11°13	20°44	26°14	23°41	2°27	3° 3	11°26	13° 1	21°28	29° 6	S 20
M21	15 52 15	29°21'35	28°58	23° 0	5°53	11°57	20°59	26°20	23°41	2°29	3° 5	11°19	12°57	21°35	29° 9	M21
T 22	15 56 12	0♊19'18	12♊ 4	22°31	7° 7	12°42	21°13	26°25	23°42	2°30	3° 6	11°14	12°54	21°42	29°11	T 22
W23	16 0 8	1°17'00	24°51	22° 4	8°21	13°26	21°27	26°31	23°42	2°31	3° 7	11°11	12°51	21°48	29°13	W23
T 24	16 4 5	2°14'40	7♋21	21°40	9°35	14°10	21°41	26°36	23°42	2°32	3° 8	11°D10	12°48	21°55	29°15	T 24
F 25	16 8 1	3°12'19	19°36	21°19	10°48	14°54	21°55	26°42	23°43	2°34	3°10	11°10	12°45	22° 2	29°17	F 25
S 26	16 11 58	4° 9'56	1♌39	21° 2	12° 2	15°38	22° 9	26°47	23°43	2°35	3°11	11°12	12°42	22° 8	29°19	S 26
S 27	16 15 54	5° 7'32	13°33	20°49	13°16	16°22	22°23	26°53	23°43	2°36	3°12	11°13	12°38	22°15	29°21	S 27
M28	16 19 51	6° 5'07	25°23	20°40	14°30	17° 6	22°37	26°59	23°43	2°38	3°14	11°16	12°35	22°22	29°22	M28
T 29	16 23 48	7° 2'40	7♍15	20°36	15°43	17°49	22°51	27° 5	23°R43	2°39	3°15	11°R15	12°32	22°28	29°24	T 29
W30	16 27 44	8° 0'12	19°13	20°D36	16°57	18°33	23° 5	27°11	23°43	2°41	3°16	11°14	12°29	22°35	29°26	W30
T 31	16 31 41	8♊57'42	1♎22	20♉40	18♊11	19♉17	23♉19	27♋17	23♒43	2♌42	3♋18	11♑12	12♑26	22♌42	29♓28	T 31

Let's go ahead with the rest of the lesson to explain what the South and North Lunar Nodes mean in a chart.

On the following page is the chart of the person born on the 29th of May 1917. The North Lunar Node is in Capricorn, and the South one is across the zodiac, in Cancer.

Remember: The North and South Lunar Nodes are directly opposed to one another. They also both represent opposed tendencies that cohabit within us. They tell us much about our life path.

The Lunar Nodes are a valuable source of information about karma, about our life path, about what we need to leave behind, to abandon, to let go, and also about where we need to go, what direction we need to take in this life.

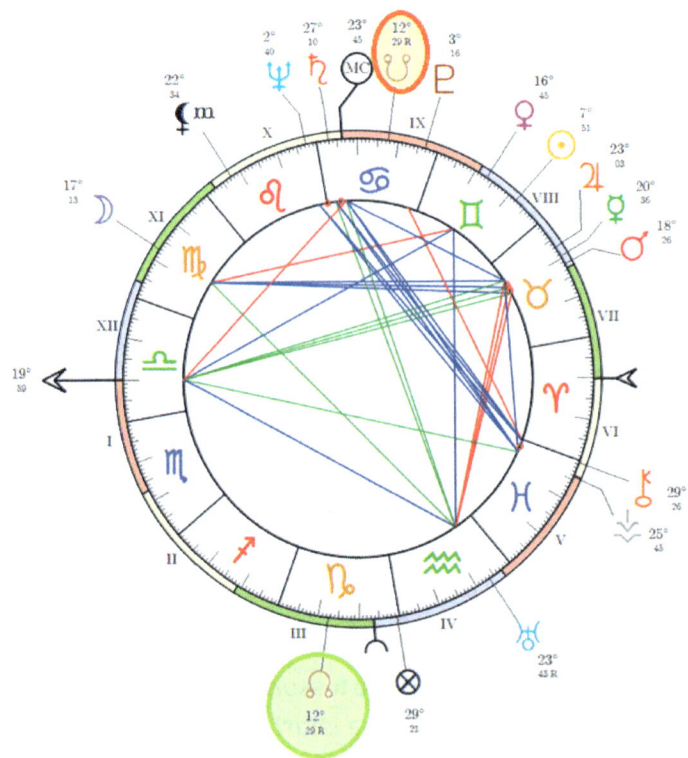

South Node in House IX - North Node in House III

The South Lunar Node in Cancer in House IX in this chart represents what this person needs to let go, to get rid of, to detach themselves from. It globally represents what has had a very strong influence in the previous incarnation, a situation where this person felt probably quite secure, so much as to become dependent on, mainly because some important facets of that person's life were favourable (or not), and consistent with the profound influence that the situation had in various ways.

How the situation in our previous life was perceived, is what matters most in today's incarnation. Hence, we have brought back an instinctive need to reproduce similar situations and a similar behaviour due to the fact that we are cosmically but unconsciously connected to them. It is therefore natural to us, and it eventually becomes a prevalent part of our personality.

The South Lunar Node in House IX that you can see in the chart on the previous page represents the karmic influence of what this House represents. It could mean, for example, that this person lived with a foreigner or in a foreign country. Perhaps this person was travelling a lot or was an explorer searching for new territories or new countries. It can also indicate that this person was very interested and absorbed by the need to study.

As you know, House IX also represents studies, higher education, universities, and anything legal and official. It represents the way we deal with society on a philosophical point of view. When the South Node is in this House, it often indicates an insatiable craving for knowledge that creates a tendency to learn constantly, not necessarily getting anything concrete from what is learned. It is learning for the sake of learning or travelling for the sake of travelling.

Therefore, the position of the South Lunar Node tells us from the example chart that this person needs to adjust and do what needs to be done with concrete repercussions and consequences so that learning is motivated by a definite goal and not just for the thrill of acquiring more knowledge. It could be done with the view of accessing to a better job perhaps, or a better situation, or to realise an important project.

In this particular case of the South Node in House IX, if learning is not linked to a concrete objective, it may be better to forget about it and just learn what is necessary to keep on going in this present incarnation.

Nevertheless, because the North Node across from the South Node is naturally in House III, opposed to House IX, it indicates a need to communicate, teach, or share the acquired knowledge. That House makes learning a source of evolution of the ability to share with others what has been learned.

That way, what the person learns becomes more concrete. It becomes more objective and rational, instead of being a useless exercise that only confers personal satisfaction while it lasts.

Therefore, the North Node in House III shows that there is a need to improve communication as an essential medium to share and put to good use what has been mastered in House IX.

The North Lunar Node represents that towards which we should be tending to go in this present life. Consequently, in House III the North Node shows that the meaning of that House is the answer to the question of finding and knowing what to learn and how to use that knowledge.

However, apart from the positions of the North and South Lunar Nodes in Houses, they are also in signs. As you can see in the example chart, the South Node is in Cancer and the North Node is in Capricorn.

It is also necessary to consider the rulers of these signs. They are called "**regents**" in accordance with their positions in signs and Houses.

Last, but not least, the **aspects** created with other elements around the chart provide more information about the true and profound meaning of the South and North Lunar Nodes.

Let's see what the Lunar Nodes in the signs have to teach us about our karma and life path.

First, you need to remember that if the South Lunar Node is in Aries, the North one is in Libra. If the South Lunar Node is in Taurus, the North one is in Scorpio. Have a look at the list presented on the following page and memorise it to spontaneously remember that the Lunar Nodes are opposed to one another and that because they are, they complement one another. It means that what you leave behind allows you to get more from life because it lightens your existential vehicle and makes it easier to drive it you where you want to go. This process is represented by the opposition between the North and South Lunar Nodes.

You will find a supplementary section at the end of this lesson to help you analyse the positions of the South and North Lunar Nodes in Houses. Use that section to read as many charts as you can until the roles of these elements become clear and meaningful. They are important in a chart as you will find out by reading the supplementary section. Once again, however, do not copy/paste my words, use them only to inspire your personal definition an interpretation with your own words.

The Lunar Nodes in signs

South Node Aries	North Node Libra
South Node Taurus	North Node Scorpio
South Node Gemini	North Node Sagittarius
South Node Cancer	North Node Capricorn
South Node Leo	North Node Aquarius
South Node Virgo	North Node Pisces
South Node Libra	North Node Aries
South Node Scorpio	North Node Taurus
South Node Sagittarius	North Node Gemini
South Node Capricorn	North Node Cancer
South Node Aquarius	North Node Leo
South Node Virgo	North Node Pisces

There is also a supplementary section about the Lunar Nodes in signs to be used in the same manner. Avoid parrot-like interpretations, repeating what you read in the book. That would not make you a valuable astrologer.

Below is a list of the possible positions of the Lunar Nodes in the Houses. Memorise it to speed up your readings and understand the bond between these two inseparable elements.

In the list on the following page, you can see that if the South Lunar Node is in House I or Ascendant, the North one is automatically across in-House VII or Descendant. If the South Node is in House II, the North one is in House VIII. If the South Node is in House III, the North one is in House IX. If the South node is in House IV, or NADIR, FC, the North one is in House X or MC, the MidHeaven, and so on and so forth.

The Lunar Nodes in Houses

South Node House I (ASC)	North Node House VII (DESC)
South Node House II	North Node House VIII
South Node House III	North Node House IV
South Node House IV (NADIR)	North Node House X (MC)
South Node House V	North Node House XI
South Node House VI	North Node House XII
South Node House VII (DESC)	North Node House I (ASC)
South Node House VIII	North Node House II
South Node House IX	North Node Gemini House III
South Node House X (MC)	North Node House IV (NADIR)
South Node House XI	North Node House V
South Node House XII	North Node House VI

Memorise this because it is essential. As soon as you find out that someone has the North Node in a certain House or a certain sign, you know immediately that the South one is across in the opposite sign or House.

As a rule, only the North Node is listed in the Ephemeris. It is sufficient to determine that the South Node is at exactly the same degree in the opposite sign. Note that the South Node is not always shown in computer-generated charts such as the one below.

The Regents of the Lunar Nodes

I have mentioned earlier something about the "**regents**". The *regents* are the rulers of the signs in which the Lunar Nodes are found. In the example chart shown at the beginning of this lesson, we can easily determine the regents of the South and North Lunar Nodes.

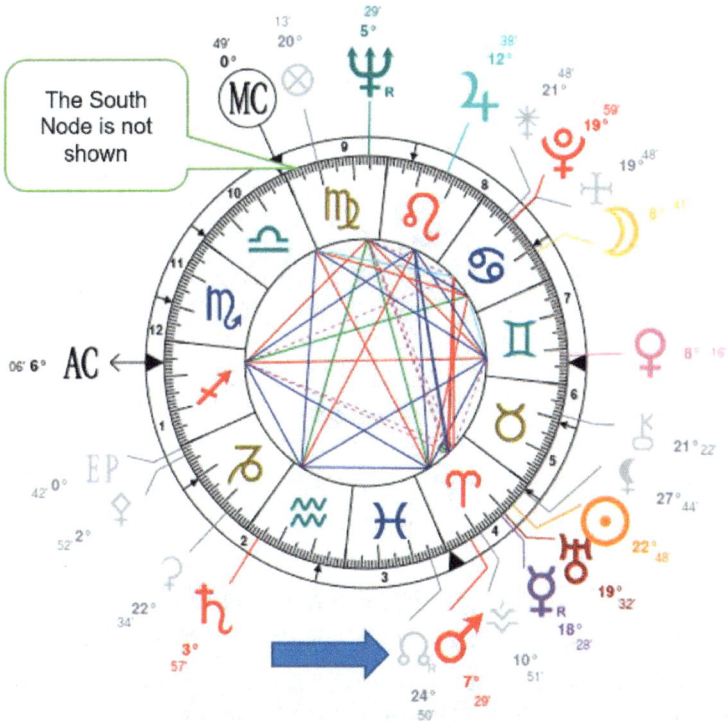

Note that the regents of these fictive points transfer the energies of the Lunar Nodes into signs where they are modified in various ways. As I explain in my "Astrology for a Better Life" book, a planet is influenced by the energy of the sign in which it stands. For example, with Mercury in Aries, the brains and the intellect work differently than with Mercury in Pisces. The same principle applies to the regents of the South and North Lunar Nodes.

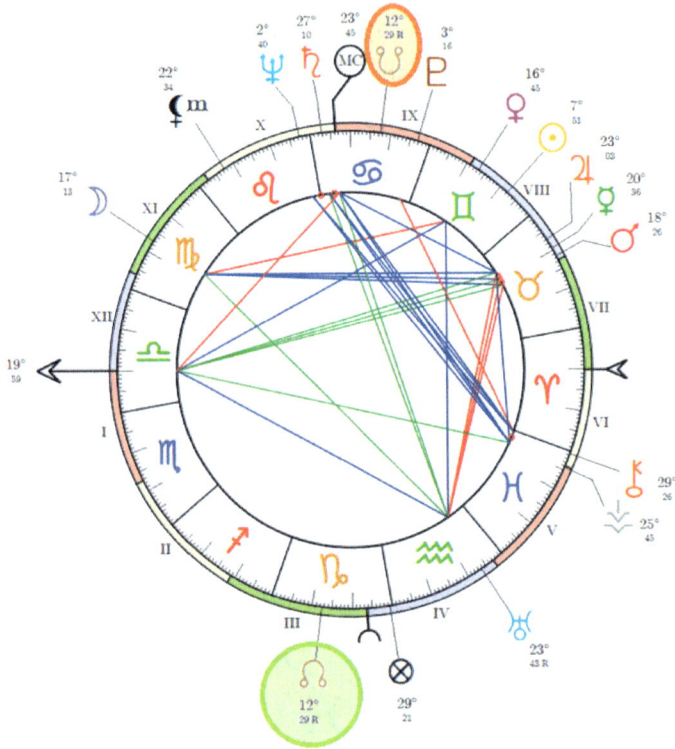

In the chart above, you see that the North Node is in Capricorn and the South one is in Cancer. As a result, the North Lunar Node is "regented" by Saturn, ruler of this sign. The South Lunar Node is under the regency of the Moon, ruler of Cancer.

Next, we need to know where the Moon is in this chart. Its position in sign allows more information on the role of the South Lunar Node in this person's life. In this chart it is in Virgo, an **Earth-Mutable** sign. Because the Moon represents the emotions, it means that this person tends to analyse and to rationalise emotions. It also indicates an emotional link with health, which is represented by the sixth sign, Virgo. That's one more element to better understand how the South Lunar Node operates.

As for the North Lunar Node in Capricorn in this chart, it is ruled by Saturn which becomes the regent of this Node. Saturn is in Cancer and Cancer is the sign where the South Lunar Node is. That complicates the process of dealing with the South Node because if it represents that from which we should strive to get away from, as soon as the person reaches out for the North Lunar Node, its energy and value are brought back in the opposite sign through the regent's position. Saturn is in Cancer in the MC (Midheaven) at the top of the chart. This position enhances the importance of Saturn but, knowing that the South Lunar Node is in Cancer as well means that Saturn is actually under the regency of the same element as the South Lunar Node, the Moon.

Because Saturn is in the Moon's sign (Cancer) it complicates the interpretation and even if we can explain what it means, the person is likely to find it difficult to adjust to the energies of the Lunar Nodes to realise important objectives or goals.

Understanding the potential of the combined influences of the regents of the North and South Nodes in Houses is as important as their positions in signs. In this lesson, you will find two supplementary sections. One about the positions of the regents in signs and a second one about their positions in Houses.

The regents provide further information about the basic influence of the South and North Lunar Nodes on our life path and on the karmic reasons behind our most important choices in life.

That's why their positions in signs and Houses, and the aspects, that we will discuss next, are so valuable to the reading of a chart from a karmic point of view. The aspects explain a lot about the way we deal with this present incarnation and where we are tending to go.

Do not forget that because you had a previous life, you will have a future life after this one. When you die, you will reincarnate in another body, another world, another country, another family, and another "you". However, you will bring back from this present life a lot of what has had a deep influence on your behaviour in various ways. Therefore, what you do in this life, what you achieve, is not just to fill out or pass the time that you spend on Earth; it is also to prepare for your next incarnation

Let's look at the example chart again to summarise what needs to be done.

- **The North Node is in Capricorn.**

- **The regent is Saturn**

- **The South Lunar Node is in Cancer**

- **The regent is the Moon**

- **The North node is in House III**

- **The South node is in-House IX**

- **The regent of the North Node, Saturn, is in Cancer**

- **The regent of the South Node, the Moon, is in Virgo**

- **The regent of the North Node, Saturn, in House X (MC)**

- **The regent of the South Node, the Moon, is in House XI**

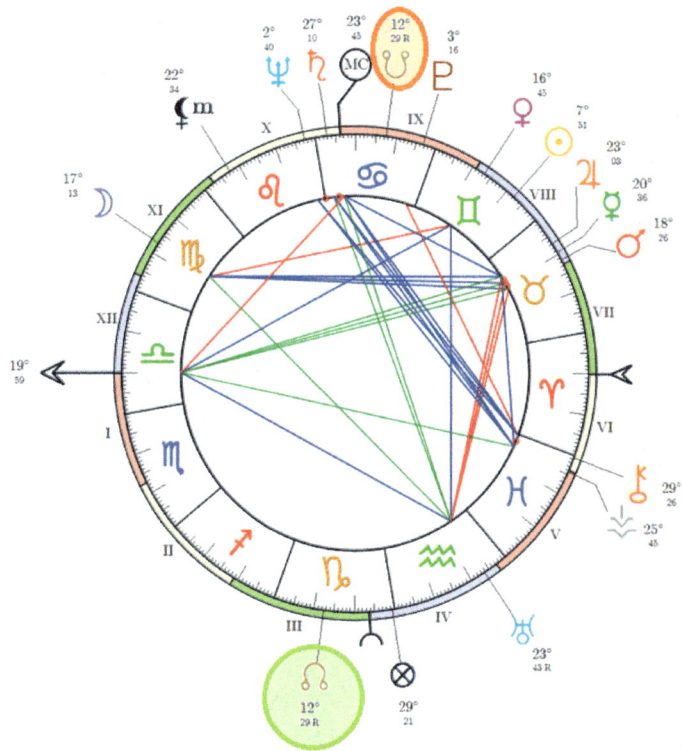

Once the list is complete, it can be analysed. Each element is addressed individually before they are blended to obtain a coherent interpretation of the Lunar Nodes.

Another task is to look for and analyse **the aspects** involving various elements in the chart with the South and North Lunar Nodes, and later with the regents of these Lunar Nodes.

To begin with, make a list of the aspects to the Lunar Nodes. They are drawn on the example chart presented on the following page.

- Saturn is sextile South Lunar Node and trine North Lunar Node.
- The North Lunar Node is trine Sun and Mars.
- the Sun and Mars are sextile South Lunar Node

- Vesta is inconjunct North Lunar Node and half-sextile South Node[1]

When the list is drawn, we can start to interpret the aspects according to the positions of the South and North Lunar Nodes in signs and House.

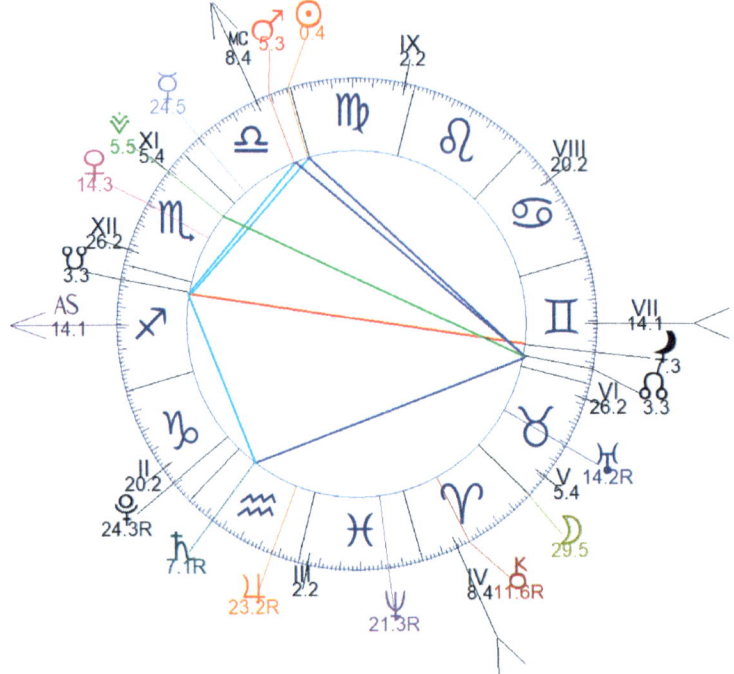

Next, we must consider the regents of each Lunar Node in signs and in Houses in aspect with other elements in the chart, as mentioned earlier.

The best way to tackle such complicated exercise, is to draw up a list similar to the one made for the aspects involving the South and North Lunar Nodes.

---

[1] In my opinion, the half-sextile is a difficult aspect and not a 'half-beneficial' one like many astrologers claim.

The picture on the previous page shows the aspects converging to the South and North Nodes. The picture below shows the aspects to the regents of the South and North Lunar Node.

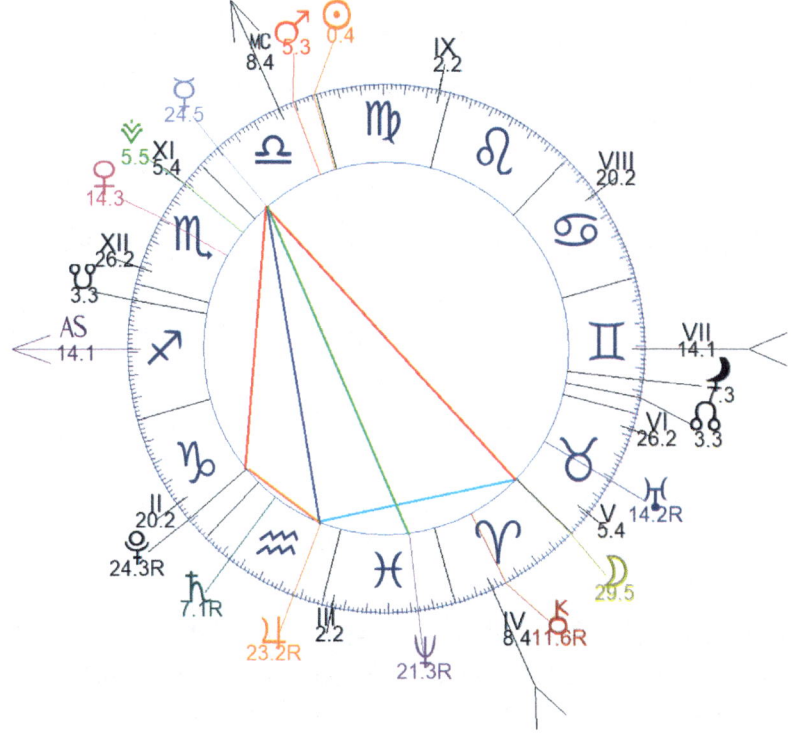

The North Lunar Node is in Gemini and its ruler, Mercury is in opposition with the Moon. There is also an inconjunct with Neptune, and a trine with Jupiter, as well as a square with Pluto.

Once again, making a list of the aspects involving Mercury is essential until you master the technique.

Jupiter, regent of the South Lunar Node in Sagittarius, is in Aquarius, half-sextile Pluto, sextile Moon and trine Mercury, a very positive aspect showing that the potential to make good use of the South and North Lunar Node is increased.

Let's go over the whole process once more to end this lesson.

1 - Assess the positions of the Lunar Nodes in signs and in Houses

2 - Determine the regents of the Lunar Nodes (the rulers of the signs where they stand)

3 - Situate the regents of the Lunar Nodes in signs and in Houses

4 - List the aspects involving the Lunar Nodes with other elements in the chart.

5 - List the aspects involving the regents of the Lunar Nodes with other elements in the chart.

This procedure represents quite a lot of work when you begin the study of this technique of astrological analysis. However, with practice, you will gradually gain confidence and speed to observe and simultaneously analyse all the factors to take into consideration in your reading.

It is like mixing colours, akin to what the artist does on a canvas. Practice is essential to master the art. The experience of the beginner is that of the teacher. The same applies to astrology and to any other skill. Acquiring basic knowledge is a tiny portion of the process. Practice does the rest. Practise, practise, and practise again because that's how you will eventually become a master in your own art.

This is the end of this important lesson about the Lunar Nodes. Use the Supplementary sections in the following pages to guide your initial readings. Avoid the copy/paste approach. Use your own words as much as possible. The short aphorisms are only meant to inspire your personal analysis of the Lunar Nodes in a chart.

The next lesson deals with Lilith or Black Moon, a most interesting constituent of karmic astrology readings.

Supplementary section

The Lunar Nodes in the signs.

South Node in Aries - North Node in Libra

Your previous life was marked by war, aggression, or martial law. Hostility prevailed in your immediate and broader surroundings. You thus developed a combative tendency to defend yourself and those around.

You may still have impulsive defensive reactions in the present incarnation although it may help you obtain positive results by channelling your energy to direct it towards the goals you want to reach. Focusing on balance and harmony will give better results.

South Node in Taurus - North Node in Scorpio

Your past life was marked by earthly needs and necessities. Agriculture, food, nature, and the good and beautiful things in life were your main sources of motivation. A materialistic and down-to-earth attitude allowed for survival and personal satisfaction.

In this present incarnation, if you are confronted to purely materialistic challenges, they are meant to detach yourself progressively from detrimental dependency on earthly matter. Optimal feeding habits also need to be assessed to allow body and mind to function properly.

South Node in Gemini - North Node in Sagittarius

Your previous life was marked by numerous voyages, changes of residence and situations, human relations, communication, and writings of various kinds. Intellectual instability and shallowness may have resulted.

In the present incarnation, you need to work on acquiring solid and profound knowledge such as is derived from higher education and studies. A foreign city, region or country may become a source of inspiration and deep motivation to settle far away from your birthplace. Politics, philosophy, and philanthropy are areas of potential success. The spiritual aspect of life is also a prominent aspect of your path to personal achievement.

South Node in Cancer - North Node in Capricorn

Your previous life was marked by major setbacks and difficulties in your family, home, and perhaps country. You have inherited from these times a greater need to identify and to connect with your roots, even though there may still be a lot to experience and learn from them.

In this present incarnation your "mission" is to part with the restricting influence of the family and the burden it generates. To take its flight and become autonomous, one day the young bird leaves the nest to realise itself and be part of the community. Your hesitations to do so are derived from negative reminiscences dating back to your previous life.

South Node in Leo - North Node in Aquarius

Your previous life was marked by a monarchic regime and an aristocratic education that included the arts, financial wealth, and the many privileges given to people of your class. However, sentimental hardship deeply affected your personal wellbeing.

In the present incarnation, you need to be more open to others in an altruistic manner that will win you much popularity and gratitude. If you hesitate in making good use of your talents and creative potential, you may not reach the level of success you deserve.

South Node in Virgo - North Node in Pisces

Your previous life was deeply marked by the burden of heavy workloads, constraints, and a kind of servitude to a despot or ruthless master. In those times, health was subject to questionable hygiene standards which were accentuated by your strong sense of responsibility that complicated your daily routine.

In the present incarnation, you need to develop a lighter and more spiritual approach to professional and personal responsibilities. Hesitations about work, hygiene, and health need to be assessed and dealt with to favour a more resolute and positive approach to such important values. Precise goals or objectives would help you accomplish your mission in this life.

South Node in Libra - North Node in Aries
Your previous life was marked by social disorders involving the justice system to the detriment of harmonious human relations. You probably had an artistic education (theatre) that influenced the way you express yourself while social tensions demanded strong reactivity when confronted to critical events or situations.

In the present incarnation, you need to develop a high level of self-discipline and individualism to avoid depending on others to achieve your goals. You may find it difficult to relate to authority but avoid being aggressive or too defensive to harmonise your relationships as much as possible.

South Node in Scorpio - North Node in Taurus
Your previous life was profoundly marked by death, sex, and magic or occultism. Painful events have left deep scars that made it difficult to find life pleasant and promising. The darker side of most circumstances prevailed over their lighter and more encouraging aspect.

In the present incarnation, you need to consider the constructive connotation of life, rather than focus on the threat of destruction due to unforeseen unfortunate or fateful events. Save, invest, and constitute a material and philosophical patrimony to preserve your personal interests and those of loved ones.

South Node in Sagittarius - North Node in Gemini

Your previous life was marked by long-distance travels, foreign countries and cultures, intellectual and philosophical pursuits to feed an insatiable need to be knowledgeable and experienced. Social success depended as much on your level of expertise than on that of the privileged social class to which you belonged.

In the present incarnation, you need to make renewed efforts to learn and acquire solid knowledge in the areas you want to master. Don't satisfy yourself with average achievements, strive to be the best, while favouring communication with simplicity and lightness of heart and mind. Consider your intellectual aspirations both from the academic and philosophical points of view.

South Node in Capricorn - North Node in Cancer

Your previous life was rather austere, but you showed authority, determination that led to social success and significant achievements in a valuable career. However, the general atmosphere did little to promote happiness and joy. You received a strict education and led a life of service to the community without questioning the reasons nor the system.

In the present incarnation, you need to cultivate a more convivial and easy-going approach to your responsibilities, at work and privately. Being close to your family and looking after your home, your community, or your country may complement your daily life and become a source of positive motivation and realisation. Apprehension in certain areas and situations come from unconscious karmic reminiscences that you have to overcome.

South Node in Aquarius - North Node in Leo

Your previous life was marked by a technical and perhaps social revolution that triggered major fundamental changes to your daily life. Disrupted by such radical events there came a crucial need for evolution and stability still reflected in the present incarnation.

In the present life, you need to assert your personal potentialities and talents rather than altering them through socialising and excessive dependence on others. You may find it inspiring but uneasy to exploit your creativity spontaneously. However, striving to impose yourself in a pleasant and altruistic manner will promote success in meaningful areas.

South Node in Pisces - North Node in Virgo

Your previous life was marked by religion, church activities and spiritual endeavours that brought more confusion than certainty in your social environment. Absorbed by the common beliefs, you found it difficult to express your own views spontaneously. Hence, you let others decide for you because it was easier and less responsible for the outcome.

In the present incarnation, you need to face up to realities and personally deal with important responsibilities and duties. Work, health, and hygiene may be a source of positive motivation and social or professional achievement. However, avoid considering academic knowledge as spiritual achievement. Spirituality needs no particular learning other than the lessons life teaches.

The Lunar Nodes in Houses

SOUTH NODE IN House I - NORTH NODE IN House VII

In your previous life you essentially functioned for yourself, in a rather selfish and self-centred way. You showed talent and your charisma allowed you to impose your conceptions and ideas. However, this "cult of personality" has set you off the path to others by seriously compromising your relationships.

In this life you must work on the idea that sharing is essential to the harmony and richness of human relationships. Your path of evolution depends on the awareness of the importance of the others in relation to them rather than in relation to yourself.

SOUTH NODE IN House II - NORTH NODE IN House VIII

Your previous life was led by the need to always have more with essentially materialistic and self-serving goals. They have used most of your vital energy to produce, in this present incarnation, down-to-earth automatisms and dominant material needs.

The idea of expanding your abilities at a higher level will provide social rewards that will entice you to collaborate rather than jealously keeping to yourself what you gain and earn from what you do. Trusting and sharing with others are necessary notions on your path to evolution and freedom from earthly matter.

SOUTH NODE IN House III - NORTH NODE IN House IX

In your previous life, you did not lack intelligence, but you did not have access to knowledge or culture through proper education. Today this can result in an inferiority complex detrimental to your ability to reach higher levels of knowledge. Trips to discover the world and studies will pose you or have posed crucial problems.

Open-mindedness must absolutely be cultivated in this present incarnation. Becoming aware of what is happening around you and being interested in it, not only for yourself but also for the people or situations concerned, would allow a faster mental evolution process.

SOUTH NODE IN House IV - NORTH NODE IN House X

Your existential journey is imbued with reminiscences of a previous life essentially devoted to the cause of family and homeland. One of your parents (your mother probably) played a fundamental role at that time and everything about this person today is a source of strong emotional load and obligations.

In this present life, frequent efforts are required to promote your social evolution rather than "sacrifice" your ability to succeed for the benefit of questionable family constraints or duties. Social success does not mean abandoning your home; they can both be reconciled.

SOUTH NODE IN House V - NORTH NODE IN House XI

Everything about love, art too perhaps, children and the pleasures of life has essentially motivated or marked your past existence. Your talents or gifts do not seem to have been sufficiently shared with the outside world. This is probably why today you lack self-confidence and motivation to live a successful artistic or romantic life.

It is by reaching out to others that you will succeed in making yourself heard, in making yourself understood, and in making yourself appreciated. It is by showing what you know that you will succeed in getting out of your cocoon and imposing yourself positively. It is requested that you act with love and spontaneity to confer its true value to your creativity.

SOUTH NODE IN House VI - NORTH NODE IN House XII

A previous life imbued with a sense of responsibility and accomplished duty has imposed all kinds of constraints. Medicine and health have also marked your past existence, either professionally or to treat or control chronic illnesses.

In this life it will be necessary to acquire a more global vision of existential challenges by rising above rudimentary questions, using your knowledge or abilities for the good of those around on a large scale rather than a small committee. Alternative medicine and humanitarian work would certainly promote positive opportunities and fulfilment.

SOUTH NODE IN House VII - NORTH NODE IN House I

You have essentially lived for people around. Everything related to personal relationship and the notion of association monopolised your previous life. You developed dependency on others that made you feel safer but prevented you from being yourself and, certainly, from imposing your own talent and potential.

In this life, you will have to work on the acquisition of independence that must not be an excuse for selfishness. It will allow you to get rid of the influence of others, in favour of the liberation of your own abilities. The "I" must be cultivated for the benefit of the "we", in the spirit of sharing and fair play.

SOUTH NODE IN House VIII - NORTH NODE IN House II

In your previous incarnation, everything about "death" and the "mysteries of life" profoundly marked your behaviour pattern. Material goods derived from inheritances, as well as the link between money and social status were at the forefront of your concerns. Sexuality has also been the source of recurrent needs that you had trouble managing and controlling.

In this life, you must remain aware of immediate realities rather than focusing on long-term projects. Daily life and personal needs are essential values that allow personal enrichment, increasing the potential for success and improve relations with others.

SOUTH NODE IN House IX - NORTH NODE IN House III

In your previous life, the law, the administration, far-distant places and foreign people, or frequent stays away from your place of birth have motivated your behaviour pattern. Setbacks with the law or with the administration are still possible in this present incarnation, especially if some issues dating back from your previous life have not been completely settled.

In the present life, it may become necessary to work on the acquisition of precise knowledge through studies and higher education. That would allow you to understand and manage societal challenges without less influence from external pressures from the social system. Travel could also be a source of multiple discoveries and knowledge.

SOUTH NODE IN House X - NORTH NODE IN House IV

Your previous life was essentially motivated by the need for social success and what it generously allows on a personal level. You have acted on valuable ambitions, but at the expense of family values and home life. It seems that your role in society has not allowed you to fully meet with your responsibilities on these levels.

In today's life, if you encounter insurmountable obstacles to social success, it may be that this kind of ambition no longer really concerns you. By avoiding far-fetched aspirations, you could focus more on building a strong and solid home life that would be a source of liberation and spiritual evolution.

SOUTH NODE IN House XI - NORTH NODE IN House V

Your previous life seems to have been heavily infused by everything related to social relationships, friends (or enemies) and worldliness. However, it all came at the expense of your privacy. You have lived so much for others that you failed to express your true worth and deeper personal feelings.

In this life you need to act so that your talents are recognised officially but, above all, so that they become sources of genuine accomplishment. To succeed in your love life, it is necessary to differentiate love from friendship to avoid unfortunate misunderstandings and chronic ambiguity in social and intimate relationships.

SOUTH NODE IN House XII - NORTH NODE IN House VI

In your previous life, you did not endorse a very specific social role. You were rather drifting between "good and evil", without ever settling down. A great dependence on beliefs based on superstitions and other legends, has not allowed you to find your spiritual path. Poor hygiene has been responsible for health concerns, both morally and physiologically.

In this life you seem to struggle to assume a specific role in society. Yet, whether it is your professional future or your health, you could certainly find it difficult to impose yourself. You may be fearing some imaginary "divine" or social dire consequences to your actions. But you know too well that they cannot excuse your own errors or weakness...

Lesson 2

Link to the video: https://youtu.be/w3tD3HlHw8U

Lilith

Welcome to lesson number 2 of this karmic astrology course with ABLAS. In this lesson we are going to investigate the role of Lilith in a birth chart. Lilith is also called the "Black Moon".

Now, what is Lilith?

There it is this is the drawing below that shows you what Lilith is. It is a point of energy which is worked out according to the position of the Earth and most especially the position of the Moon which is, as you know, orbiting around the Earth.

Lilith or Black Moon

"**Lilith**" a point that represents the direction of the actual moon's apogee. When considered as a point, this Lilith is sometimes defined as the second focus of the ellipse described by the Moon's orbit; the earth is the first focus, and the apogee lies in the same direction. It takes 8 years and 10 months to complete its circuit around the zodiac

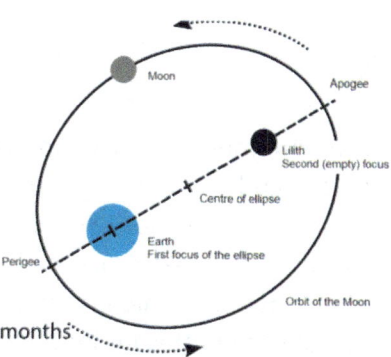

Revolves around the zodiac in 8 years and 10 months
12 September 2012 0° Gemini
18 July 2022 0° Gemini

As you can see here, the orbit of the Moon is not circular, it is elliptic. See the Earth and the Moon's perigee, which is the closest position to the Earth. Then see the apogee, the farthest position to the Earth. The position at the centre of the ecliptic is the point between the sections of the dotted line crossing the Earth on the drawing. In the middle lies what we call Lilith, the second empty focus. The first focus would be, of course, the Earth, and the second one is called Lilith. It is a complicated sort of calculation made by astronomers, but they're not sure exactly, or at least some believe that it is that type of calculation that should be made, while others think it is another type. So, it gives rise to three possible positions of Lilith that you can find in the ephemeris.

O ECL. PARTIELLE   23 ♑42 14 JAN. 20h29 68 S   43 E Magnitude 0.555
(Non-centrale) Début 18h38, 51 S 144 E - Fin 22h20, 44 S 41 W

JANVIER 1964

In the ephemeris you will find the true position of Lilith, the mean position, and the corrected position. But not all ephemerides give the corrected position. Some will just give the true and the mean positions. Most astrologers use the mean position, which is the median position, which is what I use and that is what we are going to investigate in this lesson.

In the chart on the following page, have a look at the three positions of Lilith. I call them the "three sisters". 😊

You see the "corrected position" at 28°46' in Taurus, but the other two are in Gemini. The "mean position" is at 7°40' in Gemini and the "true position" at 11°25'.

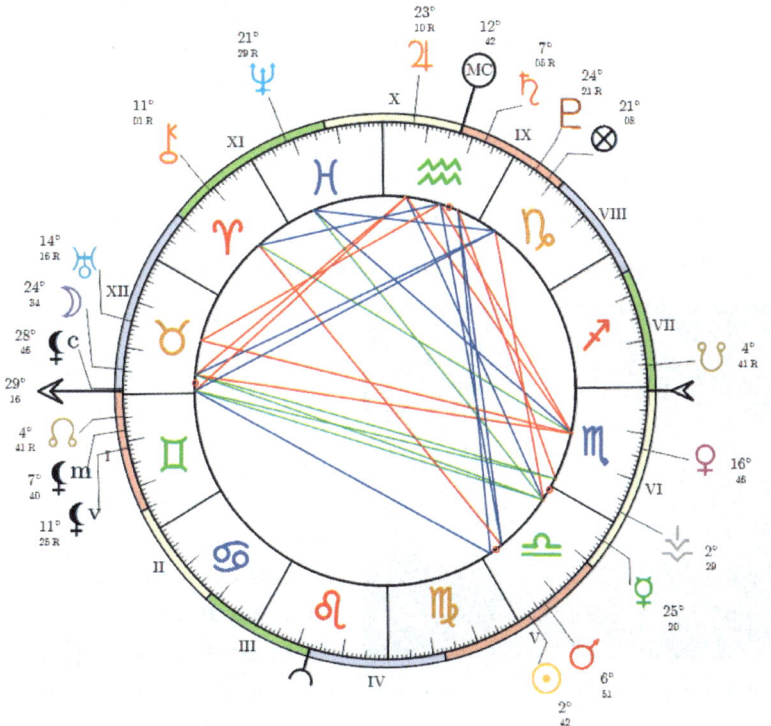

Note that the "mean position" is not the median position as such, between the true and the corrected positions, it is a position that has been worked out on a long period of time, with multiple calculations until this result was considered as being right. There is not much difference in this particular chart between the true position and the mean one, but sometimes the difference can be as much as around 20 to 30 degrees, which becomes quite important in terms of interpretation.

My advice is to use the position of Lilith that seems right for you. Have a look at the mean position (in the ephemeris or on a computer-generated chart), determine what it means according to this position, then have a look at the true position, what it means according to where it is in your chart, and according to the aspects that are created with other elements and planets.

If there are only a few degrees difference between the mean position and the true position, like in the example chart on the previous page, you can consider both as being quite similar.

What Lilith represents from a karmic point of view.

Lilith represents the dark zones, the past, karma, reincarnation, fear, shame, and what is hidden.

It represents the darker side of ourselves, it represents what we don't want to know, or what we don't want to show. It represents ambiguity, it represents what we bring back from a past incarnation during which we did not face up to our responsibilities. We tended to avoid complicated situations because we were afraid of the consequences, or because we were ashamed of ourselves. So, shame is also represented by Lilith. It is an important element to analyse in a birth chart, especially when you are dealing in karmic astrology.

Karmic astrology is very interesting not only to determine who you were and what you did in your past incarnation, but more importantly what you bring back in the present one.

You must remember that if your present life is issued from your past incarnation, it certainly prepares you for your next incarnation.

Therefore, it is very important to situate all the energy of your birth chart, going through all the planets and other elements, just like the North and South Lunar Nodes studied in the previous lesson.

Lilith represents what we are not yet quite prepared to deal with. What we tend to avoid in the area of our life either represented by the sign in which Lilith is, or by the House where Lilith is in our birth chart. And of course, the aspects and the positions of other elements close to Lilith. If there is a conjunction, for example, between Lilith and the Sun, or the Moon, or Mercury, it means something important about the way we are bound to deal with the hidden part of our personality…

Lilith in a birth chart

What is important to determine about Lilith in a birth chart?

- Its position in sign

- Its position in House.

- Determine Lilith's regent. (The regent is the ruler of the sign in which Lilith is positioned. In the example chart on the following page, Lilith is in Sagittarius. What is the ruler of this sign? It is Jupiter. So, Jupiter becomes the regent of Lilith.)

- The position of the regent in Sign

- The position of the regent in House

- The aspects to Lilith

- The aspects to the regent of Lilith

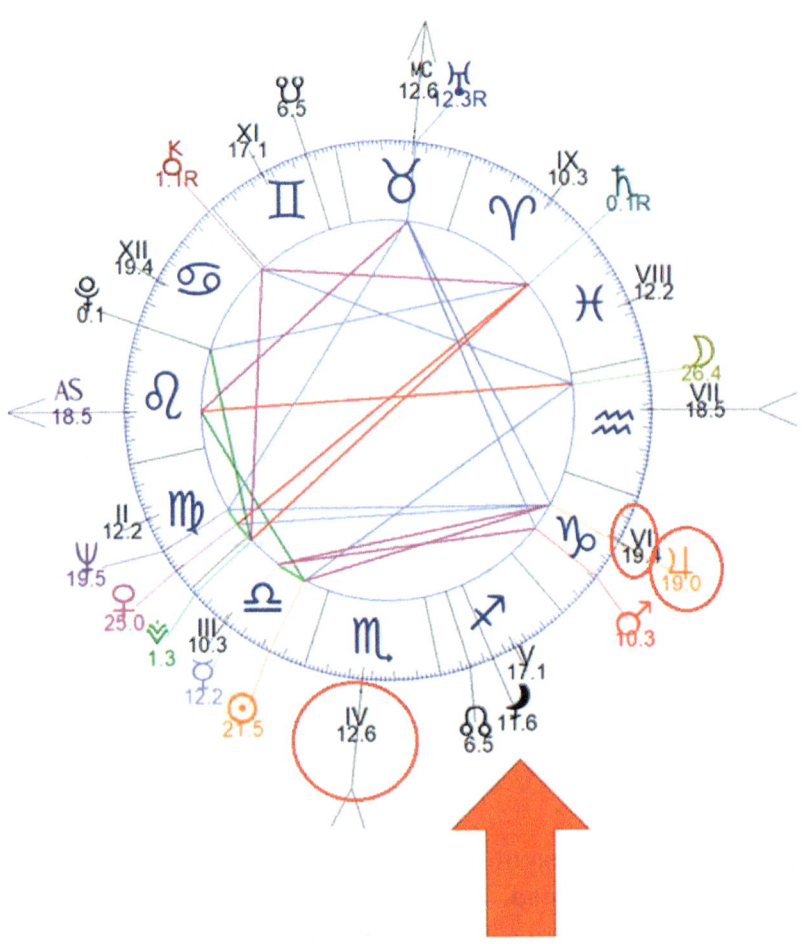

The House where Lilith is found in this chart, House IV, begins in Scorpio and ends where House V begins, in Sagittarius. So, Lilith is not in House V, but in House IV. As such, House IV is ruled by the planet that represents Scorpio, Pluto. And then, of course, we need to analyse the aspects involving the regent with other elements and planets in the chart.

The Aspects Involving Lilith

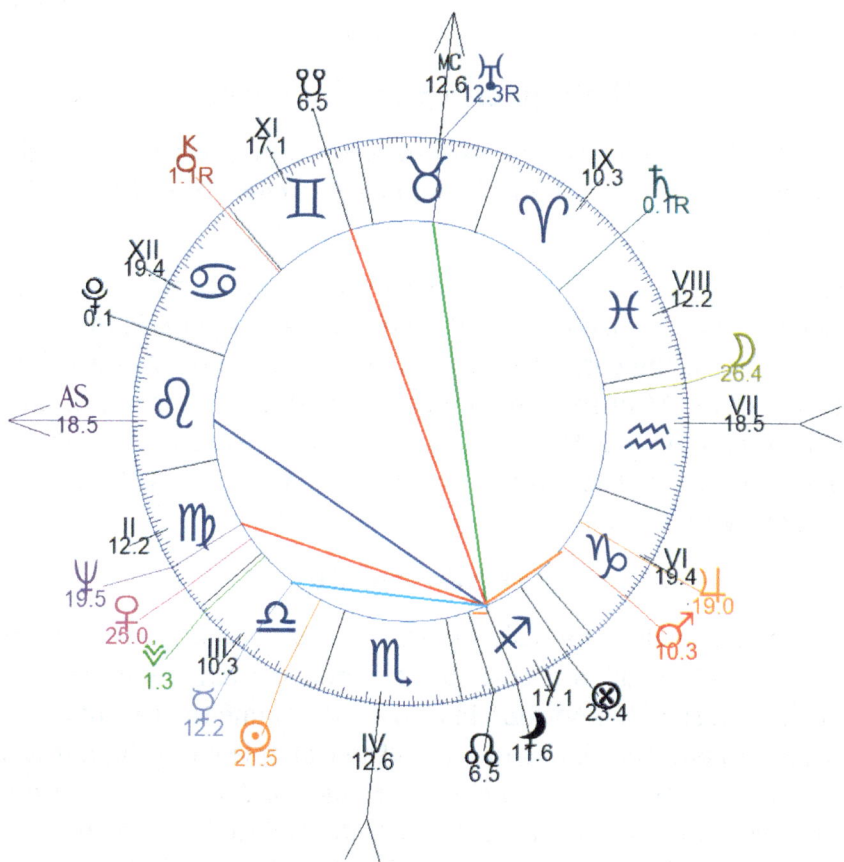

We see that Uranus and the MC at 12° in Taurus with Lilith at almost 12° in Sagittarius form an inconjunct. There is a conjunction with the North Lunar Node and a trine to the Ascendant which is at 18°, almost 19° in Leo. There is also a sextile with Mercury. Mercury is at 12° in Libra. We could consider a half sextile with Mars because it is at 10°30' in Capricorn, almost 30° from Lilith.

Once we know what aspects are linking Lilith with the rest of the chart, we can explain what the Black Moon means in that chart and, of course, in the life of the person concerned.

The aspects to Lilith's regent

Last but not least, we need to analyse the aspects between the regents of Lilith and other elements in the chart. See the drawing on the following page.

We have seen earlier that because Lilith is in Sagittarius, Jupiter represents it. It is Lilith's regent. In this chart, Jupiter is in House VI, very close to the cusp of House VI, but still in House V. It is locked on the cusp of House VI in Capricorn, and it is creating a trine with Uranus and the MC. There is also a trine with Neptune and another one with Venus. There are a couple of squares. One with Mercury and one with the Sun.

The Procedure

When you analyse the role of Lilith in a birth chart, you need to make a list of all the criteria explained earlier, determine the position in sign, the position in House, determine the regent and in what sign and House it is found. In the example chart, Jupiter is in Capricorn, in House V, very close to House VI. You will find it useful to make a list of the aspects to Lilith and to the regent. This procedure will help you understand and track the meaning and the role of Lilith in your birth chart and in any other person's birth chart.

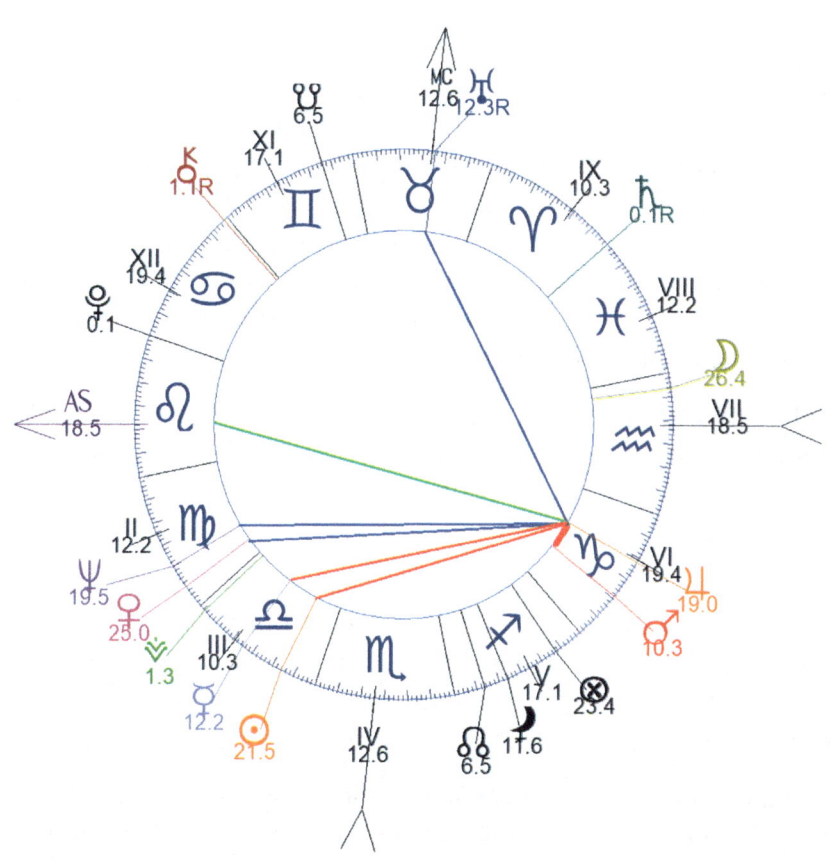

Lilith in signs

Let's concentrate on what Lilith means in the example chart...

First of all, we must assess the role of Lilith in sign. It is in Sagittarius where it shows that honesty, generosity, and the social system to which the person belongs are a source of ambiguity and turmoil that delay important deadlines and reduce the potential to succeed...

That doesn't sound like good news, but it is a fact. Jupiter represents our ambition to succeed in life, to acquire either knowledge, material possessions, or fame perhaps, as well as whatever we want to achieve in this world. If Lilith is under the rulership of Jupiter, it means that we must assess objectively what needs to be done, what we need to face as far as rational responsibilities are concerned, to favour success. That's what one is striving for with Jupiter regent of Lilith. That's what seems to have been the case in the previous incarnation, because if Lilith is linked to karma, it is linked to the past lives. It means that with Lilith in Sagittarius, in the previous incarnation the person would have been too honest, maybe too generous, and too dependent on the social system.

With Jupiter regent of Lilith, in the past life, the person didn't do enough to deserve the wealth and all the privileges they enjoyed due to their rank or to their social status. They expected everything effortlessly.

Consequently, in the present incarnation, it is likely to be quite different. If they don't face up to their responsibilities, waiting for the good things to come instead of going to them, this person won't deserve the success and the satisfaction that goes with it, they will not be rewarded. That is what Lilith indicates in this particular case.

If you want to find out more about the meaning of Lilith in signs in a birth chart, read the supplementary section "Lilith in signs" included at the end of this lesson.

Lilith in Houses

The next step is to deal with the position of Lilith in Houses. As we've seen earlier, in the example chart, Lilith is in House IV. It means that the origins may be a source of confusion and doubt. The person finds it difficult to accept trials involving family, home, homeland, or the mother. Hiding from the truth increases its negative impact.

Controversy is often a source of inner growth. That is something to remember, controversy and difficulties, obstacles, constraints, restrictions, and whatever is unpleasant, are a source of inner growth. But it all depends on how we deal with that dissatisfaction represented by this type of difficulty. Read the supplementary section called "Lilith in the Houses" included at the end of this lesson to get a hint of what the position of Lilith in your chart means.

The Aspects Involving Lilith

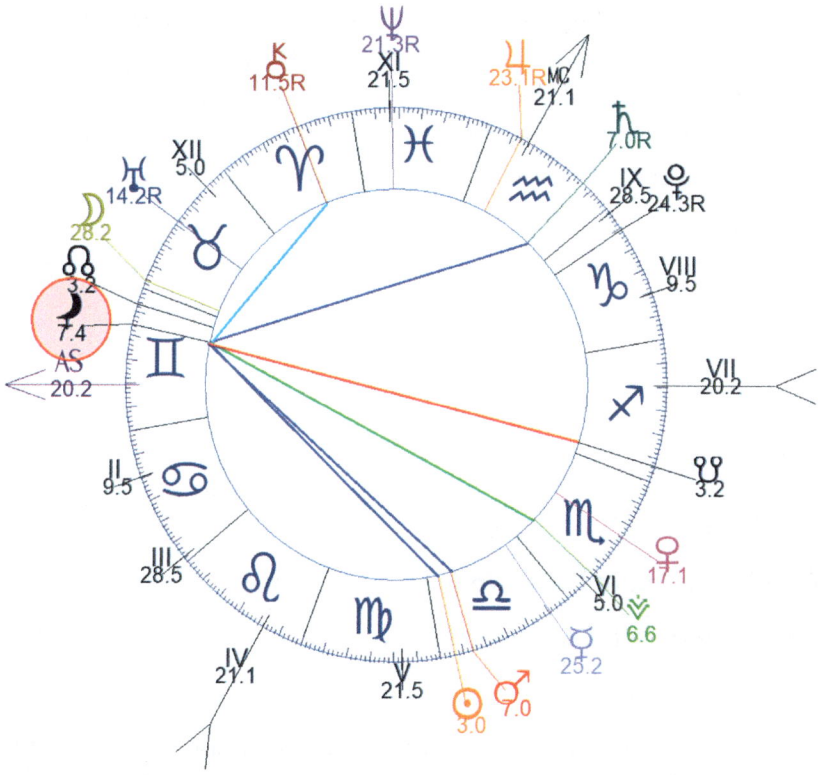

Here is another example chart. This one has Lilith at 7°40' in Gemini. What we can do is a list of the aspects involving Lilith in this chart. You can do so for any other chart you wish to analyse.

Drawing that list will help you avoid forgetting some of the aspects. Once you've drawn the aspects or once the aspects have been drawn by the computer program or application you are using, you can make a list of them to analyse each one separately, and then combine, mix, or blend all the information together.

That synthesis represents the role of Lilith in the birth chart in relation to the other elements. All planets and other elements involved in the aspects represent something to deal with, a challenge in the life of the person concerned. It is very important to do so because Lilith is making it either very difficult or very easy for the person, spontaneously easy, effortlessly, if beneficial or harmonious aspects involve Lilith in the chart...

Let's have a look at what we have in the example chart on the previous page. Lilith is:

- Sextile Chiron

- Trine Saturn

- Trine the Sun

- Trine Mars

- Opposition South Lunar Node

- Conjunction North Lunar Node

- Inconjunct Vesta

There are no squares, only one opposition, and one inconjunct that are indicative of difficulties. Each aspect must be analysed separately, then in relation to the others.

If you are following this course or simply reading this book, I assume that you already know how to analyse aspects. It means that you have already studied at least the first section of the course dealing with the basics of astrology and have learned how to analyse a birth chart. Although it is not on a karmic point of view, knowing how to read a chart is essential.

For example, in karmic astrology, the Sun represents power and authority. Mars represents the warrior and combativeness, and how we can use it to defend ourselves. There is a great potential shown in the example chart to instinctively use both energies of the Sun and Mars to fight and defend the person's own interests and perhaps their own life.

Saturn renders more responsible and quite rational about what needs to be done. Saturn represents our ability to face up to our responsibilities. If that person did not in their past incarnation, the trine involving Lilith with Saturn shows that now they can. Saturn is showing the role of education and personal experience that have helped this person face up to their responsibilities in the present life, thus dissipating ambiguity.

Saturn helps that person get more from other aspects. For example, we've seen that there is a sextile with Chiron which represents anything that has to do with health and the potential to analyse, to observe, to focus on details, and to understand in a very intricate manner. Chiron helps here once again. It is in Mars's sign in Aries, from where it relays its influence into this sign, while the double trine confers strength, willpower, authority, and whatever else is necessary to create a positive energy useful to obtain the best results.

There is an opposition with the South Lunar Node because there is a conjunction with the north one. The conjunction with the North Lunar Node indicates a tendency to be in doubt as far as where this person should go. As you've learned in the previous lesson, the South Lunar Node represents that which we should let go. There seems to be some difficulty in accepting that direction, that destination, or that objective because Lilith here is in House XII, where the North Lunar Node is, where the Moon is, where Uranus is as well.

The past, represented by House XII, plays a very important part in this person's life. In the past and also in the past incarnation represented by House XII lay the answers to the existential questions that this person may ask during the reading of the birth chart from a karmic point of view. House XII is the subject of lesson 4.

The Regent

The next step is to assess the position of the regent of Lilith. It is Mercury because Lilith is in Gemini, and Gemini is ruled by Mercury. Mercury is in Libra, in House V. It means that there is a link between what happens in this person's life and their past incarnation as far as House V and Libra are concerned because Mercury is in this sign. Libra represents personal relationship and partnership, because it is the seventh sign as you learned in the first section of the course dealing with the birth chart.

House V represents love, romance, creativity, children, and everything that is nice, for example holidays. It means that there is an instinctive need to connect with such areas of life, to connect unconsciously, of course, with what this person went through in their past life. It seems even more important in this case because this person's Ascendant or rising sign is in Gemini. Therefore, the ruler of this person's Ascendant is the same as the regent of Lilith, Mercury. This indicates a close link between the person's inner personality represented by the Ascendant and by Mercury, while Lilith is also represented by this planet.

We can conclude from this analysis that the ambiguity is probably stronger, therefore more difficult to deal with because Lilith is in House XII, known as the "locker House" where much is hidden or forgotten. It also represents the unconscious mind. The fact that the ruler of the Ascendant and the regent of Lilith is the same planet amplifies its troubling role in this person's present life.

The Aspects

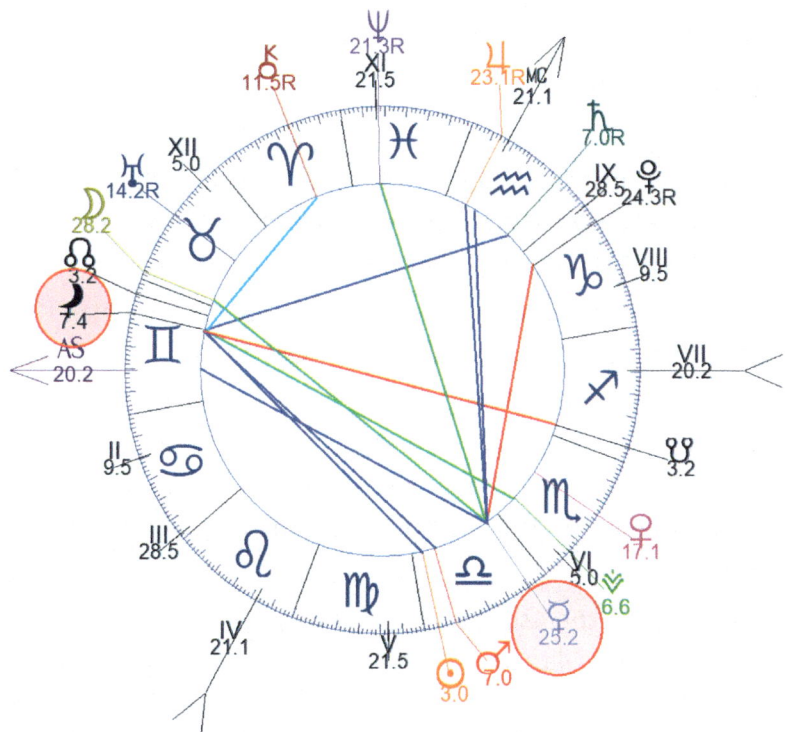

Next, we must determine the aspects involving the regent of Lilith with other elements in the chart. Then, we add up the aspect between Lilith and the other elements in the chart to the aspects between the regent and the other elements in that same chart. The reading greatly benefits from that addition of valuable information.

In this chart, between Mercury and the other elements there are the following aspects:

- **A trine with the Ascendant**

- **A trine with the MC or Midheaven**

- **A trine with Jupiter**

- **An inconjunct with Neptune**

- **An inconjunct with the Moon**

- **A square with Pluto**

It is a good idea to make a list of the aspects in your chart between the regent of Lilith and the other elements similar to the above one. Make sure you don't forget any. It would have a detrimental influence on the quality and veracity of your reading.

I am not going too far into explaining the aspects, of which I hope you can understand the effects and analyse them. They affect the chart, just like Mercury regent of Lilith does by itself.

For example, the square with Pluto means that there is an underlying influence of the idea of death that can confer a nihilistic approach to life for this person in situations where ambiguity prevails.

But the trine with the Ascendant is very positive because it amplifies the trine between Lilith and the Sun and Mars. Such configurations should make it easier for this person to communicate about personal issues revealed by the position of Lilith in the birth chart.

Mercury represents the ability to communicate about what is going wrong in life, thus helping this person to find solutions and deal with difficult or ambiguous situations represented by Lilith.

Then, there is trine aspects with Jupiter and the Midheaven. They are very promising in terms of social and professional success. This person can use the ambiguity symbolised by Lilith to succeed in this present life by communicating and understanding inner doubts and confusion.

What happened in this person's previous incarnation is likely to be helpful in the present life, both personally and for others, thanks to communication skills. Jupiter represents the potential to successful relationships because in this chart it represents House VII in Sagittarius, and it is high in the chart, right on the cusp of House X. Relationships and partnerships promise to be a source of great achievement.

The inconjunct involving the Moon has to do with motherhood, family, and emotional states. The inconjunct with Neptune represents the influence of religious belief and the spiritual side of life. It confers a tendency to be influenced by other people that needs to be addressed in the reading to improve this person's ability to deal with it and perhaps to build on it, rather than be a victim of spiritual confusion represented by the inconjunct.

If you want to find out more about the inconjuncts, you will need to read my paperback, **Astrology for a better life**. Note that it gives access to sixteen videos made to support the reader's study of the *materia astrologica* described in this book. It is available from the Amazon website in your country, but you can also order it from your local bookstore.

The work to do after what we went through is to blend homogeneously the meanings of the position in sign and House, that of the regent in sign and in House, the aspects involving Lilith and the aspects to the regent.

That represents a lot of information that needs to be blended because some of the information may contradict others, due to the fact that we are all filled with contradictions as you know, but it is nice to be able to determine what may be beneficial and what may become a source of issues. The aspects involving Lilith explain how the ambiguity, the "dark zones" of our inner personality and what we don't want to recognise or what we don't know and are not really prepared to share with others, what we keep as secrets.

Lilith and the aspects indicate how the hidden facets of our personality, where lie many secrets perhaps, and much information about our past. This is very useful to find out because it helps understand the why and how of this position of Lilith in our birth chart.

Thanks to this book, I hope that you will soon be able to correctly analyse the position of Lilith in your birth chart or in any other person's chart. Use the supplementary sections mentioned earlier to guide your first readings. I have not included a supplementary section about the aspects because they have been dealt with in my "Astrology for a better life" book, which you may have acquired and read by now. They should be enough to help you analyse the aspects between Lilith and its regent with the other elements in your chart.

This is the end of lesson 2. Lesson 3 deals with the "Part of Fortune". Before you continue on to the next level, make sure that you have gone through everything that I have explained in this lesson and applied the information to your own birth chart or anybody else's.

Remember, you must practise, practise, and practise again until you master the role of Lilith according to what has been developed in this lesson.

Supplementary section

Lilith in signs

IN ARIES

Latent aggressiveness and impulsiveness increase the risk of human conflicts triggered by an unconscious need to lead, direct, defend, and impose oneself to the detriment of close relationships.

IN TAURUS

You show an attraction to earthly foods, to art and to nature without taking advantage of them as you should. Carnal impulses are sources of inner controversy and doubt.

IN GEMINI

You are punctually faced with communication difficulties, problems with siblings, and obstacles that can delay the progress of your studies and your intellectual achievements.

IN CANCER

Ambiguity in relation to your family, your mother, your homeland, or the history of your country is at the origin of a latent emotional anxiety that you cannot understand rationally.

IN LION

You often show excessive pride and susceptibility. Such behaviour generates affective ambiguity in dealing with those around you. Frustration may stem from unfulfilled creativity.

IN VIRGO

Ambiguity is present in the context of work, in your conception of hygiene, and in health matters. It may lead to irrational fears and a strong need to protect yourself even when you are safe.

IN BALANCE

Ambiguity manifests itself mainly in personal relationships and in situations requiring close collaboration with others. Doubt can become a source of failure when irrational fear intervenes.

IN SCORPIO

Your relationship with money, sex, and death is ambiguous. You often fear the worst for no concrete or rational reason. A tendency to paranoia could result and produce moral discomfort.

IN SAGITTARIUS

Honesty, generosity, and the social system to which you belong are a source of ambiguity and turmoil that delay important deadlines that can reduce your potential to succeed socially or privately.

IN CAPRICORN

Ambiguity is shown in your relationship with authority. Your actions to fulfil your personal ambitions and impose yourself professionally and socially are unclear and filled with doubt.

AQUARIUS

Friendship, social relationships, your role in society, and the way you communicate with others are marked by inner confusion and doubt that you find difficult to understand and to manage.

IN PISCES

Ambiguity about religion, medicine, and physiological or spiritual health causes inner confusion and errors of judgment that are difficult to understand and to address rationally.

Lilith in Houses

IN House I

Ambiguity is essentially noticeable in the expression of your intimate and deeper self. This could result in a lack of direction. To counter doubt, uncertainty, and a lack of self-confidence, follow strict rational rules and do your best to apply them constantly.

IN House II

Personal finances and material assets are a source of ambiguity and confusion. Trials should be seen as useful lessons to encourage you to deal with your resources more objectively and rationally to avoid squandering them unnecessarily.

IN House III

If communicating with those around you is a source of inner confusion, try to express yourself more clearly and rationally. Friendship is a source of various upsets for obscure reasons. Being direct and fair with others will bring rewards.

IN House IV

Your origins may be sources of confusion and doubt. You find it difficult to accept trials involving family, home, homeland, or your mother. Hiding from the truth increases its negative impact. When tackled, controversy is a source of inner growth.

IN House V

Your artistic leanings and creativity deserve more attention, but you lack the necessary confidence to fully express what inspires you. Love and children could also become a source of confusion and disorders. In love, total sincerity is essential.

IN House VI

Work and duty are sources of preoccupations that make daily responsibilities heavier and less enjoyable. Do not neglect your personal hygiene and the quality of food you eat. Regular exercise allows better control of body and mind at all times.

IN House VII
Ambiguity is noticeable in the way you deal with important relationships. Doubt and lack of confidence in the other person produce insidious disorders over which you have almost no control. Objectivity and trust are the keys to relational success.

IN House VIII
Sexuality, death, and money are sources of doubt and confusion. You like money but you also despise it, which creates financial ups and downs. Be more rational and sincere in business and love rather than secretly yearning for wealth and the laxity it entails.

IN House IX
Your approach to social rules and laws leaves quite a lot to be desired. Philosophical ambiguity is a source of inner doubt. You are usually eager to study and travel, but fate seems to place obstacles in your way for obscure reasons that you cannot understand.

IN House X
Ambiguity shows in your dealings with authority. The relationship with your father may be the source of confusion. It can cause a lack of social or professional stability. The benefits from rationality and self-discipline come from accepting realities to succeed durably.

IN House XI
Social interactions and friendship are a source of confusion that you cannot objectively understand. This results in errors of judgment and doubt about others. To improve your social life, consider human relationships more openly and spontaneously.

IN House XII
Physical health is just as important as spiritual wellbeing. Doubt and inner confusion lead to moral destabilisation and insidious

repercussions on body functions. Follow high-level mental and body hygiene rules to preserve your vital energy and inner balance.

The regent of Lilith in signs

IN ARIES

Your previous incarnation was marked by confusion and doubt due to stressful situations that created a defensive attitude in this present life. Hence, your reactions are not always understood nor as efficient and constructive as you would like them to be.

IN TAURUS

Your previous incarnation was deeply marked by a lack of good food and material realisations. It may have created in the present life a need to accumulate wealth and an attraction to nature's goodness to protect yourself and your family against undesired privations.

IN GEMINI

Your previous incarnation lacked proper education that caused you to miss out on learning how to communicate and express yourself. In the present life, knowledge may be an upmost need to counterbalance ignorance and reach higher intellectual goals.

IN CANCER

Your previous incarnation was deeply troubled by family feuds and various problematic situations involving your home or your city, or country of residence. In the present life, you need to dissipate all doubts in these areas by fostering direct and positive interactions.

IN LEO

Your previous life was sentimentally difficult and confused due to lack of opportunities and a tendency to hide to avoid disappointment in intimate relationships. In the present life, overcoming your fear of failure is the key to romantic realisation.

IN VIRGO

In your previous life, you lacked proper hygiene and had to deal with long periods of unemployment and poverty due to adverse circumstances. In the present incarnation, striving to do your best all the time allows to overcome innate fears of failure and shame.

IN LIBRA
During your previous life you relied too much on others, which created much confusion determining your personal talents. In the present incarnation, you may feel the need to avoid being affected by the group but rather impose yourself for what you truly are.

IN SCORPION
In your previous incarnation you were deeply affected by epidemics, death, sex, and mysterious events that made you fear the worst for yourself and others. In the present life, avoid reactions that would damage your moral and physical wellbeing.

IN SAGITTARIUS
Your previous life was marked by legal actions, political turmoil, and philosophical confusion. In the present incarnation, you need to overcome your dislike for the system and encourage a clearer approach to your societal and moral responsibilities.

IN CAPRICORN
In your previous incarnation, you didn't really know how to climb up to the top of the social or professional ladder, you lacked the necessary education and motivation. In the present life, you need to assert yourself and accept hierarchical differences to succeed.

IN AQUARIUS
Your previous incarnation was disturbed by social confusion, strikes, demonstrations, riots, or revolution which forced you to hide for protection. In the present life, you need to appreciate others more to derive more pleasure and benefit from friendship.

IN PISCES
Your previous life was marked by spiritual confusion due to strict

religious rules that made it difficult to find rational answers to lofty questions. In the present incarnation, you need to search for the divine truth without being told what to do to find it within.

The regent of Lilith in Houses

IN House I

The influence of your past life is shown in the way you express your inner self. There is a need for authenticity in spontaneously exploiting your natural talents and potential to succeed both privately and socially. Fears and doubts must first be overcome.

IN House II

The way you conceive and deal with the material plan is closely linked to periods of uncertainty in your previous incarnation. The lessons learned should now be put to good use if you really want to obtain the best results in your search for satisfactory stabilisation.

IN House III

Your past life was marked by uncertainty and doubt in an area that is having a subtle influence on the way you express yourself and communicate in the present incarnation. Friendship and fair play are derived from the ability to learn and to share knowledge.

IN House IV

The uncertainty shown by Lilith in your past life tends to create doubt and confusion in family relations, making this present incarnation a must regarding the home and quality of residence, motherhood, and the need to belong and identify with siblings.

IN House V

Romance and creativity in the present life are subtly linked to the uncertainty and confusion you felt in your past incarnation. Your existential mission is to put forward your innate talents and potential to achieve what you previously missed out on.

IN House VI

The influence of what you had to deal with in your past life due to various setbacks and lack of self-confidence, may produce a strong need to do your best in the present incarnation in terms of work, service, health, and hygiene to the benefit of personal wellbeing.

IN House VII

The way you deal with personal and other important relationships is subtly linked to a degree of confusion, doubt, and self-deficiency observed in your previous life and that you unconsciously strive to offset and bravely defeat in the present incarnation.

IN House VIII

The way you handle your finances derives from unfulfilled material needs and confusion in your past incarnation. Sex and death are awkward subjects to deal with due to inappropriate involvement in magic or other types of esoteric practices in your previous life.

IN House IX

The role of moral values is important as it contributes to making self-realisation possible or difficult. Lack of integrity or a tendency to rely on the system may have induced in this present life a strong need to comply and do your best to be ethically irreproachable.

IN House X (MC)

Your perception of success, authority and power is subtly derived from the inconsistency of your past life in areas that were a source of doubt and confusion. In the present incarnation, you strive to reach higher levels of perfection to succeed satisfactorily.

IN House XI

Friendship and social life were linked to a lack of realism and objectivity that fed human relationships with doubt and confusion in your previous incarnation. In this one, you need to consider others with integrity and share with them various pursuits joyfully.

IN House XII

Spiritual confusion was linked to a lack of confidence in the greater levels of awareness that prevailed in your past incarnation. The present life needs to repair the damage done to your soul by reaching out to your higher self to rise above uncertainty.

Lesson 3

Link to the video: https://youtu.be/hV2d54w1C6Y

The Part of Fortune

Let us not be mistaking, the Part of Fortune does not represent the chances we have to "make a fortune" in one area or another. Unless we apply this term directly to matters of money, in this instance, "fortune" means happiness, self-realisation, deep satisfactions. That is what it is all about. Beyond the basic earthly material interests or constraints that motivate most of our actions in our capitalist societies, the simple pleasures, the joys of a moment, and everything that can bring a ray of Sunshine into a greyish life, must be cultivated as sacred flowers in an intimate human garden...

We too often forget that the seed exists and that it is only waiting to germinate, then hatch, producing all kinds of wonderful colours! We only care about what is important, the problems posed by our everyday life that must be solved without delay. Our thoughts are monopolised by myriads of necessities that too often take us away from our inner wonderland that we neglect because we lose the motivation to find the best way around.

The Part of Fortune is there to remind us that there is a secret door through which we can enter the heart of a paradise that it is up to us to discover and appreciate. Its position in the chart indicates that a karmic "gift" was given to us at the time of our birth, perhaps for having the courage to reincarnate. Search around the foot of the "tree of life" and take its gift. It is yours to enjoy! Astrology is at our service to help us achieve this feat. Let us find out how...

In the example chart below, the Part of Fortune (PF to abbreviate) is in Capricorn, in House IV. It is represented by this symbol: ⊗ Its regent is Saturn, ruler of Capricorn, in Pisces, in House VI. Note that this position of the PF in Capricorn, in House IV is identical to that of the North Node. They almost form a conjunction.

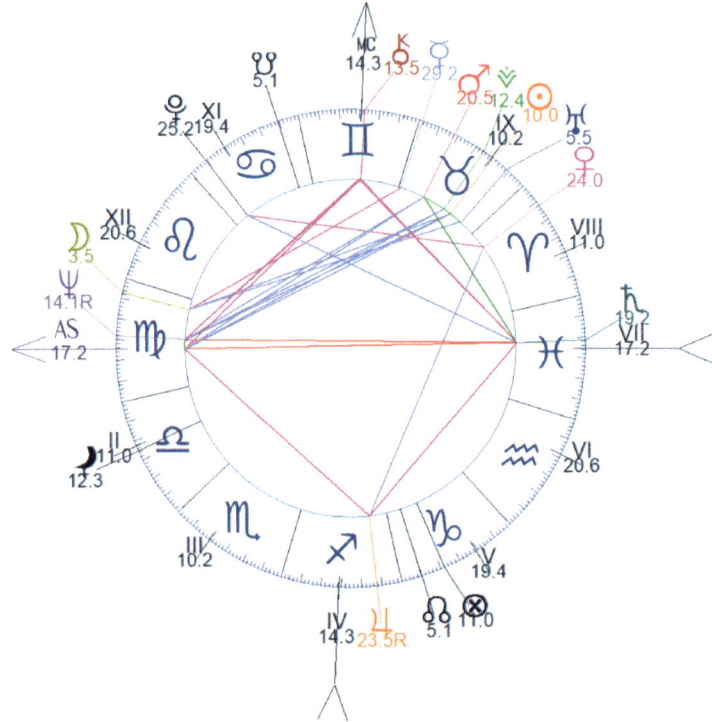

This "coincidence" reinforces the idea that this person must "tend", in this life, towards all subjects related to the family, the home, the place of residence. Happiness, peace of mind and personal comfort and achievement depend on those values.

Strangely, despite a very strong attachment to her mother, son and sister, this lady never really founded a real home, preferring a rather bohemian lifestyle to the stability and safety of a well-established situation. Multiple sentimental and relational setbacks have gradually kept her out of her "path".

This brings us back to the notion of "free will". We decided our destiny to a large extent before we were born, but despite our abilities, gifts or talents, we rarely choose the best path to achieve the various goals we set for ourselves. Should we believe that we fall into the traps set by fate because we unconsciously refuse the ease out of the need to "suffer" to better "purify" our karma? I leave it to you to meditate on this before answering this important question for yourself...

The PART OF FORTUNE's position does not promise unavoidable success. It is a tool at our disposal that we must use as best as we can or want to. To render it valuable, we need to be aware of this potential, accept it and verify its worth. Only then will it be possible to derive real results and deep satisfactions...

Determining the position of the Part of Fortune

First, we have to recognise the Part of Fortune in a chart, recognise its symbol. It is drawn like this ⊗. It is a cross inside a circle.

How is its position worked out in a chart? It is simple. You take the distance from the Sun to the Moon, and you add it to the position of the Ascendant.

If, for example the Sun is at 10 degrees in Aries and the Moon at 20 degrees in Taurus, the difference between the two is 40 degrees. If the Ascendant is at 5° in Gemini, 40° away from that 5° position puts the Part of Fortune at 15°s in Cancer, the following sign. That is the position of the Part of Fortune.

Note that some astrologers consider two Parts of Fortune, one for daytime births and one for night-time births. The first is calculated as I've just shown, and the other is worked out according to the difference between the position of Moon compared to the Sun's. There is an example chart about this in the following pages. Personally, I don't use that second position, I only use the "normal" Part of Fortune because to me it is good enough to explain quite a lot about what the Part of Fortune means in a chart, what the karmic gift is...

In the example chart presented a couple of pages earlier, the Part of Fortune is in Capricorn, a sign ruled by Saturn. Therefore, Saturn becomes what we call the "regent" of the Part of Fortune in House IV in the sign of House V. The regent of the Part of Fortune, Saturn, is in Pisces in House VII.

That's the kind of work needed to understand the true influence, the role of the Part of Fortune, to understand the person's gift from a past incarnation. The House where that "gift" is, represents an area of life where the person can find some sort of wellbeing, happiness, serenity, peace of mind, and so on. And, of course, because the ruler or the regent of the Part of Fortune is in House VII it means that the gift and the satisfaction that comes from that gift are also put to good use in a relationship, in a personal relationship, and in all sorts of other important relationships.

It is interesting because we move from House IV to House VII which means that because Saturn is in Pisces, its influence is biased by a square from Jupiter and one from Chiron and the Midheaven, the cusp of House IV, an opposition with the Ascendant and Neptune, ruler of Pisces, therefore regent of Saturn.

The opposition means that the gift may be a source of satisfaction in the area represented by House IV (family, home environment, place of residence) but perhaps somehow difficult or confused because of Neptune, which also acts in personal relationships. However, it is also an area where this person is going to try their best to obtain the satisfaction that is derived from the influence of the Part of Fortune.

More examples

Now, let's have a look at the difference in the positions of the Part of Fortune for two people born the same day but not at the same time.

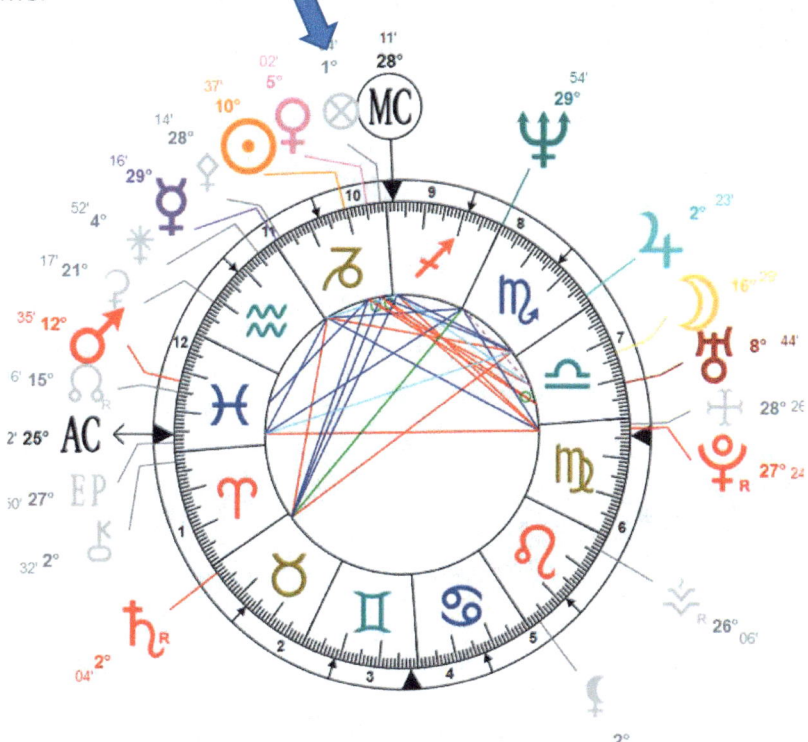

The first person was born on the 1st of January 1970 at midday in Paris. The other one was born on the 1st of January 1970 just like the first one, but at 10 p.m. also in Paris.

For the first one, the Part of Fortune is in Capricorn at about 1° in the sign. For the second person, the Part of Fortune is at 26° in Scorpio, next to the cusp of House IV, in House III.

There is an important change of position of the Part of Fortune in both charts which is essentially due to the different time of birth that affects the position of the Ascendant, from where the Part of Fortune is positioned according to the calculations mentioned earlier.

In the first chart, the Moon is at 16°29' in Libra and the Sun at 10°37' in Capricorn. The difference between both positions is 276°. Added to the position of the Ascendant at 25°in Pisces, it puts the Part of Fortune at 1°34' in Capricorn.

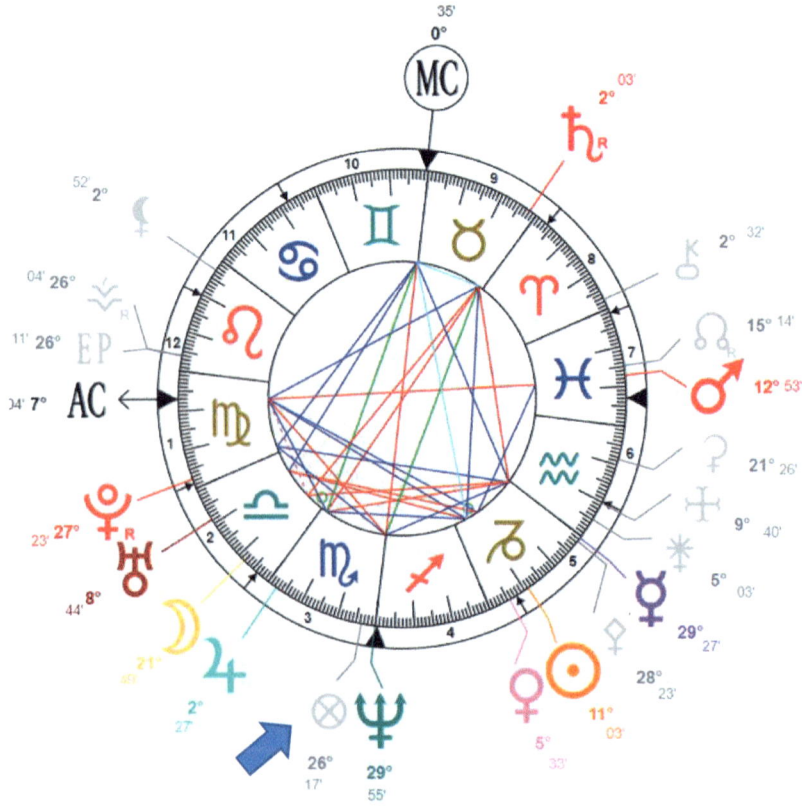

In the second chart, the Moon is at 21°49' in Libra and the Sun at 11°03' in Capricorn. The difference is 79°. Added to the position of the Ascendant at 7°04', it places the Part of Fortune at 26°17' in Scorpio.

This demonstration shows how the time of birth affects the position of the Part of Fortune due to the fact that it determines the position of the Ascendant, the starting point to define the position of the Part of Fortune.

In the chart above, there is no Part of Fortune. Do you know why? The reason is simple... There is no Ascendant and no Houses because the chart was established without a time of birth.

Therefore, it is not possible to attribute a rising sign and other Houses to this chart.

In the following example, the Ascendant is at 3°45' in Scorpio, the Sun is at 10°18' in Libra, and the Moon is at 26°3' in Cancer. The difference between the Sun's and Moon's positions is added to the position of the Ascendant and it puts the Part of Fortune at 19°30' in Leo, in House X, Midheaven, MC.

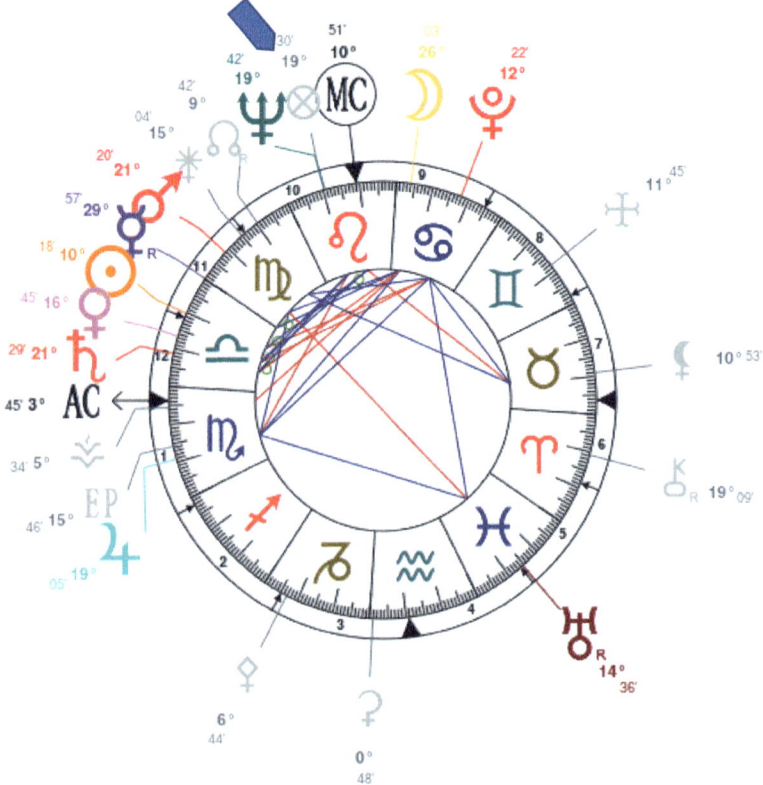

Let's see a couple more examples to help you understand how to determine the position of the PF. In the following chart, the Sun is at 11°24' in Capricorn and the Moon is at almost 22° in Taurus. The difference between both position of the Sun to the Moon is 131°. Added to the position of the Ascendant at 11°24' in Capricorn, the Part of Fortune should be placed 131° away at almost 22° in Pisces. However, in this chart, the Part of Fortune is found at 1°02' in Cancer. Why? Is there a mistake? The reason for this position is the different calculation method linked to a night-time birth. This is what we call a "nocturnal" Part of Fortune. It is determined by adding the difference between the Moon's and the Sun's positions, rather than between the Sun's and the Moon's positions. This is probably linked to the idea that the Sun is a daytime object, while the Moon is our night-time natural satellite.

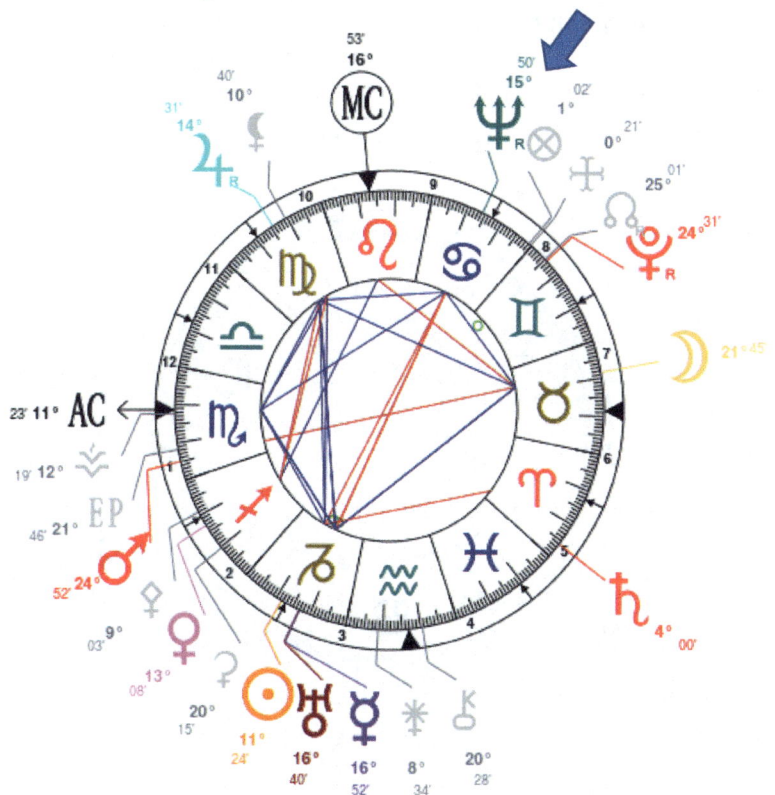

You can see that this person was born at night because the Sun is positioned below the horizon, which is determined by the line crossing the chart from the Ascendant to the Descendant (House I to House VII). Therefore, Houses I to VI are nocturnal Houses, while Houses VII to XII are diurnal Houses.

The next and last example is a daytime birth. It's easy to understand even if you haven't been told the time of birth. A position up near the MC corresponds to midday. We can then assume that the birth time is approximately 11 00 a.m. which places the Sun in House XI. The Moon is right across, forming an opposition with the Sun. This is what we call a Full Moon.

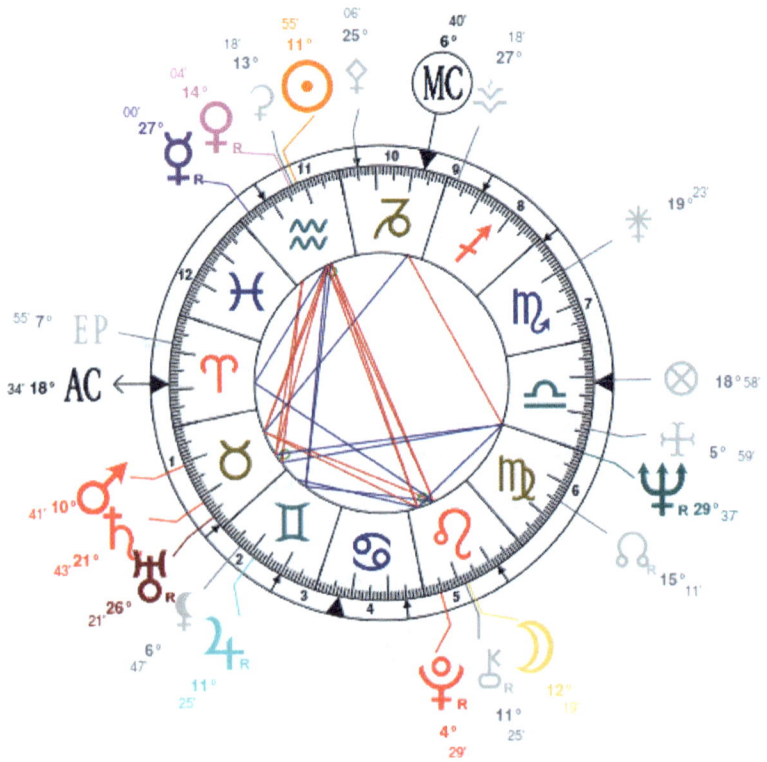

Consequently, there is also an opposition between the Part of Fortune and the Ascendant. As you know, the opposition is an angle of about 180°, which is the difference between the Sun's and the Moon's positions in this chart. Adding this difference to the position of the Ascendant automatically produces an opposition PF/Ascendant, placing the Part of Fortune near the cusp of House VII.

Let us carry on with the lesson...

First of all, to analyse and understand the role of the Part of Fortune in a chart you need to consider it according to the sign where it is found, because the sign gives its "colour" to the Part of Fortune. It determines how the person is going to act and react to take advantage of the "karmic gift" derived from a past incarnation. It also provides basic information of the type of gift received. The Part of Fortune in Aries, for example, has a much different meaning than in Libra, Scorpio, or Leo.

Read the supplementary section at the end of this lesson to understand how the Part of Fortune is treated according to its sign position in a chart. The supplementary section is made up of twelve short texts to explain the role and the energy of the Part of Fortune in every one of the twelve signs. But of course, the aphorisms are only meant for you to begin with. You will have to add your own personal touch as you go along and as you get used to analysing the position of the Part of Fortune.

Then, of course, we also need to analyse the position of the Part of Fortune in the Houses. As we have seen earlier, the Part of Fortune can be in any sign and in any House. Its position in a House represents the area where the karmic gift is found, together with the satisfaction that stems from it.

The areas of life where the gift is put to good use vary according to the House concerned. It has a different kind of application that depends on its House position in a chart.

I have also added a supplementary section at the end of this lesson so that you understand a bit further the influence of the Part of Fortune in each one of the twelve Houses.

Determining the "regent" of the Part of Fortune.

In the example chart on the following page, the PF is in Libra. ABLAS method considers Vesta to be the ruler of this sign. Therefore, Vesta is the regent of the PF.

In the second example chart, the PF is in Leo, which is ruled by the Sun. Therefore, the Sun in Libra is the regent of the PF in Leo.

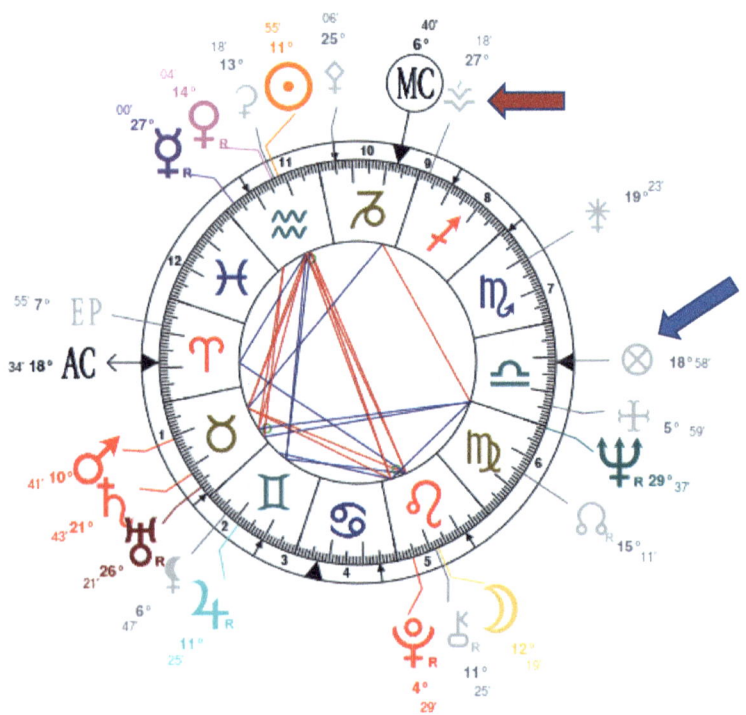

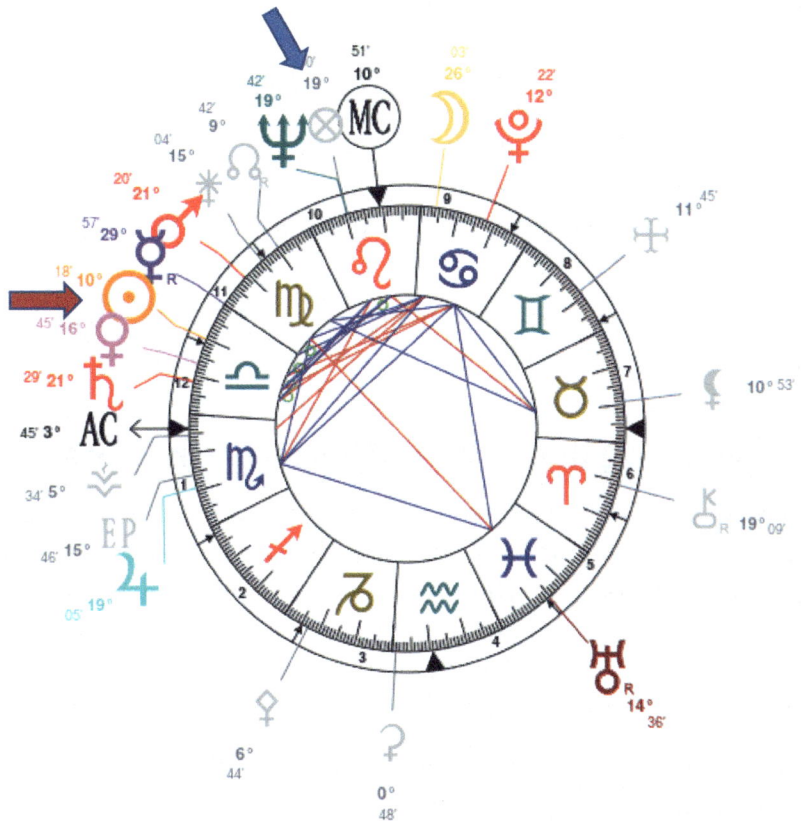

Analysing the position of the regent in sign

Adding the position of the regent in sign allows more understanding of the PF because the regent carries the energy of the PF "somewhere else" and the sign in which it stands represents another type of energy. But the regent planet itself signifies another type of energy. Taking the regent into consideration is essential to understand the PF and to get the most out of the karmic gift it represents.

The further we go to analyse the position of one element the more we travel around the chart to get a deeper insight into its true meaning. It goes for the Part of Fortune as for any other element in the chart, applying the same circular technique.

As seen earlier, in the first chart Vesta is in Sagittarius. This position is useful to enrich the reading and the understanding of the PF in Libra. The same applies to the PF is in Leo with the regent (the Sun) in Libra.

Read the supplementary section included in this lesson to discover what the regent of the PF in sign represents in your chart or any other chart.

Analysing the position of the regent in House.

We have seen earlier in the first example chart that Vesta was in Sagittarius, but it must also be analysed according to its House position, here House IX. This position provides more information on how the PF can be used, represented by its regent's position in sign, then transferring that influence into certain areas of the native's life. In this example, areas represented by House IX.

Read the supplementary section at the end of the lesson for more information.

In the second example, the PF is in Leo, a sign ruled by the Sun, which is in Libra, in House XI, close to the cusp of House XII. That tells us a little more about the role of the PF in this person's life.

It is important to find out exactly what we can get out of the PF. If it is a "karmic gift", we should appreciate it and get the most out of it. The more we discover about it, the more we can appreciate it, and the more we can put it to good use in our daily life to improve it.

In conclusion, the Part of Fortune represents areas of our life where we can create ideal conditions to feel better, to heal our wounds, or to give our natural talents a chance to develop in a positive and satisfying manner. But that's not all! Next, we need to consider the aspects between the Part of Fortune and other elements in the chart.

The Aspects Involving the Part of Fortune

In the following example chart, I have drawn the aspects involving the PF in Libra. There is a trine with Venus and with the Sun. There is another trine with Jupiter and one with Lilith. There is an inconjunct with Saturn.

These configurations mean a lot to better understand the role of the PF in someone's life. However, you will not find supplementary sections about the aspects to the PF or its regent in this lesson. For that, you will need to read my "astrology for a better life" book where numerous supplementary sections are proposed to analyse the aspects. You can also put your own knowledge of the aspects if any, to analyse the aspects involving the PF with other elements in the chart.

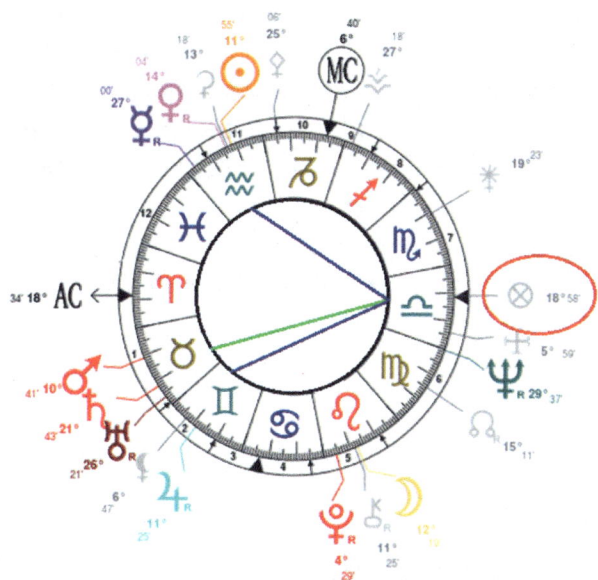

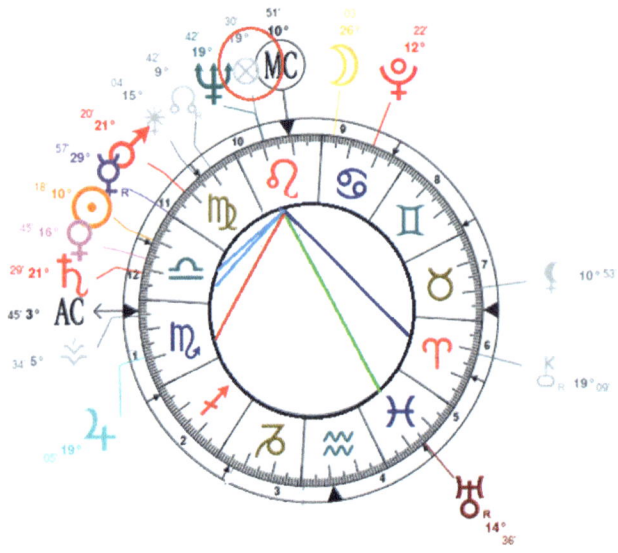

In the second example chart, the PF is in Leo. There is a trine with Chiron, an inconjunct with Uranus, a square with Jupiter, and two sextiles, one with Venus and one with Saturn. There is also a conjunction with Neptune. These aspects need to be assessed to understand how to make good use of the PF. The more you know about it, the better your life is going to become because you will get the best out of this important element of profound karmic implication. Once the aspects involving the PF are analysed, there is still one more step to take, and it's a most important one.

The Aspects Involving the Regent of the Part of Fortune

In the first example chart below, the regent of the PF is in Sagittarius, in House IX. It is involved in a sextile with Mercury, a square with Neptune, a trine with the cusp of the Ascendant, and two inconjuncts, with Saturn and Uranus.

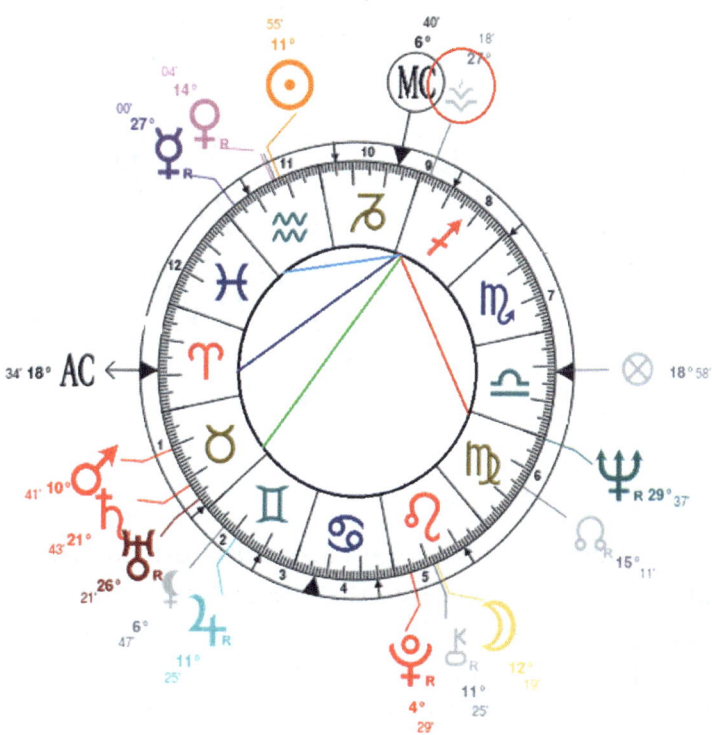

In the second example chart, the Part of Fortune is in Leo with the Sun for regent. There is a sextile with the Midheaven, a square with Pluto, an inconjunct with Lilith, an opposition with Chiron, and another inconjunct with Uranus. There is also a conjunction with Venus.

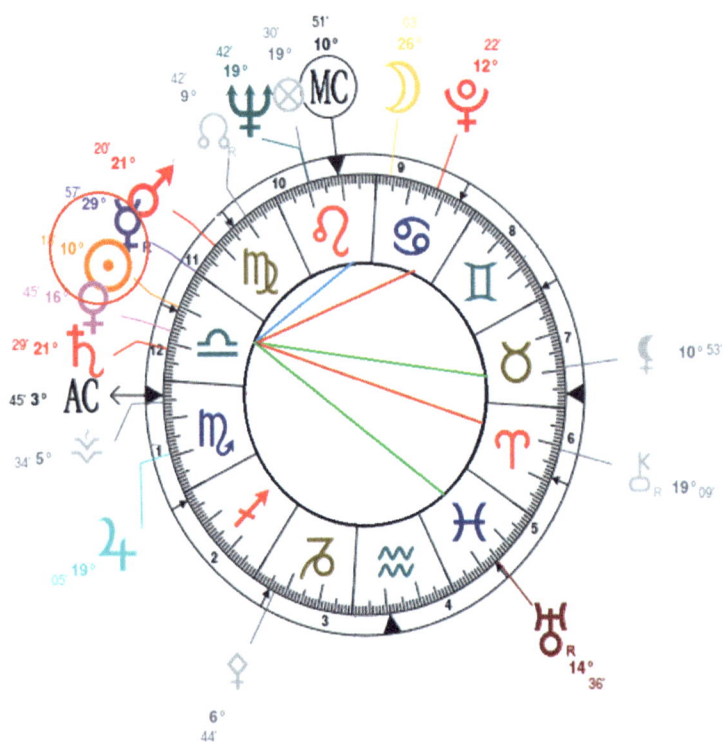

The last step is to blend the collected information to make the reading coherent and useful. That's an essential task. No reading is of any significant value without this last step. Mixing elements from which a profound understanding of the Part of Fortune emerges is the astrologer's mission, one that takes many years of regular practice to master...

Once you've understood the context of this lesson, you can carry on to the next one. Lesson 4 deals with House XI, a very interesting area of the chart from a karmic point of view. Don't hesitate to use the following supplementary sections to guide your analysis of the PF.

Supplementary section

The Part of Fortune in Signs
(The tool for joy and wellbeing)

ARIES
Action is the key to your success. Enterprising, making decisions, strong will, and overcoming irrational fears and prejudices help you succeed. Appreciate others without preconceptions.

TAURUS
Material possessions are at the origin of many desires and as many problems. By cultivating an altruistic approach to earthly needs, you will achieve positive management of the good things of life.

GEMINI
Communication, studies, travel, reading, or writing confer all kinds of personal satisfactions. Learning allows a smarter approach to life by avoiding superficiality and biased preconceptions.

CANCER
The family, home, place of residence, and motherhood should always be sources of joy and satisfaction. Then, they can motivate and promote success as long as a positive approach is the favoured rule.

LEO
Art, love, and the simple pleasures of everyday life are sources of strength to overcome many obstacles and solve many problems in various ways. Put your creativity to work, it will be rewarded.

VIRGO
It is in work and respect of the tasks imposed on you, and by cultivating a healthy lifestyle that you will find the positive motivation to carry on until duty is done and goals are reached.

LIBRA

Thanks to the ability to preserve harmony in human relationships, common wellbeing makes it possible to accomplish much more than on your own. Others become a source of strong motivation.

SCORPION

The need to 'transcend' yourself is expressed in the area represented by your PART OF FORTUNE's position in House. Sublimated sexuality and sharing earthly goods are sources of deep joy.

SAGITTARIUS

It's a strong position that indicates a positive approach to life promoting success in the areas represented by the House where the PART OF FORTUNE is found. Travels, discoveries, studies are sources of joy.

CAPRICORN

This position shows that a great deal of personal wellbeing is derived from work and effort. The satisfaction experienced by building with patience and insight helps achieve the highest goals.

AQUARIUS

Socialising produces a strong potential to succeed and intimate moral and spiritual satisfaction. Helping or guiding others is a source of positive energy despite the obstacles to overcome.

PISCES

God is in all sentient living and his light is warm to your heart. Your relationship with life is a source of great joy when you focus on the brighter side of your soul and that of those around you.

The Part of Fortune in Houses
(Latent potential transferred in the areas of life)

House I (Ascendant)
Personal talents and potential represented by the Part of Fortune in sign have favourable repercussions on the expression of your inner self by promoting a line of conduct that allows you to impose yourself in a generally pleasant and effective manner.

House II
Material and financial pursuits are sources of personal satisfaction that stem from the influence of the Part of Fortune in sign. The good things in life, food, romance, art, music and singing may increase chances of social success and inner satisfaction.

House III
You will get all kinds of positive returns from human relations. Studying, writing, reading, travelling, and meeting people are some of the many means to personal achievement. Deep joys and lasting success depend on our readiness to seize the best opportunities.

House IV
The family, the home, the place of residence are sources of joy and achievement when their importance is realised and assumed. The resulting wellbeing is a source of renewed motivation. The mother or motherhood has a positive influence on personal growth.

House V
Art and all areas in which creativity can be exercised are sources of joy and potential success. Love and affection expressed by close ones motivate positive actions and allow to move mountains when concrete consequences are realised and assumed.

House VI
Self-assertion is derived from work and duty. The need to be of

service to others is essential to generate inner joy and personal growth. Health, medicine, and/or domestic animals are likely to be sources of strong motivations to succeed in various ways.

House VII
Maintaining balance and harmony in personal relationships is a must to produce the inner joy and satisfaction needed to feed the positive energy stemming from them. The potential to self-realisation greatly depends on constructive partnerships.

House VIII
Stripping away from the core values of earthly food is one of the many transcending approaches to your inner wellbeing and personal growth. Money, sex, and the mysteries of life may become strong sources of motivation to regenerate and progress.

House IX
Studies, travel, social interactions, philosophy, and all topics that arouse intellectual interests are sources of satisfaction and potential success. The legal and moral aspect of human relationships motivate positive initiatives with fulfilling results.

House X (MC)
Success and the notion of climbing to the top are sources of positive actions needed to feed the need for inner satisfaction and growth. A positive self-image helps achieve the greatest goals often based on the importance of a prosperous home life.

House XI
The potential to personal success and satisfaction lies in your ability to give to others to relieve them of their burdens so that they can enjoy better days. Nothing stimulates you more than to perceive in the eyes of those you help this spark of eternal gratitude.

House XII
Life is perceived in relation to what we understand and conceive of

the forces governing the universe with the notion of divinity that ensues. If the infinite truth, the light in darkness attracts and fascinates it becomes the upmost source of positive inspiration.

The Regent of the Part of Fortune in signs

ARIES
Show initiative, measured authority and firmness. This will not only allow you to impose yourself, but also to appreciate your capacities and to benefit from them in all circumstances.

TAURUS
Nature's inexhaustible energy potential allows you to recharge your batteries and get the physical, mental, and spiritual strength necessary to overcome obstacles and succeed in your projects.

GEMINI
Express yourself in whatever ways you think are relevant and that you can use best. Inform yourself, study, travel and do not hesitate to reach out to others. Curiosity is a source of discoveries.

CANCER
It is within a stable, warm, and comfortable home that you can draw the necessary strength to carry out your projects and to become aware of your potential, your talents, and your abilities.

LEO
Art may be a source of extraordinary creations if you accept to use your expertise to increase your own talents and inspiration. Appreciation of love will open the secret door to your inner truth.

VIRGO
A meticulous and measured approach to work and health would allow you to detect subtle details that would serve you to fuel your quest for perfection and reveal you real potential to succeed.

LIBRA
Trust your partner and develop your collaborative skills. This will allow you to combine your strengths and qualities with those of your loved ones with whom you will discover the path of truth.

SCORPIO
The attraction for the mysteries of life and the hidden forces which govern this world can lead you beyond the limits you have set for yourself. What you discover will surely motivate you deeply.

SAGITTARIUS
It is perhaps abroad or by cultivating a generous, sincere, and honest attitude that you will succeed in raising yourself high enough so that your inner gaze can discover your true potential.

CAPRICORN
By adhering to sound principles and working to achieve highly desired goals, you will understand the value of life as it should be lived so that the truth is your only and best ally.

AQUARIUS
People, friends, and social causes are likely to lead you on the path to find your inner truth and reveal your best facets. Observe, listen, and take advantage of the most pleasant situation life can bring.

PISCES
To believe is to be convinced without needing proof. What you believe must be cultivated because your intuition and sensitivity can guide you on the path to the truth that will fulfil you.

The Regent of the Part of Fortune in Houses

HOUSE I
This position favours the expression of your inner self and your ability to impose yourself as you really are rather than as others expect you to be. The efforts you make in this direction are likely to bring happiness through authenticity and true interactions.

HOUSE II
This position promotes positive relationships with the material world and the good things it can bring. Money, but also everything related to art, nature, and food, will be a source of success if you accept your potential, talents, and ability to reach the top.

HOUSE III
Your intellect and communication skills in areas relying on contacts in various ways are your best tools to succeed. Learning or teaching may prevail. A sibling may have a positive role to play if you recognise the potential of such relation and its deeper value.

HOUSE IV
It is in the family, home, or place of residence that you can derive the energy and motivation to grow and succeed. From there, you can truly express and make good use of your potential and innate talents. Your mother (or similar person) has a positive role to play.

HOUSE V
It is by becoming aware of your potential that you will be able to express and exploit them. Your creativity will serve you as much as your affectivity. Other's appreciation of your true value is a source of strong motivation. Art or children have a positive role to play.

HOUSE VI
It is through diligent and well-organized work that you can assert and exploit your potential while deriving deep and lasting

satisfaction from the results you obtain. Health-related subjects or innate skills in medicine have a positive role to play.

HOUSE VII

It is in intimate relationships or collaboration with others that you can express and exploit your true potential and succeed in the areas represented by the position of your Part of Fortune in House. Your partners or close collaborators have positive roles to play.

HOUSE VIII

Thanks to your ability to regenerate and question earthly values, you can exploit more effectively your potential to succeed in the areas represented by your Part of Fortune in House. Material, philosophical, or intellectual inheritance plays a positive role.

HOUSE IX

Asserting yourself through studies, and travel, you can gain a worthy position in society. From there, you will exploit your innate potential and talents in the areas represented by the House position of the PART OF FORTUNE. A foreign place may have a positive role to play.

HOUSE X

It is by working to achieve a lofty goal and by cultivating thoroughness and a strong, determined mind that you will be able to harness the potential in areas represented by your PF in House. Your father (father figure) has a positive role to play.

HOUSE XI

Thanks to the positive influence of your social environment, and to your relationships with friends and acquaintances, you will be able to exploit the potential in areas represented by your PF in House. Human interaction has a major positive role to play in your life.

HOUSE XII

It is by cultivating a spiritually elevated attitude and by devoting your inner strength to the good of others that you will be able to harness the potential in areas represented by your PF position in House. A spiritual guide has a positive role to play in your life.

Lesson 4

Link to the video: https://youtu.be/MU8ILnwi5OY

House XII

In this lesson we are going to deal with House XII. There are 12 Houses around the zodiac. House I is the Ascendant and House XII is the last House. But House XII precedes the Ascendant or House I and, as such, it represents what laid in the past, before the baby was born. So, it represents the period during which the baby was in the mother's womb in preparation to be born. Further than that, it also represents the 'past incarnation' and, more than the past incarnation in its entirety, it represents the atmosphere, the period during which the person was alive and dealing with all the situations, problems, and joys of life then, during that previous incarnation.

So, House XII is a very interesting subject, as far as I consider karmic astrology anyway. It is my opinion, because, to me it reveals many interesting facts to know and discover when analysing a chart on the basis of karma.

You can rely on House XII to provide precise and significant information about the person's previous incarnation. That is what we're going to investigate now in this fourth lesson.

As I just mentioned, House XII represents the past period of incarnation. Have a look at the example chart on the following page. From this chart, we can understand quite a lot about House XII.

First of all, we assess the position in sign because it corresponds to a certain period in time, the atmosphere, and everything that may have become important for the person in that previous incarnation.

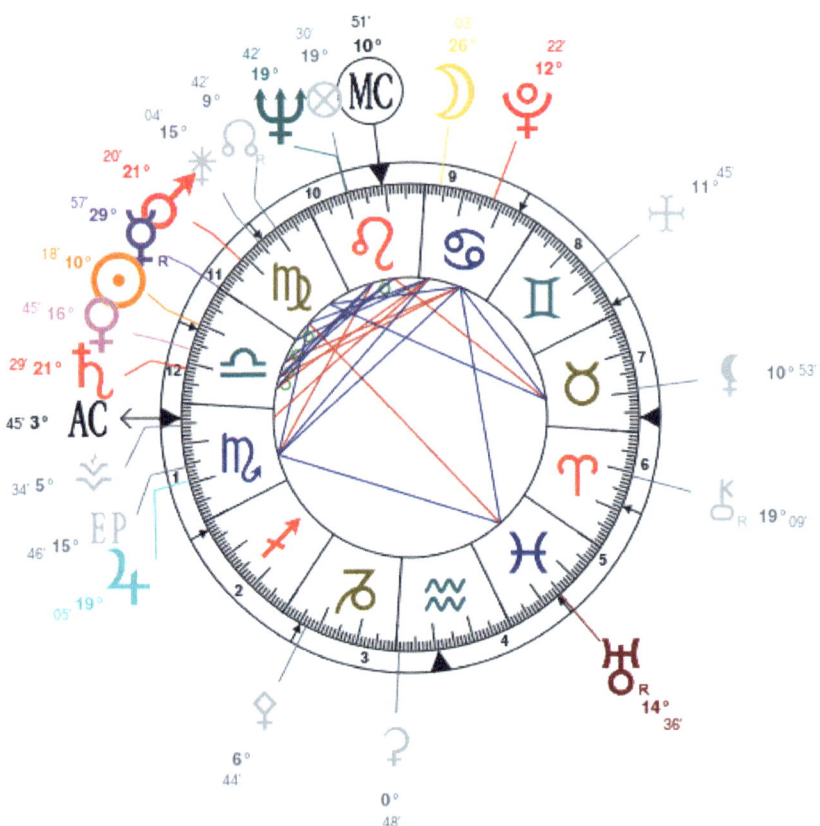

From a karmic point of view, the theory is that we bring back what we went through in a previous incarnation as far as our own individual life is concerned, but also as far as the social (historic) period is concerned.

In the example chart, House XII begins in Libra, the sign of justice. It represents the need to preserve or restore harmony, balance, and by extension, wellbeing. Thus, having House XII in Libra indicates that the person went through a very interesting period as far as the evolution of justice and the preservation of harmony and equity were concerned.

Then, we need to go a bit further than that by having a look at the planets that may be in House XII. In this chart, we see the Sun, which actually is not in House XII, but stuck on the cusp of House XII. It is only about one degree away from the cusp of House XII.

When you're in a situation like that, you must always wonder if the time of birth is exactly right, because the Ascendant and all the Houses cusps progress or regress by one degree every four minutes in time. It means that if you were born four or five minutes after or before the time that was recorded then, the Ascendant and all the other Houses cusps would move by one degree either way. That can make a difference. That is why, when we have a position of a planet or other element very near the cusp of a House, we must consider that this planet or element belongs to both Houses concerned.

In the example chart, the Sun would belong to House XI because it is in House XI, but also to House XII, because it is conjunct the cusp of House XII.

That's interesting because in karmic astrology, the Sun represents the nature of power, the quest for being powerful. It indicates that this person, in their previous incarnation, most probably held a high position in society. Perhaps this person was a judge for example, because we've seen that House XII is in Libra, and the Libra influence has to do with justice. Knowing that this person was born under the sign Libra, increases the potential to bring back unconscious memories of the previous incarnation when this person was in power or help a prominent social status.

This position therefore indicates that this person probably strives to preserve as much as possible what he or she considers as being just and unjust to find the right balance to preserve or restore harmony and wellbeing...

Venus and Saturn are also in House XII. Venus represents love and creativity. It represents what is nice, the good things of life, good food and carnal pleasures, sexuality, and sensuality.

That's interesting because next to Venus is Saturn, and Saturn does not represent joy as such, it represents limitations, constraints, and everything that is difficult, and not really nice to deal with. It represents fate, obstacles, difficulties, and of course, with Saturn in House XII, it indicates that this person is bringing back the unconscious knowledge that life was not meant to be easy. This knowledge or conviction may become a tool with a positive influence on the ability to deal with difficulties. However, it can also produce a degree of negativity in the way this person deals with love (Venus) and power (the Sun).

In astrology, House XII represents 'what' we tend to hide, or 'where' we tend to hide. In the example chart, House XII is inhabited by Venus, Saturn, and the Sun. The Sun represents light, Venus represents creativity, love, and anything that is nice, Saturn represents difficulties. This tends to indicate that this person hides in a secret, private, or secure area comparable to the foetal area before birth, the mother's womb, where the baby feels protected, and safe. Later in life, when one feels unwell, the need to be alone motivates the choice of a special place. It can be a room, the child's room, or it can be any other place, a physical place, or a psychological, or mental place.

That place where we tend to hide ourselves from the madding crowd perhaps, and hide what we don't want to show, what we are not prepared, or not ready to share with other people is represented by House XII.

Whatever the gift may be, if it is kept locked in a cupboard or other secret and safe place, it becomes worthless. Therefore, that beautiful tool, or whatever it is, loses its fundamental value. With time, we even tend to forget that it has ever existed, we forget that we have that potential, that we have that special talent, that innate gift, that ability to obtain such concretely positive results. We have locked it in so well perhaps because at some point in our life, we felt that we had to hide it, to protect ourselves, or to protect what we had received, what belonged only to us...

House XII is a very interesting area of the chart. From a karmic point of view, Saturn represents what the person is bringing back to this present incarnation as far as difficulties and the notion of not being easy (life wasn't meant to bet easy...) that is represented by this planet. Next to Venus, which represents love, affection, creativity, and the good things of life, it may indicate that this person is holding back or unable to enjoy the good things of life represented by Venus.

Then, the Sun in House XII indicates that the strength of the person, which was a major asset in the previous incarnation, is there also to help the person shed some light and open the cupboard so that what is hidden comes true somehow, to benefit the person's life...

If you don't find any planet or other element in House XII, there is still a House XII in the chart. Of course, you cannot analyse the positions of the planets in this House, but you can rely on the position of the **ruler of House XII**.

In the example chart, House XII is in Libra. According to my personal approach of astrology, Libra is represented by Vesta. And where is Vesta in this chart? It is in the Ascendant, stuck on the cusp of the Ascendant. It means that there is a strong link between that person's karma and the present life, an awareness and natural connection with what happened in the previous incarnation. There is an innate potential to bring back valuable information that can help that person deal with the karmic load spontaneously and effectively to preserve or restore inner harmony and wellbeing (Vesta and Ascendant)...

Next, we need to know in what sign the ruler of House XII is. In the example chart, it is in Scorpio and, as seen above, in House I. In Scorpio it indicates that there is a need to go deep into what is felt as being true. The truth. What is just, what is unjust. These notions have a deep influence on the inner nature of this person who may have gone through difficult situations, as seen earlier, in the previous incarnation. They may be associated to death because death is linked to Scorpio through Pluto. Pluto is the ruler of Scorpio, as you know...

Furthermore, we must consider the aspects to the ruler or rulers of this House. In this chart, we see a square between Vesta and the Moon. **However, it is what is called a false or hidden aspect**. Why? Because the Moon is in Cancer, and Cancer is a water sign just like Scorpio. Water signs, Air signs, Fire signs, Earth signs, are all complementary. So, this square here indicates that there is an obstacle. The obstacle is emotional, it may have to do with family background, it may have to do with what is represented by House IX, where the Moon is. House IX represents foreign countries or places, it represents the law, justice, and the philosophical perception of life.

We have seen that House XII is in Libra, a sign that represents justice and Vesta represents harmony. So, the notion of harmony, and the search for balance and wellbeing, are somehow in conflict with the emotional nature of that person. Such tendency needs to be dealt with, of course, and explained, in order to obtain more information about what we can derive from such configurations and to, of course, improve the life of the person concerned through the reading of the birth chart from a karmic point of view...

From the example chart presented earlier, we are now going to go through what needs to be done step by step.

—First of all, the position in sign.
   House XII in Libra.
—The planet/s in House XII.
   Venus, Saturn, and ~ the Sun
—The ruler or rulers of House XII in sign.
   Scorpio
—The ruler of House XII in House.
   House I (the Ascendant)
—The aspects.
   A conjunction with the cusp of the Ascendant.
   A ~ square with the Moon (false, hidden aspect)

Note that a 'hidden aspect' is often not assumed. Therefore, if this person is told something like 'your emotions are strong but in contradiction at times with the search for wellbeing, balance, harmony, and happiness', that person may reply: 'No, no, no, I'm not like that, I'm not like that at all!' because they may not realise it. It is a hidden aspect; it is not something obvious…

The importance of the regent/s of the ruler/s

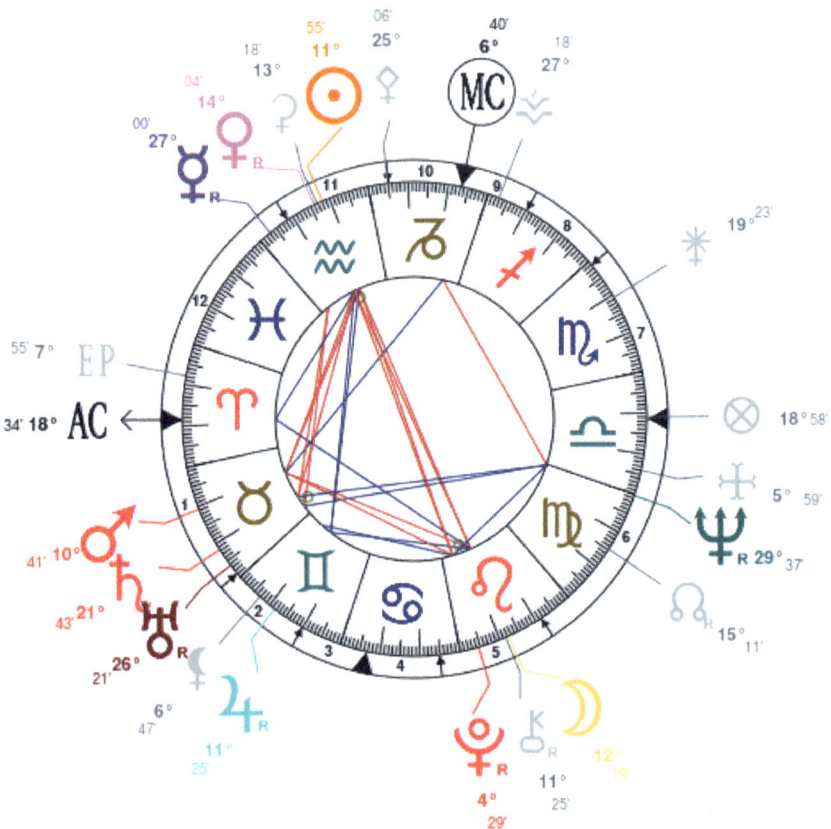

The chart presented above shows that House XII begins in Aquarius, and it overflows Pisces, with the Ascendant's cusp in Aries. Therefore, Aquarius and Pisces belong to House XII. Not Aries. Even though there is a part of it that belongs to the space occupied by House XII, we don't include it, it is not included in House XII because that is the sign where the Ascendant begins.

In the example chart on the previous page, House XII has two rulers, Uranus for Aquarius, and Neptune for pieces. Uranus is in Taurus, is in House I, and Neptune is on the last degree in Virgo in House VI.

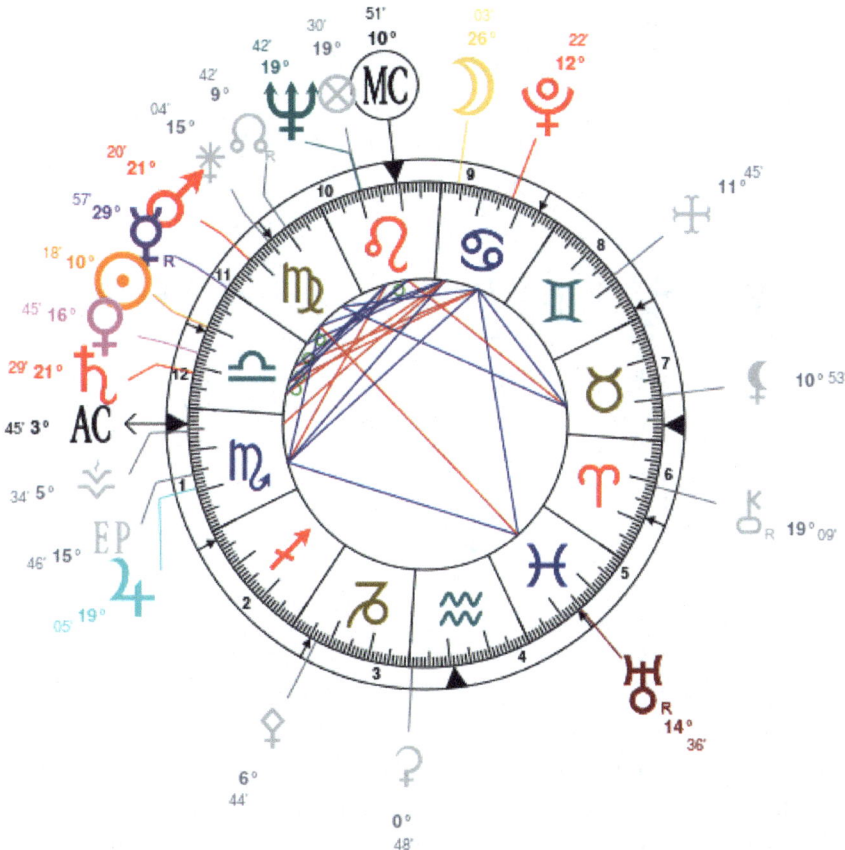

This is the example chart that we discussed earlier in this lesson. The Sun is in Libra, and the ruler, Vesta, is in Scorpio, in House I. So then, the regent of Vesta is Pluto, ruler of Scorpio. Once again, the regents are the planets ruling the signs where the rulers are.

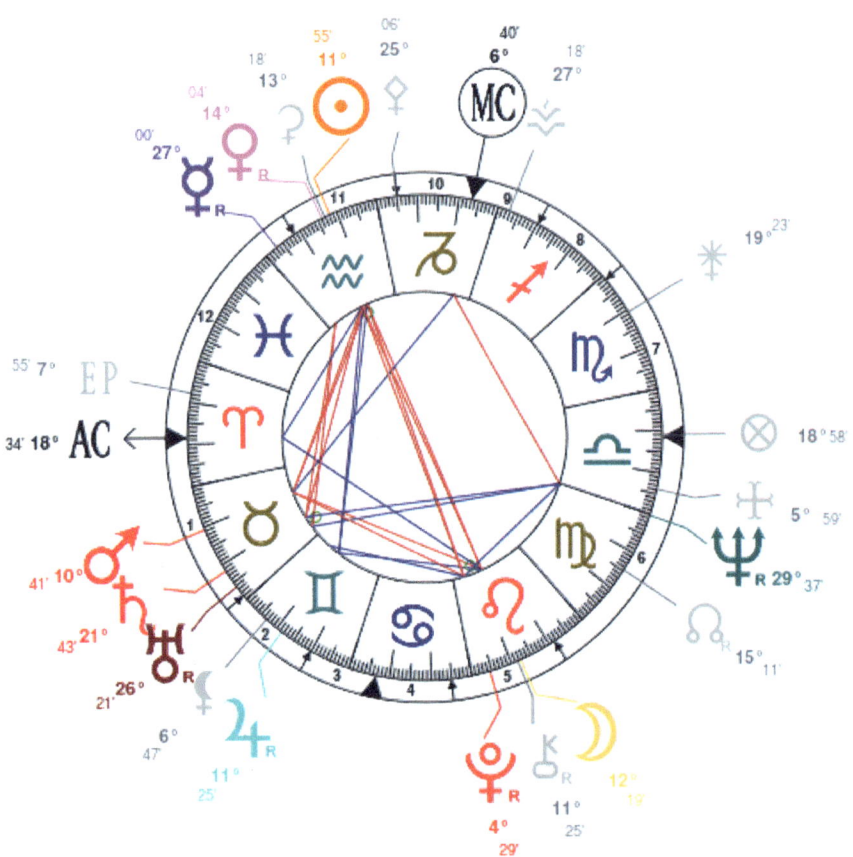

In the chart above, Uranus is in Taurus. The ruler of Taurus is Venus, as you know. So, Venus becomes the regent of Uranus. Next, we need to find where Venus is. It is in Aquarius. Therefore, in Uranus's sign. It means that there is an 'exchange of residence' for both planets. Venus is at Uranus's place and Uranus is at Venus's place. That is an important piece of information as far as the meaning of this configuration is concerned.

Uranus is square Venus, an interesting to analyse. It also forms a square with the Sun. These aspects indicate how the person is dealing with the karmic load brought back from the previous incarnation.

Then, Neptune… Neptune is in Virgo on the last degree in Virgo, at 29° 37′   in Virgo, a sign ruled by Chiron in my practice of astrology. Chiron next to the Moon in Leo. Leo is a sign represented by the Sun. The Sun is in Aquarius, a sign represented by Uranus, etc.

These configurations show a strong karmic link with what this person is going through in the present life. However, the 'solution' is represented by Neptune because, even though there is a square with the MC, there is very beautiful trine with Saturn and Uranus. There is also a sextile with Pluto. The Moon being close to Pluto, we can say that there is an element of positive energy flowing from Neptune through Chiron, the Moon, and Pluto.

Therefore, the solution lies with Neptune. Neptune represents the connection that we all have with the spiritual dimension of life. That is what this person needs to cultivate in order to free themselves from the burden brought back from a past incarnation…

The other chart shows an easier karmic load because there is only one ruler, Vesta. It is here in Scorpio, a sign ruled by Pluto. Therefore, Pluto becomes the regent of Vesta, regent of the ruler of House XII. Pluto in Cancer involved in beautiful aspects with Jupiter in Scorpio and Uranus in Pisces. There is also a sextile with the North Lunar Node, therefore a trine with the South Lunar Node, and another sextile with Lilith. All that is helping this person deal with the karmic load despite difficult aspect with the Sun, Venus, and Saturn, indicating, because Venus and Saturn are in House XII, that this person must have gone through romantic or sentimental turmoil. It may be the death of someone close, someone dear, and a burden to carry, perhaps because this person felt responsible for the loved one's death, or for the problems in the relationship…

As you can see, the analysis of the positions of the rulers and of the regents helps a lot to understand the deeper meaning of House XII in a chart.

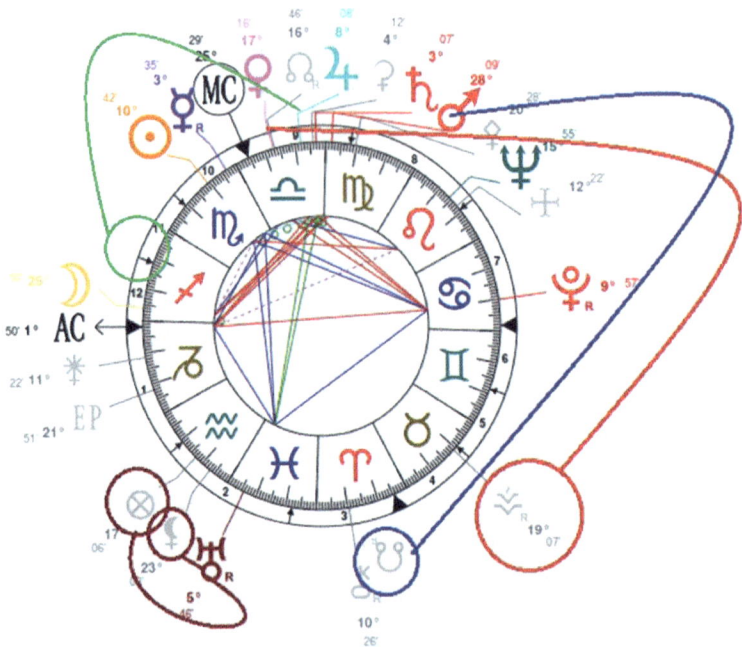

Have a look at the chart above. It shows the links to track rulers and regents. In this chart, House XII is in Sagittarius, a sign ruled by Jupiter. Therefore, Jupiter becomes the ruler of House XII. Following this line from the cusp of House, we find Jupiter. It is in Libra, a sign ruled by Vesta. Following the red line from Jupiter, we find Vesta. It is in Taurus, a sign ruled by Venus which we find in Libra, a sign ruled by Vesta. This gives a lot of importance to Vesta because it is the regent of Jupiter and Venus.

The same process is applied to the Part of Fortune. It is in Aquarius, a sign ruled by Uranus, which becomes the regent of the Part of Fortune, and the regent of Lilith, also found in Aquarius...

That's how you have to proceed. When the chart is drawn, do what I have done, to help you find the way to the regents and the rulers. Begin with the ruler of House XII and find the way to the regent of the ruler of that House.

Recapitulation

Let's summarise what has to be done. Note that what follows applies to all planets and other elements you analyse in a chart. I call it the '*family tree*'.

Starting with the element to analyse, put it at the top of this family tree. It can be in House XII, it can be a planet, it can be the Part of Fortune, or any other element.

Going down from the top to the left of the tree, take note of the position in sign. It represents the behaviour according to the element in question. If it is Venus, if it is in Aries, it means that the love principle represented by Venus expresses itself through the energy of Aries.

Then, of course, the position in House shown in the pink circle to the right of the tree. It represents the area of life where the energy of Venus in Aries, for example, is going to behave and be used in accordance with its position in sign.

Then, the fact that this element (Venus for example) is in a sign means that the ruler of this sign becomes the regent of Venus.

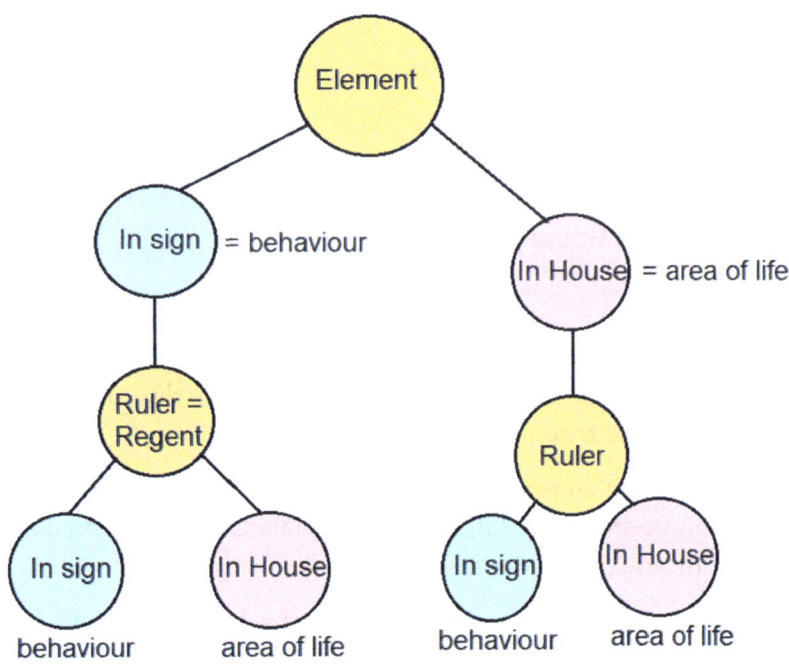

That regent, of course, is in a sign, and it is in a House as well. To the left of the tree. The regent in sign (behaviour) and in a House (area of life concerned or affected).

To the right of the tree, we return to the House. It has one or more ruler(s) depending on the size of this House in the chart. The ruler is in a sign (behaviour) and in a House (area of life concerned or affected).

Once you understand that, once you visualise this 'family tree', then it becomes easier to analyse a chart and to understand all the links that are created, not only through this family tree, because you also have to consider the aspects, not included in the incomplete family tree presented above.

The aspects represent more branches of this family tree from which other elements are going to come into play. That is why the reading of a birth chart is quite complicated. To the beginner, taking one element after the other, and then synthesising the data derived from the family tree guarantees better results.

Never lose sight of the primary values of the planets. For example, despite what House Mercury rules in the chart, it always represents mental activity. Venus always represents love, affection, and creativity. The Sun always represents the energy, the vital energy. The Moon represents the emotions, and so on.

This is the end of lesson 4. Lesson 5 deals with the influence of Chiron, a very important element, as you will soon discover.

In the following pages I have written a series of aphorisms designed to help you analyse the positions of House XII and of its rulers in signs. Once again, do not copy/paste, use your own words to describe the role of this House in a birth chart, and don't forget to look at the regent of the ruler of House XII, as explained in this lesson.

Supplementary section

House XII or its ruler in signs

In ARIES

Your previous life was marked by war, aggressiveness, hostility, or martial rules. The army attracts or repels you due to unconscious past-life memories. In the present life, the management of aggressiveness and anger is a source of occasional challenges.

In TAURUS

Your previous incarnation took place in a rather peaceful context, in a rural environment, concerned with agriculture, good food, visual arts, or music. You value the good things in life, but you also depend on what you imagine that love and money can bring.

In GEMINI

Your previous incarnation took place in an urban area. Moving, communicating, and travelling were in vogue, but you didn't take enough advantage of it all. In the present life, writing, speaking, learning, or teaching, are sources of inner challenges and setbacks.

In CANCER

Your previous incarnation was marked by a social context that relied essentially on family, patriotism, or tribal values. In this life, motherhood, emotional needs, and homeland may become a source of setbacks and inner uncertainty or confusion.

In LION

Your previous incarnation took place in a monarchical context. Art, painting, and sculpture were major values. You were very sensitive to richness and pleasure and sought approval from others. In this life, managing ego and social success may be sources of challenges.

In VIRGO

Your previous incarnation was more proletarian than aristocratic. Hard work and daily routine prevailed. Hygiene was a major issue that may have left deep karmic scars. In the present life, managing your responsibilities and your health is part of the main challenges.

In BALANCE

Your previous incarnation took place in an artistic context, from where you brought back an innate acting talent. Justice also played a dominant role in the way social life was organised. In the present life, fairness and morality are some of your challenges.

In SCORPIO

Your previous incarnation took place in a difficult context, marked by epidemics, degradation of social and sexual values, death, occultism, or witchcraft. In the present life, these areas attract or fascinate you, but are a source of confusion and inner doubt.

In SAGITTARIUS:

Your previous life was led in a rather bourgeois environment. Faraway places, long journeys abroad, studies, religion, and laws prevailed. In the present life, these areas attract and repel you at the same time, producing occasional inner doubt and confusion.

In CAPRICORN

Your previous incarnation took place in an authoritarian social context led by a dictatorship or other monarchical, or tyrannical regime. Senior officials imposed draconian rules that produce in the present life inner doubts and a lack of trust in hierarchy.

In AQUARIUS

Your previous life was marked by a revolutionary social context. Great discoveries have prompted radical changes in various ways. Freedom and independence are today still particularly important values. However, they cause occasional inner doubt and confusion.

In PISCES

Your previous life took place in a context where religion and the spiritual aspect of existence largely dominated. From the period of the Great Crusades or the beginning of the Christian era perhaps, you brought back a latent awareness of the presence of the soul that causes occasional inner doubt and confusion.

supplementary section

The ruler of House XII in Houses

In House I
In your previous life, you essentially acted to preserve or to protect your personal interests at the expense of your higher self. Selfishness and egotism prevailed as a means to survive. Today, you must promote the development of your inner potential and exploit your talents in a concrete and positive manner.

In House II
In your previous incarnation, the money and diet were sources of various disorders not necessarily due to a lack of means. It seems that you missed out on proper education to better manage your affairs. In this present life, you have to show rationalism regardless of your wealth and your attraction to luxuries.

In House III
In your previous incarnation, fraternal relationships, and communication with those around were marked by confusion that manifests itself in this present life by unspoken and grey areas in important human interactions. A karmic link with a loved one may become a matter of spiritual challenge or trial.

In House IV
In your previous incarnation, family relations, motherhood or maternity were the cause for various disorders. In this life, these sectors require special efforts to remain objective and rational, understanding that any family dispute has a spiritual meaning to it and a degree of inner discovery that should not be neglected.

In House V
In your previous life, sentimental life, art, and creativity were the

sensitive sectors in which confusion or lack of concrete motivation caused various complications. A determined, Cartesian, and compassionate approach is now necessary to accept and deal with occasional trials and take advantage of them on a spiritual level...

In House VI
It seems that you have been quite laxist about work or other duties in your previous life. Poor hygiene may have caused health issues due to living in rather unhygienic conditions. In the current life, you may develop a tendency to either neglect or be overly concerned with cleanliness, work, and daily duties for spiritual reasons.

In House VII
In your previous life, the management quality of private and social relationships was not exemplary. You relied too easily on others rather than on your own ability to succeed. That's perhaps why you're struggling to impose yourself in the present life, in major relationships or important social or professional partnerships.

In House VIII
Sexuality, inheritance, money, death, and parallel sciences played a troubling role in your previous life by creating a morbid approach to your own existence. You found refuge in the occult without understanding its deeper value. In the present incarnation, your challenge is to manage your darker side in a realistic and open way.

In House IX
The law, foreign countries and cultures, politics, and higher education prevailed during your previous life. It seems that you leaned on the social system in place from which you took advantage, neglecting its deeper value. That is probably why you find it difficult to deal with these areas in this present incarnation.

In House X
Notoriety, hierarchy, paternity, personal ambitions, and

leadership strongly motivated you during your previous life. However, you relied more on the system for assistance than you acted to impose yourself. That is why your social, professional, and family situations need to be bravely tackled in the present life.

In House XI
In your previous life, social acquaintances, friends, and many favours obtained from such relationships created dependence on others and a lack of personal initiative that deterred your potential to succeed. In the present incarnation, you need to concretely define your landscape, both human and geographical.

In House XII
Illness, hospitals, prison, isolation, and religion prevailed in your previous life, creating dependence on theories that induced the idea of fatality instead of motivating you to understand and free yourself from unrealistic beliefs. In the present life, a rational and enterprising spirit is necessary to deter misfortune and succeed.

Lesson 5

Link to the video: https://youtu.be/8c1cRiA7tzo

Chiron

Chiron is a very important element to take into consideration when you analyse a chart on a karmic point of view as you will find out in this lesson.

Chiron is an asteroid. It orbits between Saturn and Uranus, and it takes about 50 to 51 years to complete a full circle around the Sun and, as you can see on the drawing below, the orbit of Chiron is quite elliptic compared to that of Saturn, Uranus, and Neptune. Chiron's orbit is distorted by the attraction of Saturn and Uranus. It is trapped between the two giant planets and astronomers say that it could be a comet residue rather than an asteroid as such.

That's why Chiron takes a lot longer to transit through some signs. In Aries, for example, it will remain eight years, and in Virgo it's going to take Chiron about two to two and a half years to transit through the sign.

Such differences make it difficult to guess the sign where Chiron is in a birth chart based on the year of birth. That's because Chiron's orbital period of 50.71 years does not correspond to twelve equal periods of transit in each zodiac sign.

Chiron has a very interesting influence in karmic astrology. It represents the *inner doctor, the healer, the guide.* That applies to health but it has other meanings on a spiritual point of view.

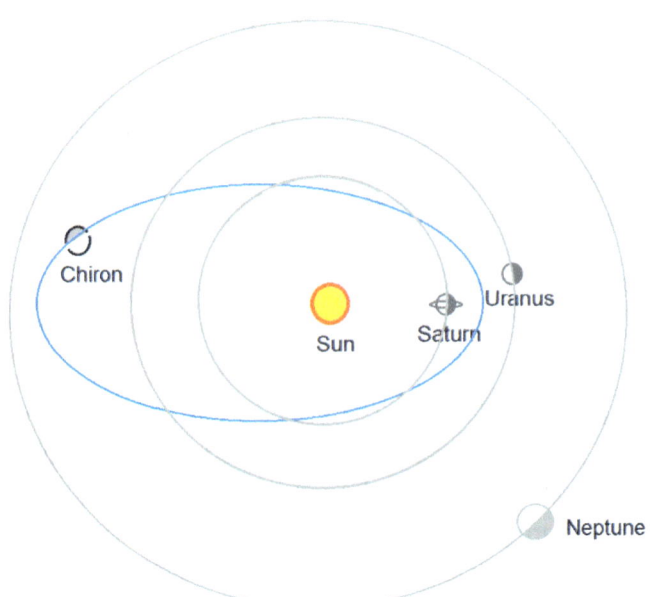

To begin with, let's investigate what Chiron can tell us about our health. Our karma or karmic load also includes a health record. There is something registered or saved somehow from our past incarnation. A period during which perhaps we haven't behaved as we should have to preserve or restore optimum state of health.

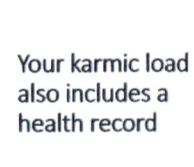

Your karmic load also includes a health record

Chiron represents what we have done right or wrong in the previous life and what we brought back in the present life on a health point of view. It represents a potential pathological terrain for the development of some illness that we could avoid if we are, of course, conscious of what Chiron is telling us in our birth chart. It also shows what organ or function we should look after more than others.

Apart from our health Chiron also represents challenges that we need to overcome, to deal with. It represents a complicated. Our own efforts, of course, make all the difference and, if we can overcome the obstacle, we are rewarded by succeeding in an area of our life where we were not expected to succeed.

However, Chiron is not acting alone. It needs to be referred to in accordance with the other elements in the chart.

The first element is the sign in which Chiron is found in the chart. It has to do with health naturally, but it also has to do with the challenges that we need to overcome, to deal with, as seen earlier.

Let's have a look at what we can derive from the position of Chiron in a zodiac sign.

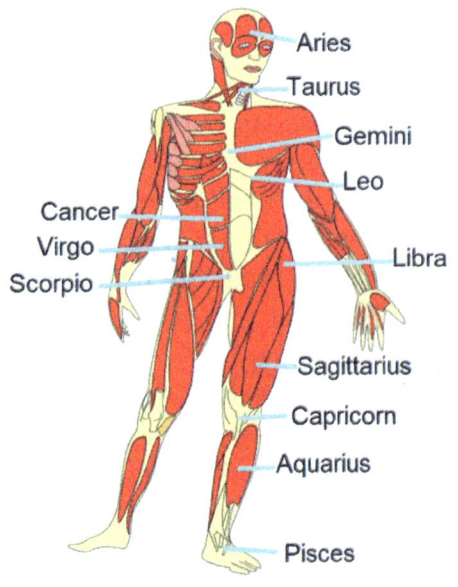

Here is a human body on which the signs have been written from the top to the bottom. Each sign is linked to a part of the body.

Aries represents the head.

Taurus represents the throat and the neck section.

Gemini represents the chest and lungs, the shoulders, and the arms.

Cancer represents the stomach, which is the primary digestive system.

Leo represents the heart, the spine, and the vision of the eyes.

Virgo represents the intestines, the secondary digestive system.

Libra represents the pelvis and, of course, the urinary function and kidneys.

Scorpio represents the reproductive organs and colonic function.

Sagittarius comes next with the thighs and the hips.

Capricorn represents the knees and the bone structure as well as the skin and the joints.

Aquarius represents the calves and the lower section of the leg.

Pisces represents the ankles and the feet.

Chiron indicates how it performs according to the sign in which it is

found. However, Chiron does not act alone. Its influence also depends on the other planets and elements in the chart that may have a determining incidence on Chiron's primary influence in a sign. Such interaction must be considered as a provider of valuable information about Chiron's truer influence and deeper influence.

After having taken into consideration the sign in which Chiron stands, we need to also have a look at the House where Chiron is positioned.

Take note that Chiron can be in a sign a House that begins in the previous sign. Chiron would still be in the House in question but not in the sign where the House begins. All the same, Chiron does affect the House where it is positioned. It does so according to the derived influence of the sign. Just like other planets, Chiron's nature relies on the energy of the sign where it is found.

And of course, just like it is done for the Part of Fortune, the Lunar Nodes, and Lilith, Chiron's *regent* in a sign and in a House is used to broaden the information gathered to better understand its role in our present incarnation in relation to the previous one.

Let's take an example to help you understand how to proceed and what you can achieve from the process of analysing Chiron.

In this chart on the following page, Chiron is in Aries, in House VI which begins at 25° 51′ in Pisces and ends at 20° 20′ minutes in Aries. Chiron is in Aries but it's not in this House VII, it is in House VI.

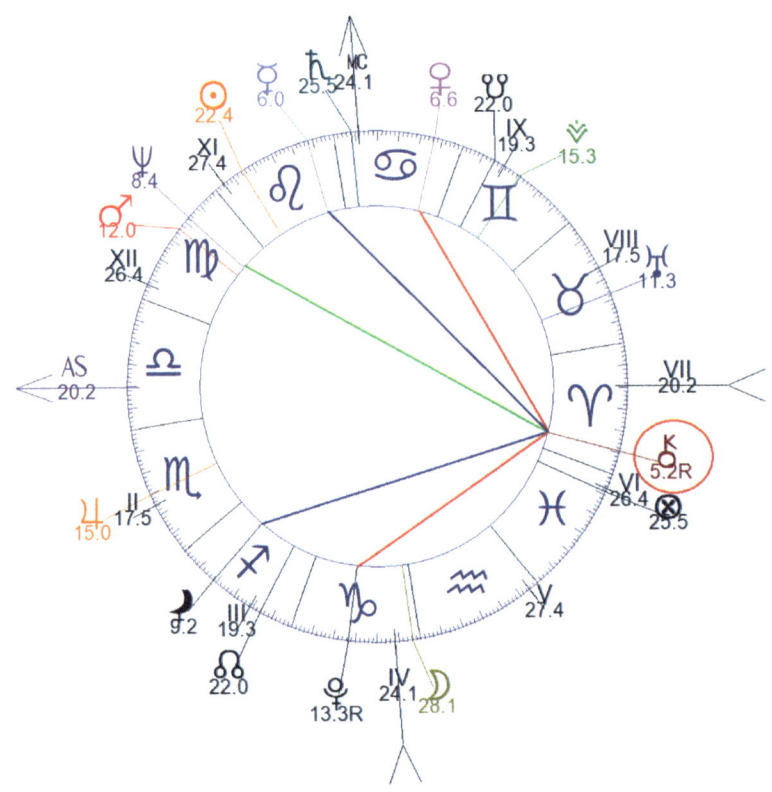

Chiron's regent, Mars, is in Virgo. That's interesting because, as you know, perhaps if you read my *'Astrology for a Better Life'* book, Chiron is Virgo's ruler in the way I practise astrology. It therefore means that Mars is in Chiron's sign Virgo, and Chiron is in Mars's sign, Aries. There what we call an 'exchange of residence' which makes the influence of both planets much stronger.

There is also an inconjunct with Mars and another one with Neptune which forms a conjunction with Mars. It is an important aspect because Neptune represents House VI which begins in Pisces. That makes Neptune quite important because it is in Chiron's sign, Virgo, next to Mars that gives strength and combative energy to this configuration. It also indicates that the person needs to be careful about anything that could affect the head, the skull, the nose, the orbits of the eyes, the mouth, the teeth, the skin, and the bones around the head, the jaws, and the ears may become a source of sudden incidents.

Meanwhile, Mars, the regent of Chiron is in Virgo which represents the secondary digestive system, the intestines, of course, it has a troubling influence that increases bowels and digestive conditions brought back from a past incarnation during which mistakes were made. Feeding habits may have become a source of health concerns to the extent that this person died from Cancer of the digestive system. Coming back in the present incarnation, it is not surprising to note that this person suffers from weakness and various disorders of the secondary digestive system.

Mars and Neptune are in House XI which represents the social environment. Their presence in this House means that the social environment can become a source of problems. The influence of other people is likely to affect food choices and preferences with negative consequences on the secondary digestive function.

The question is to determine how to take care of Chiron's influence and bring this person to understand that there is something to do to preserve the secondary digestive system from potential ailments.

Then, we must analyse the other aspects. There is a square with Venus. It indicates a link between this person's sentimental state and health condition which can deteriorate suddenly with violent and painful symptoms shown by the influence of Mars and Aries where Chiron is. Mars represents the speed with which incidents or accidents can happen, especially when this person is under sentimental or effective pressure.

However, we see in the chart a very nice aspect, a trine from Mercury. Mercury represents the brains and what we can get out of our ability to think and to analyse. Therefore, if this person is conscious of the influence of Chiron, then perhaps the potential disturbances will become easier to deal with it. Indeed, understanding a problem often helps find the solution.

There is also a trine from Lilith. That's an interesting aspect because Lilith represents that which we ignore or want to ignore. It is the darker zone, a place, or areas of life where we know there is something troubling enough to hold us from going there. We may be afraid, or we couldn't be bothered to find out what is wrong. Such an approach makes things more blurry, uncertain, and confused.

Lilith is in House II (House 2) forming a trine with Chiron. It shows the ability to bring light on whatever could otherwise become a source of problems. House II represents food and feeding habits. Thanks to the trine from Lilith, this person understands and sees what is wrong in the way certain people feed themselves, thus avoiding wrong habits. But keep in mind that this person can still be influenced by other people as we have seen earlier.

The last aspect is a square with Pluto, which could be worrying because Pluto represents death. Of course, we know that we all are going to die one day, that's for sure, but the later the better and if we can stay in good health until very late perhaps until the end of our life it's even better. Pluto represents what needs to be destroyed therefore it represents what we need to consciously get rid of, to avoid problems because Pluto can represent the risk of being contaminated. Food poisoning can be represented by Pluto and all sorts of contamination are represented by Pluto.

Pluto is in House III which represents our brains, our intellect. We have seen earlier that Mercury is playing a very positive role. It makes it possible for this person to understand what may become a source of health issues. Pluto in House III indicates that there is a need to abandon or destroy a certain way of thinking that could become a source of problems rather than a source of solutions. Solutions are represented by Mercury; problems are represented by Pluto.

But of course, we can go even further in this reading because Pluto is in Saturn's sign, Capricorn. Therefore, Saturn should also be considered. Then, Mercury in Leo, the Sun's sign. The Sun is in Leo, in its own sign. Venus is in the Moon's sign, while Mars and Neptune are in Chiron's sign. And of course, Lilith is in Jupiter's sign.

That means that we can connect, as we go along analysing one aspect or two or three or four with other planets, with other elements in the chart. That is because a planet has a regent according to the sign in which it is positioned and that regent is in another sign which also has a ruler which becomes the regent of that regent, and so on. I agree that it may be quite complicated for the beginner to proceed in this way, but the more you get used to analysing an aspect and an element in the chart in this way you will go a lot further, a lot deeper into the reading of such chart.

Now, let's have a look at what we have to do to understand and analyse the position of Chiron as such and in relation to any other element or planet around the chart. Here is how to proceed.

1 – Take note of the position in Sign

It reveals the type of energy derived from Chiron and what needs to be done to deal with past life issues.

2 – Take note of the House position

It reveals where (in what areas) challenges are likely to be most operational.

3 – Take note of Chiron's regent in Sign

It reveals the manner of expressing and using past life experiences in the present incarnation.

4 – Take note of Chiron's regent in House

It reveals where (in what areas) challenges expressed by Chiron in Sign are likely to be transferred.

5 – Take note of the aspects involving Chiron

They reveal how past life motivations interact with various elements in the present incarnation.

6 – Take note of the aspects involving Chiron's regent

They reveal how the derived influence of Chiron in the present life interacts with other energies.

Step by step

Let's see each step one by one to better understand how to proceed. In the example chart reproduced on the following page, you can see that Chiron is in Aries. The position of Chiron in a sign reveals the type of energy derived and what needs to be done to deal with past-life issues. In Aries it means that challenges and the tools to deal with such challenges depend on behaviour in presence of such challenges. In Aries it has something to do with energy, with aggressiveness, perhaps combativeness. The way the person acts and reacts is perhaps too strong. It indicates that in the past life something violent happened. That's why this person is unconsciously on the defensive, in reaction to what happened in a past incarnation.

Understanding that the tendency to be violent, too spontaneous, or too aggressive and impulsive affects the way this person feels and deals with life in general has health-threatening consequences surely helps deals with such tendency.

The organs and function concerned

We have seen that Aries represents the head and that Mars, regent of Chiron, is in Virgo, a sign representing the secondary digestive system, the intestines. If Chiron is the 'inner doctor' how can it help? It can help through understanding what Chiron means in the chart, not forgetting the aspects involving Chiron. They play a major role to decrease or increase its primal influence.

The House Positions

Then, there is the House where Chiron is found. In this case Chiron is in House VI where it affects the area of work and health represented by House VI. It is therefore likely that this person becomes interested in medicine and anything that has to do with health and will perhaps work in health care or medicine. It also indicates that this person may always feel unwell all the time.

However, this position of Chiron in House VI must be deepened. Simply knowing that Chiron is in this House gives only basic information on its real influence. To enrich the reading, we need to turn to the regent of Chiron.

The Regent

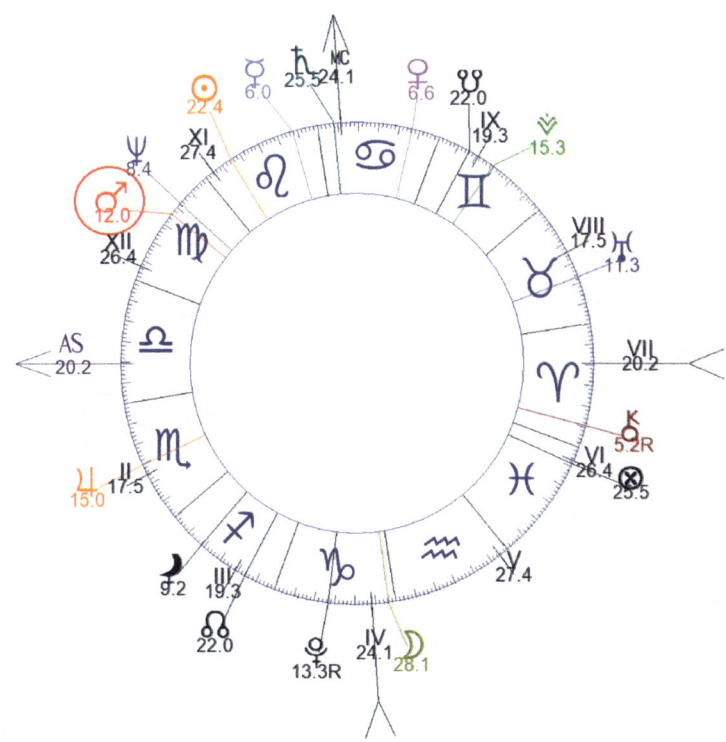

Chiron is in Aries. Mars is its regent. It is found in House XI. This position transfers the karmic challenge represented by Chiron in the person's social life and friendship. Chiron represents extra effort to make in order to overcome an obstacle. We don't know what this person does for a living, what sort of work, but from the position of the regent in House XI we can see that this person's karmic challenge has to do with the social environment. It therefore indicates that there may be an innate interest medicine and various forms of therapies to help people, to cure people. Mars shows a very intense motivation.

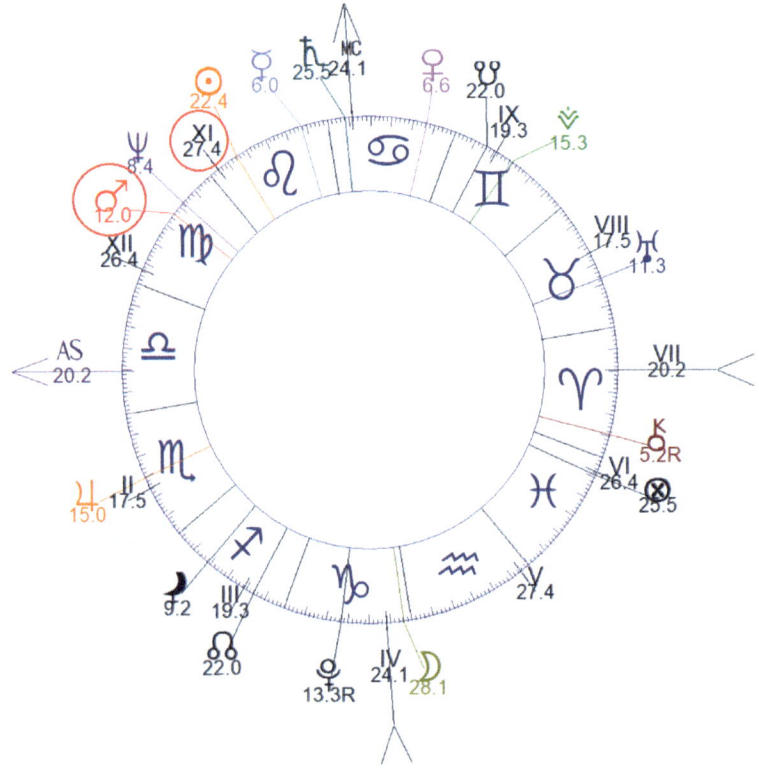

Next to Mars is Neptune. It represents the spiritual dimension of life, and it rules House VI in Pisces. This position of Neptune next to Mars puts the emphasis on the fact that this person could choose to work in the medical area to help people who would, in return, become useful to themselves and others again.

Now let's turn to Chiron's regent it reveals the manner of expressing and using past-life experiences in the present incarnation. Mars is Chiron's regent as we've seen earlier. It is in Virgo in House XI. This means that this person's past life experiences can be put to good use in the area represented by House XI, namely, the social environment. We have just seen that it was probably the case and that this person had to overcome many professional and relational challenges. Sustained effort is necessary to obtain the best results on a social point of view (House XI).

Next to Mars is Neptune, ruler of House VI as we've just seen earlier as well. Neptune's role is therefore to put a lot more emphasis on the idea that this person needs to put a lot of effort to get right health-wise but also humanely wise with others around, because on a human point of view and on a social point of view, or on a philosophical and spiritual point of view, the influence of Chiron linked to the regent next to Neptune in House XI, itself linked to House VI is, of course, representative of what this person needs to do to overcome the global challenge of this present life.

Although already mentioned, the position of Chiron's regent in a sign and a House is important to take note of seriously. Chiron is in Aries which should immediately trigger in your reading the fact that it is linked to Mars. Therefore, the first thing to do when you see Chiron in a sign is to instantly have a look at where the regent is because its position will give you an important information that may actually contradict what is derived from the position of Chiron in sign.

Health is a very important area to analyse, of course, but the position of Chiron's regent in House XI has a different meaning and not the same purpose as if Mars, regent of Chiron in Aries, was in any other House. That is because every House represents certain areas of life affected by the position of the regent of Chiron, and also by the position of Chiron itself.

The Aspects

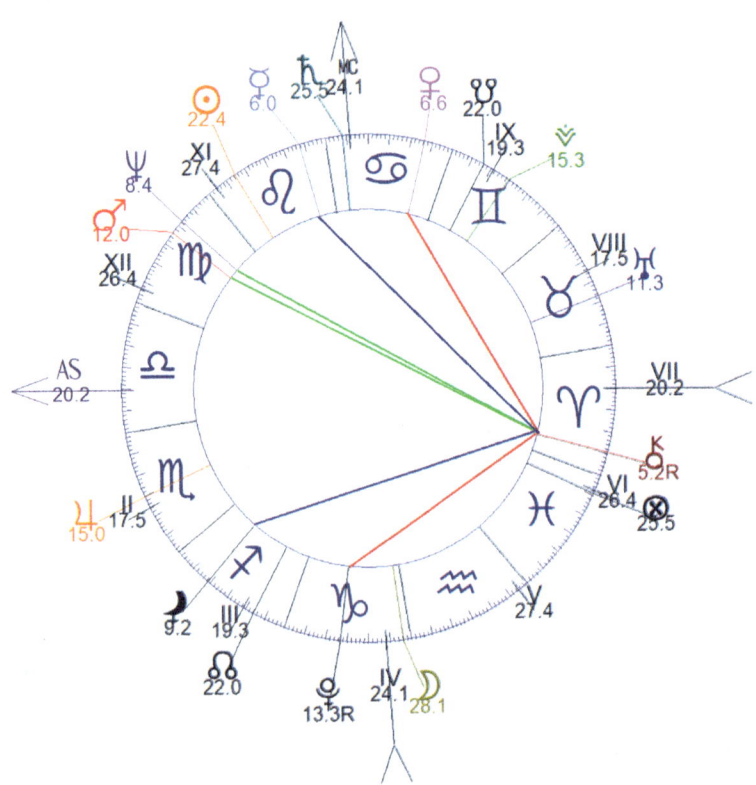

Then, of course, we need to have a look at the aspects. We saw earlier that there was a square with Venus, a square with Pluto, a trine with the black Moon or Lilith, a trine with Mercury, and two inconjuncts, one with Neptune and one with Mars.

Every aspect needs to be analysed individually according to the plane or element concerned as well as according to the position of the planet or element concerned.

In the chart displayed on the previous page, Venus is in Cancer, Mercury is in Leo, Mars and Neptune are in Virgo, and Lilith is in Sagittarius, while Pluto is in Capricorn.

Venus is in House IX, Mercury in House X, Mars and Neptune in House XI, Lilith in House II, and Pluto in House III. They all come into play individually and in relation to the other planets to do a proper reading of the influence of Chiron.

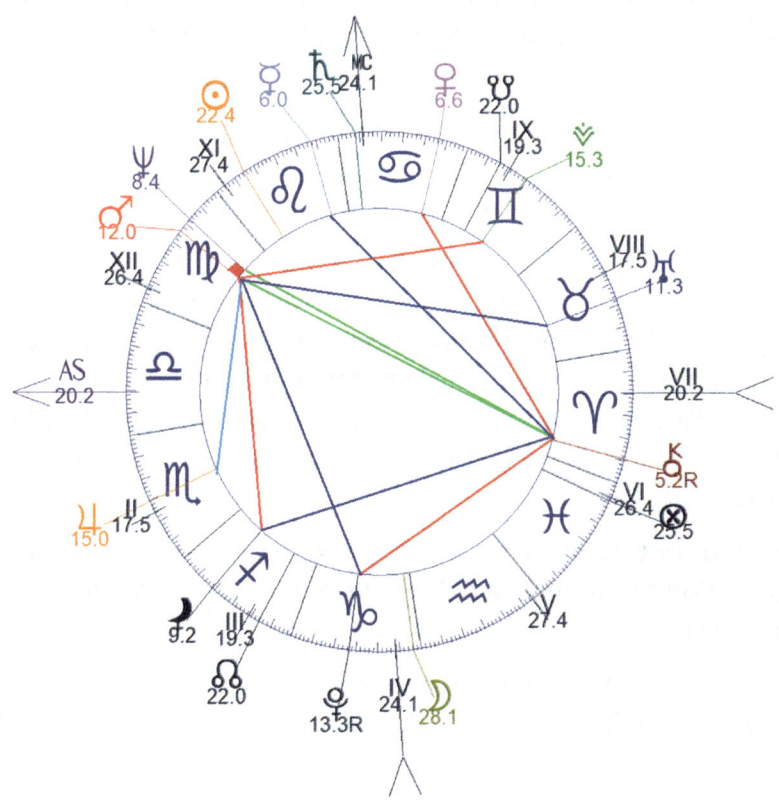

Simultaneously the regents must be considered. For example, the regent of Mars is also involved in various configurations (aspects). We must take note of the aspect involving Mars with the other elements and planets around the chart.

Not forgetting, of course, the aspects involving Chiron in sign with other elements and planets around the chart. The information provided is richer, thanks to the global number of aspects to analyse. Their meaning is very useful to understand more precisely how this person must deal with the influence of Chiron. Is a major influence and the way you analyse it can be very superficial or very deep depending on how you approach it. The deeper the better, and the greater information you will derive from Chiron's influence in a birth chart.

In fact, what you see in the birth chart about Chiron and its regent, including the aspects is a very important source of information to realise a correct, precise, and useful reading.

To complement this lesson and make it more useful for you, use the **supplementary sections** included to analyse the positions of Chiron in signs and in Houses. You will find the meanings of the aspects involving Chiron in my '**Astrology for a better life**' book. Don't hesitate to get it from the Amazon website in your country to further the analysis of the influence of Chiron in any chart you choose to analyse.

Last, but not least, you will have to synthesise the bulk of information to obtain the right picture of what Chiron means in a birth chart.

This is the end of lesson 5. In the next lesson, you will learn how to deal with the influences of the slower planets from Saturn to Pluto.

Supplementary section

Chiron in signs

CHIRON in ARIES

The earthly karmic mission represented by Chiron in this sign is linked to the challenge of dealing with and controlling impatience, impulsiveness, and precipitation. Analysing the possible consequences of hasty decisions and reactions allows for fewer mistakes to be made and fewer incidents to deplore. Excessive authority often hides a latent inferiority complex resulting from painful incidents or accidents dating from the first year of life. Health issues tend to centre around the head: the skull, the hair, the ears, the teeth, the skin of the face or the orbits of the eyes.

CHIRON in TAURUS

Hat the Earth provides in food and other good and beautiful things, are part of the karmic mission. Money and personal possessions become a source of concerns and ruminations. The pleasures of life attract and repulse at the same time. The challenge is to accept the concept of the physical confronted to the metaphysical. It also seems important to decide if the present is more important than the future to which it is tightly attached. Health issues are likely to affect the neck area, the throat, the lips, the mouth, as well as the breasts and the thyroid glands.

CHIRON in GEMINI

Communication is one of the main challenges to take on as a karmic mission. There is an obvious need to master the art of talking, writing, and sharing thoughts and ideas. The intellect allows us to reflect and ponder on facets of the self to tackle a natural tendency to loftiness or arrogance. A shallow approach to human relationships can lead to moral errors that affect popularity negatively. Knowledge is a quest issued from an intellectual inferiority complex resulting from early-life limitations. The brains and the lungs are the main areas for health concerns. The nervous system and the upper limbs may also be

CHIRON in CANCER

Family, home environment and motherhood are essential parts of the karmic mission. Deep personal feelings are marked by unpleasant situations resulting from difficult relationships with loved ones. There is a need to better control emotions to avoid an inner sensation of vulnerability with its unfortunate consequences in personal life. Analysing irrational emotive reactions allows better understanding of their origin. Childhood holds the answers to irrational fears and anxieties. The stomach, the lymph, the body fluids, and the left eye may become health concerns.

CHIRON in LEO

Ego is a question of survival; it is essential to being alive and aware of the self. The need to be the centre of attention initiates various behaviour patterns that may produce contrary effects to what is anticipated. Analysing the reasons behind a tendency to 'show off' is useful to understand a suppressed inferiority complex caused by unpleasant childhood situations and events. Artistic creativity helps exteriorise the awkward and distasteful. The cardiovascular system, vision in the right eye, and the spine may become causes for health concerns.

CHIRON in VIRGO

Work and duty are essential parts of the karmic mission. An innate interest in health and medicine may motivate a career or profession. Serving, guiding, and helping others are a source of constant inspiration. The ability to observe, analyse and diagnose contributes to success. It can also enhance a predisposition to excessive worry about health, hygiene, and physiological wellbeing. Focusing on details tends to conceal the broader picture on which they depend. The digestive function, the intestines and the nervous system are causes for health concerns.

CHIRON in LIBRA

Partnerships and personal relationships are essential to life on Earth. Karmic ties have a profound influence on behaviour patterns. Wanting to preserve harmony may result in hurtful disappointment. Looking after a partner's or relative's health requires strength and self-abnegation to the benefit of the person's wellbeing. The earthly mission is to preserve, protect or restore close relationships and to serve as a mediator to get people to connect genuinely. Unstable urinary and kidney functions, and lower back pain may become sources of health concerns.

CHIRON in SCORPIO

Death, sex, the obscure, and the mysteries of life are a source of philosophical interest and motivation to shed light on the unknown. There is a tendency to sink deep into sombre phases, perhaps due to an innate need to discover what it is 'on the other side'. Unfortunate events may leave deep scars in the heart and the soul. There is an attraction to morbid phenomena and an innate interest in strange and unusual experiences. The physical body can spontaneously reject what it does not like and what it does not want. This process favours physical regeneration.

CHIRON in SAGITTARIUS

To study, to teach, to travel, to learn, and to share thoughts and ideas are essential to the achievement of life's karmic mission. Struggles with formalities and conventions are due to philosophical differences that cannot be resolved. There is a need to heal and to lead others to a better life. Being profoundly attached to moral and intellectual principles may attract adverse outside reactions. Feeling misunderstood enhances the desire to convince by becoming an example to others. The liver, blood circulation, and blood pressure may cause health concerns.

CHIRON in CAPRICORN

Social status is important. There is a karmic need to prove that getting to the top is possible and accessible to the brave at heart and the hard worker. Education plays a major role to enhance or annihilate self-esteem and innate gifts and natural potential. Climbing the social ladder may take longer than most but determination and patience help to get to the top. Time should be considered an ally, not an enemy, even though difficulties, setbacks, obstacles, and delays require more energy to get the job done. The bones, the joints, the knees, and the skin may become health concerns.

CHIRON in AQUARIUS

Socialising and social work are parts of the karmic mission. There is a need to help others in various ways. Involvement in humanitarian activities may be a means of achieving the ultimate goal of life. Rational observation helps find better solutions to the most difficult problems and situations. A natural tendency to criticise is derived from an innate ability to pinpoint defects and focus on how to repair them. Restoring, mending, and curing complement the various potential derived from Chiron in this sign. Blood circulation, the lower limbs, and the nervous system may become sources of health concerns.

CHIRON in PISCES

Beliefs are an essential part of the human's mind. Connecting with the soul or with the spiritual dimension of life to which we all belong, allows for a deeper understanding of the reasons behind life on this planet. The ability to link the physical body with the higher spirit promotes efficient rational holistic treatments to many ailments. To embrace universality rather than individuality enhances natural talents and potential. Intuition is a guide, a source of inspiration. There is great sensitivity to music and to subtle vibrations.

Supplementary section

Chiron in Houses

In House I
Health may be a cause for concern during the early years of life. Later, an interest in medicine or health care may develop and contribute to a career choice. The ability to analyse and need to understand, allow diagnostics in various areas. Position comparable to Chiron in Aries.

In House II
Food may be a source of concern during childhood. Later, the material aspect of earthly life and money may have been considered either as poison or as medicine. Earning a living in therapy may be a way to heal oneself somehow. Position comparable to Chiron in Taurus.

In House III
When the first cry is a cause for concern, later, communicating may require more effort. A profound need to understand, to investigate and to analyse develops. It may be a way to heal oneself from forgotten traumas during childhood. Position comparable to Chiron in Gemini.

In House IV
The first encounter with the mother is essential for the newborn to feel 'at home' and safe. If this moment is not right somehow, one may develop an uneasy feeling within or about family life. Health may also play a part in domestic difficulties. Position comparable to Chiron in Cancer.

In House V

Love is essential during childhood. Later it makes private relationships come easy, enhancing creativity and the appreciation of the good and beautiful things of life. There is a strong need, but a tendency to doubt and worry too much. Position comparable to Chiron in Leo.

In House VI

Work, duty, and health are major concerns. There is a karmic need to take up the number of responsibilities imposed daily. Chiron is strong in this House. A tendency to worry, making problems worse than they really are, is observed. Position comparable to Chiron in Virgo.

In House VII

If personal relationships are uneasy or ambiguous, it is perhaps due to the quality of the first encounter with other people shortly after birth. Later, it can make it awkward to relate to others freely as a need to observe and analyse prevails. Position comparable to Chiron in Libra.

In House VIII

From the moment of birth, we know that we are going to die. The concept motivates the way we lead our earthly voyage. If health is a major concern during early childhood, later, it creates a tendency to worry too much about minor issues. Position comparable to Chiron in Scorpio.

In House IX

Learning is an essential part of life. The more we know, the more we want to discover. When the potential to study is disrupted during childhood, it creates intellectual awkwardness and an insidious need for knowledge and adventure. Position comparable to Chiron in Sagittarius.

In House X
The father image is a factor of motivation to succeed in life. If adverse circumstances temper the perception of this major influence during childhood, it creates awkwardness and doubts that may alter the ability to climb up the social ladder. Position comparable to Chiron in Capricorn.

In House XI
Friendship and social relationships are important. If adverse circumstances during childhood hinder the natural need to relate to others, later it produces a lack of self-confidence or social interest, favouring tedious rather than joyful ties. Position comparable to Chiron in Aquarius.

In House XII
What happens during the gestation period resonates deeply into the foetus in formation. Cellular memory stores uneasy information that can create strange reactions linked to forgotten events. A strong need to connect with the past ensues. Position comparable to Chiron in Pisces.

Lesson 6

Link to the video: https://youtu.be/7BxCs0GQxQA

Saturn and the trans-Saturnian planets

Welcome to lesson number 6 which is going to deal with the influences of the slow planets. The first one is Saturn, then comes Uranus, followed by Chiron (we've already seen what Chiron meant in the previous lesson), then come Neptune and, last one but not least, Pluto. Let's begin with the study of the potential influence of Saturn in a chart around the zodiac, and in other aspects as you will find out by watching the video and reading this lesson.

- Saturn: 29.5 years

- Uranus: 84 years

- Neptune: 165 years

- Pluto: 248 years

Saturn takes 29 and a half years to complete a full circle around the zodiac. Uranus needs around 84 years to complete the same circle, Neptune takes 165 years, and Pluto, the father's planet from the sun, takes 248 years to circle the zodiac. But for now, let's begin with the influence of Saturn.

As seen earlier, Saturn's cycles last for about 29.5 years. Saturn represented death before Pluto was discovered in 1930. Today, it represents old age, experience, and wisdom. It also represents the karmic connotation of some particular events occurring during one's lifetime. Hence, Saturn's cycles have a profound meaning in various ways that we will discuss in this lesson. Saturn represents what we deserve, the results of our personal efforts and determination. It does not represent the presents that life offers us occasionally. We will discuss that as well.

29.5-year cycles

Saturn represented death before Pluto was discovered in 1930.

Since then, it represents old age, experience, and wisdom.

Events associated with Saturn have a deep Karmic connotation.

Saturn's cycles have a profound meaning in various ways.

Saturn represents the results, not the presents.

With Saturn, we receive what we deserve, no more, no less.

The House ruled by Saturn is primarily concerned.

About Saturn's cycle

You see in the example chart on the following page that Saturn is in Pisces at 19 degrees. It is in House VII (7) which begins at 17° in Pisces. Every time Saturn comes back on its original position, a new cycle begins. Saturn's cycles are quite long. They last for 29 and a half years. That means that the first one occurs when the person is 29.5 years of age. It actually begins to have an influence between

28 and 30 years of age depending on the position of Saturn in the chart. The following one occurs 29.5 years later, and so on until the third one. There's very rarely a fourth return of Saturn because of the time that Saturn takes to revolve around the zodiac.

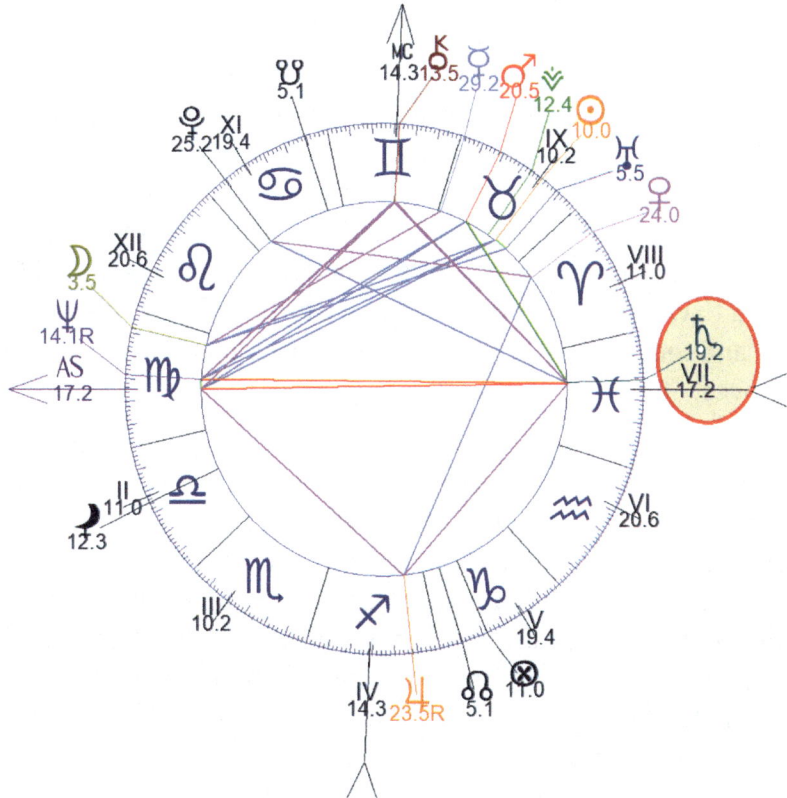

Every time Saturn comes back onto its original position or on any other element or planet position in the chart, it brings back something that has its roots in what happened during the previous occurrence. In the case of the first return, there is no 'before' but in a way that 'before' is in fact the beginning of life because a person's birth chart is drawn for the day, time, and place the person was born.

Therefore, in the example chart, it is the position where Saturn was when the person was born.

You can see that this position is connected to the Ascendant and Neptune, Chiron and the Midheaven, there is also one with Jupiter and with House IV (4) the Nadir as we call it in astrology.

In fact, every time Saturn comes back on its original position or other elements mentioned, it brings back something that has to do with what happened when this person was born and with what happened during the years that succeeded the moment of birth. Saturn's first return is a crucial moment. At around 29 or 30 years of age, the person is ready to get involved concretely in life according to what happened before, since birth, through schooling, primary and secondary education, work, and various other personal experiences.

In fact, very often, at that age, important events happen. It may be the birth of the first child, the purchase of the first home, or the moment when you get involved on a career path. Very often, what is decided then, when Saturn comes back onto its original position, has long-lasting repercussions that can last for 29 to thirty years. Bear in mind that the karmic connotation of Saturn plays a very important part as well. What we can see in the example chart, if Saturn has to do with karma, is that it is in House VII (7) which indicates that there is a karmic load to carry as far as personal relationships are concerned, collaboration, partnerships and other forms of relationships represented by House VII. And because it is in opposition with Neptune and the Ascendant, and all the other aspects that I mentioned earlier, they allow to extract from this position of Saturn valuable information to help the person understand their life path and how to readjust to benefit from the influence of Saturn rather than feeling blocked or slowed down by it. This is unfortunately very often the case. Indeed, Saturn represents the amount of work and effort needed to surmount obstacles and to deal with our karmic load.

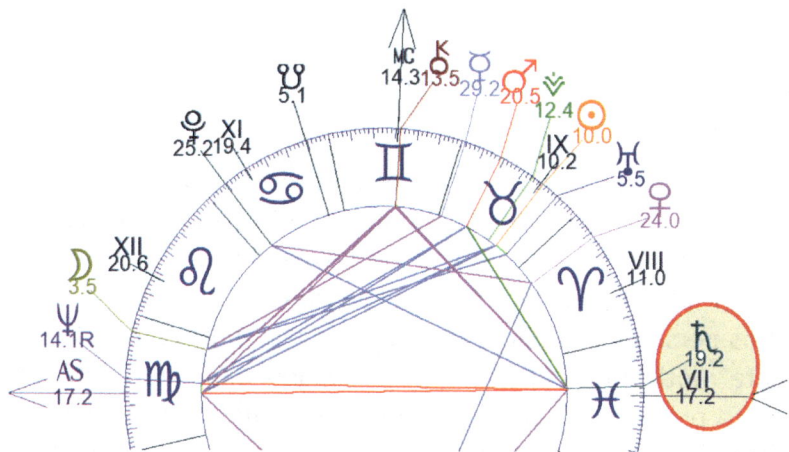

It is important to consider Saturn from the sign and House position points of view. In the example chart, we see that it is in Pisces, a sign that represents beliefs, the usual human need to believe in something, in God or in anything else. Therefore, it represents the spiritual connection with the spiritual dimension of life. When Saturn is in Pisces, then, it indicates that this connection is based on a very rational type of approach which may make it more difficult for this person to adapt quickly and to have the necessary intuition to help determine the best action to take in times of crisis. With Saturn in Pisces, it seems that the intuition has to be linked to a rational response. Religion may have a limiting influence on this person's ability to expand and to progress.

And then, we see that Saturn is in House VII which represents partnerships, marriage, personal, social, or professional relationships. Whatever links us to others is represented by House VII. So, the fact that Saturn is in this House indicates that this person has to carry a karmic load as far as personal relationships in general are concerned. Saturn may make it difficult for this person to adapt to any kind of important partnership because Neptune represents the spiritual dimension of life as well as the idealistic approach to what partnerships. It is important, of course, to be in harmony with the other person, or other people depending on the type of partnership, but when Saturn is in House VII it seems to make it more difficult.

From a karmic point of view, it means that this person may have to repay a debt somehow, a situation that reflects on the type of partnership this person is going to get involved in so that the debt is repaid. That is happening unconsciously, of course, but it could make this person quite dependent on the relationship. It indicates an innate motivating need to give more and more in a concrete manner to protect and be there all the time and perhaps assume the other person's responsibilities.

Saturn in House VII indicates that there is some weight to carry, which could be the partner or the partnership. The load usually becomes heavier with time. The older this person is going to get, the heavier the load is likely to be felt. Therefore, Saturn in this House means that there is work to do in this important area of life. Indeed, although the partner may be a 'karmic load', this person could also have a restricting influence on such partner or partners. The rational approach to the relationship may be felt as pressurising and limiting to the other person involved. Saturn here shows that there is a karmic need to let the relationship expand in a freer, more spontaneous, and lofty way.

Saturn's regent

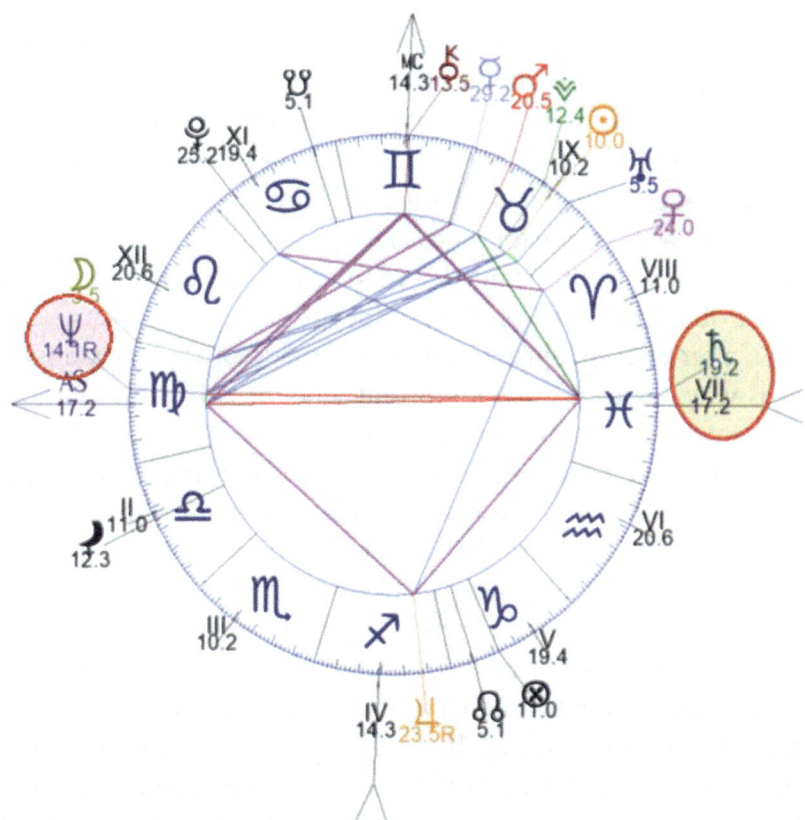

Question: 'Can you see Saturn's regent? Can you determine what planet it is? You know how to recognise a regent now. So, what planet is it? ...

Saturn is in Pisces, and we know that the ruler of Pisces is Neptune. In the example chart, Neptune is in Virgo in House XII (12), near the Ascendant. The fact that Saturn is in Neptune's sign which becomes Saturn's regent, and the fact that Neptune is in opposition with Saturn is a configuration we will explain later. For now, we must investigate what Saturn's regent in Virgo and in House XII means. It intensifies what I've explained earlier about being rational.

We know that Neptune does not represent the rational side of our personality, but rather the intuition and the inspiration, therefore what is intangible and immaterial. At the same time, Virgo is an Earth sign, which makes Virgo-born people rather rational or at least who need or want to be rational. However, there is a Pisces influence in a Virgo person because Virgo and Pisces are opposite signs. As such, Neptune has a very strong influence on Virgos because it is the ruler of their opposite sign. Pisces represents Virgo's alter ego; it represents the other side of their personality. That is why Neptune is so important when it is found in Virgo. It means that although this person concerned by the example chart may have a very rational and concrete, perhaps materialistic approach to life, there is also something very spiritual in some way which is emphasised by the position of Neptune in House XII. Why? Because House XII is 'naturally' linked to the twelfth sign, Pisces. Neptune, ruler of Pisces in House XII, increases its influence to make this person intuitive and perhaps prone to religious beliefs of some sort? But, because Neptune is in House XII, beliefs are kept inside, not spontaneously shown. This person is not prone to sharing personal beliefs with others due to a need to appear rational, a behaviour emphasised by the rising sign or Ascendant in Virgo. The Sun in Taurus which is also an Earth sign increases the rational side of this person.

To synthesise the karmic load represented by Saturn in House VII, it can be said that there is a strong link with a past incarnation represented by House XII. It means that what this person brings back from a previous incarnation resides firstly in the Sun's position because it rules House XII in Leo, and secondly in the moon's position in Virgo, also in House XII. And of course, it also resides in

Saturn's regent, Neptune, ruler of House VII and positioned in House XII.

From this position of Saturn, we understand that what this person is going through on a partnership point of view is strongly linked to a karma. We can also assume that this person most probably lives with someone who has shared this person's life in a previous incarnation during which this person has perhaps not behaved appropriately to preserve the relationship. Both have therefore come back in this present life to fulfil and succeed where they failed previously.[2]

Aspects involving Saturn

Although this needs to be done simultaneously with what has been explained above, the aspects involving Saturn and the aspects involving Saturn's regent also need special attention.

Let us begin with the aspects involving Saturn itself. However, remember that when you analyse a chart you must let your eyes explore it rapidly. Therefore, when you analyse the influence of a planet or other element, the sign in which it stands has a ruler that becomes the regent of the element or planet in question.

In the chart below, Saturn forms an opposition with Neptune and the Ascendant. There is also a square with Chiron and House X, the Midheaven (MC), a square with Jupiter and one with the Nadir (House IV), a sextile with Mars, and a trine with Pluto.

---

[2] *I have known these people for over 30 years, and I can assess the karmic nature of their relationship.*

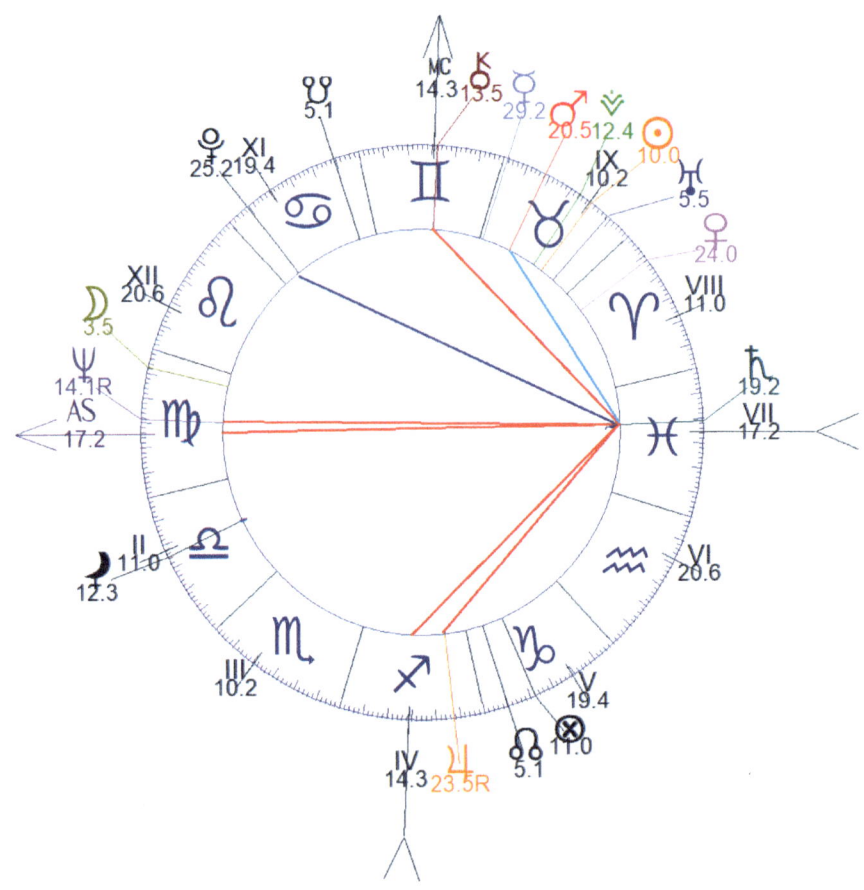

Such aspects need to be analysed separately and together because if you analyse them separately you will find that some aspects contradict others. In the chart above, for example, the opposition between Saturn and Neptune, makes Saturn weaker because Neptune interferes with the concrete influence of Saturn which represents the rational, sceptical, analytical side of the personality. It also represents prudence with its detrimental incidence on spontaneity. Rationalising intuitions that Neptune represents, as well as the natural connection with the spiritual dimension of life, the opposition in this chart means that the person may behave in a rational way, being quite strict and authoritarian. At the same time, Neptune represents moments in this person's life when rationality disappears allowing all kinds of excesses and involvements in regrettable relationships shown by the rulership of Neptune over House VII in Pisces.

To illustrate the fact that some aspects contradict one another, the opposition of Neptune makes Saturn somewhat weaker, but the trine with Pluto makes Saturn a lot stronger, not forgetting the sextile with Mars in Taurus making Saturn even stronger. This example shows that it is imperative to blend all aspects together to realise the best portrait of the person analysed. Of course, we know that we all have inner contradictions. So, at times this person behaves through one configuration, like the trine from Pluto which will help recover after an illness, or to surmount difficult obstacles. That is because Pluto represents the potential to long-lasting efforts and sufferings. At the same time, Mars indicates positive energy, will power, and determination to obtain what is desired or wanted. Therefore, at times this person can be extremely efficient and combative, and other times the aspects between Neptune, Jupiter, and Chiron make it more difficult because they make Saturn weaker, and when Saturn is weaker it is difficult for a person to assume daily responsibilities effectively.

Aspects Involving Saturn's Regent

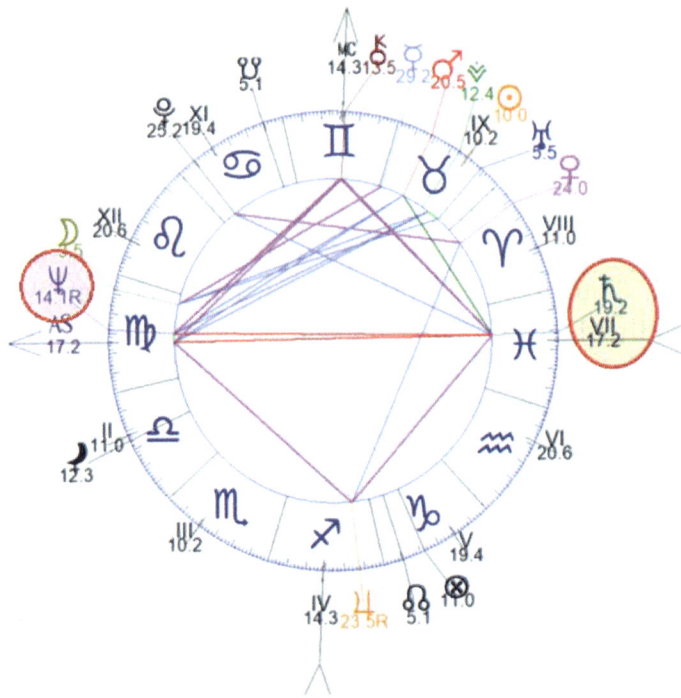

In this chart you can see that the regent is Neptune, as we have seen earlier. It is in House XII, in Virgo. It forms the same aspects with Saturn as far as the squares are concerned. And there is a trine with the Sun and another one with Vesta, which is next to the Sun, an interesting aspect because it amplifies the potential for Saturn to be what Saturn is, namely the rational side of our personality. All this means that this person can be rational and totally irrational at times, because of the Saturn/Neptune opposition. But Neptune is in harmony with the Sun and Vesta, indicating a potential to harmonise, thanks to the person's intuition, belief in being good, being a good person, being a spiritual person. However, although this person doesn't really share their belief with other people. In times of trouble such belief is still there, and it helps this person comes up with spontaneous efficient solutions to various existential problems. Hence, Neptune counterbalances and restores or preserves harmony in the areas represented by the House where the Sun and Vesta are, in House VIII, very near the cusp of House IX. It indicates a positive relationship with the legal and philosophical approach to life. House VIII represents money and the ability to invest with a potential to benefit from such investments.

However, other aspects may contradict this positive analysis. For example, Jupiter increases generosity and optimistic investments that are likely to be more costly than a source of positive returns.

There is also a square here with the Nadir as well as with the Midheaven (MC) which creates chronic difficulties to deal with the family situation as opposed to the career or social status.

There is also a square with Chiron, which was already mentioned in lesson 5. It indicates that anything to do with health may intervene to the detriment of this person's wellbeing, while having an adverse influence on the potential to realise their dreams.[3]
Use the supplementary sections included in this lesson to guide your interpretation of the influence of Saturn and of its regent in your chart and anyone else's you wish to analyse. Don't forget the aspects that you will find in my 'Astrology for a better life' book. If you don't have it, you will easily find it on the Amazon website in your country. Lesson number seven deals with the influence of Uranus. Thank you for your attention and for your interest in astrology.

---

[3] Dreams and Hope are represented by Neptune in astrology.

Supplementary section

Saturn in signs

SATURN in ARIES

The fire-cardinal energy of Aries makes Saturn uncomfortable in this sign. It confers a tendency to hesitate rather than to act or react spontaneously. However, taking time to attend to daily routines contributes to more constructive results. Saturn in Aries produces surges of energy that are sometimes difficult to control. It creates counter-reactions when time has come for major decisions. The positive side of this position is the ability to ponder and reflect instead of rushing to conclusions. Authority, impulsiveness, and aggressiveness have a karmic connotation that needs to be dealt with without compromise.

SATURN in TAURUS

The karmic value of this position is closely related to the materialistic earthly side of life. Food, money, and possessions may be considered as primary sources of concern and difficulty. Saturn here increases a tendency to dread the consequences of wrong decisions or inappropriate behaviour. Self-restriction stems from an innate need for self-protection. Financial reluctance and apprehension undermine creativity and the spontaneous expression of love and affection. Peace of mind and economic coherence depend on patience, endurance, and determination.

SATURN in GEMINI

Saturn here absorbs some of the lighter aspect of the sign of the twins: eternal youth. In appearance, at least... Intellectual development and communication are the main missions to accomplish in this life. A tendency to self-underestimation reveals that knowledge requires learning and that learning takes time. The quality of human relationships depends on the ability to express and share personal and communal thoughts and ideas. Feeling uncomfortable in the presence of others undermines the potential to build meaningful relations.

SATURN in CANCER

This karmic position of Saturn opposite its sign of rulership is often considered negatively in astrology. If it often indicates a life path or 'mission' in relation with the home, family affairs and the ethnic or social background, it also confers a more rational approach to realities, difficulties, and emotional challenges. The mother or mother figure deeply influences the choices made to deal with personal and family hardship. However, once emotional ties to past events are overcome, determination, patience, and endurance favour a more enjoyable second part of life.

SATURN in LEO

The nature of Leo is linked to the need to accomplish, to impress and to become the centre of attention. Saturn here imposes more time to reach the desired level of performance and realisation. Although it may take longer to prosper, once achieved, the outcome is often exceptionally long-lasting. The creative quality of Leo enhances Saturn's influence on personal ambition and determination to obtain the best possible results. It is a matter of ego. However, the time factor may be a source of discouragement and alter the necessary drive to achieve life's mission.

SATURN in VIRGO

Despite obstacles and restrictions, Saturn's influence on the ability to succeed exclusively depends on work and duty. Virgo instils its fastidious and rational approach of life to Saturn's seriousness and determination. There is an innate need to undertake commitments, no matter how long it takes and how difficult they are. Progress is viewed on more personal than social angles. To remain at the bottom of the ladder or reach the highest level makes little difference to the way work, and responsibilities are perceived and accepted. Health and medicine may be part of the motivation to realise life's mission.

SATURN in LIBRA

Human relationships often have a profound karmic connotation. Saturn here emphasises the need for long-lasting personal involvement, privately, socially, and professionally. Such alliances may be sources of hardship, frustrations, and limitations. They are nonetheless a must to progress and to achieve long-lasting concrete results. Personal ambition depends on the quality of the other person or people involved in a joint venture. Unable to do it solo, it appears necessary to share and split the overall tasks and efforts to assume the time factor with more determination and avoid solitude.

SATURN in SCORPIO

Sexuality, death, and the unknown have a deep karmic connotation. Self-limitations and personal dissatisfaction make it difficult to accept fate to lessen the emotional weight and build on the ashes of past errors and misfortunes. Sexual Drive nourishes determination and the purpose to deal with and overcome life's unpleasant circumstances. A constant shadow seems to limit existential brightness and happiness. More fatalistic than adventurous, Saturn enhances resignation to undergo a later life path marked by solitude and a degree of austerity.

SATURN in SAGITTARIUS

Philosophy, religion, and karma are closely linked to become a source of reflection and acceptation of the limitations and burdens that earthly life imposes to foster moral progress. Time is viewed as a necessary process to understand and accept its lofty meaning.

Restrictions may be self-imposed to assess one's determination and endurance. Travelling and connecting with foreign places and people have a common spiritual purpose. The energy used to deal with hardship helps face up to reality with a smile and a positive approach that favours the realisation of long-term projects.

SATURN in CAPRICORN

In its sign of rulership, Saturn enhances the natural connection with time. It is a strong position that improves patience and determination. Hardship is viewed as one of the unavoidable realities of earthly life. Long-term projects are sources of inspiration, although not joyfully expressed or anticipated. Social and professional realisation is a goal that may take many years to reach. A fatalistic rather than opportunistic thought pattern may alter the excitement and motivation to succeed. However, Saturn in Capricorn is often found in the charts of high-level executives and successful individuals.

SATURN in AQUARIUS

A karmic tie with humanity has a profound influence on the development of social life. People are considered as much a source of motivation and satisfaction than disillusion. Major efforts are needed to build solid and meaningful relationships. The diversity of human beings makes it exciting to participate in collective long-term projects with a common goal. Patience is required to deal with those who may be so different that it becomes a problem to connect with them. Unexpected changes are not appreciated; the nature of Saturn being more sedentary than mobile. However, major changes being considered fateful and part of one's destiny, they are usually dealt with successfully.

SATURN in PISCES

The natural connection between body and soul depends on life's difficulties and the necessary effort and time required to deal with them. A lofty approach allows for better results. Effort is considered from a spiritual rather than purely terrestrial point of view. Earthly life is made easier by accepting its many challenges. Saturn here confers more inspiration and intuition to concretely realise earthly projects. Saturn's realism impregnated by the heavenly influence of Pisces confers the ability to give time a chance to show the way to concrete and long-lasting success.

Supplementary section

Saturn in the Houses

In House I

This position indicates patience and determination, but a low consideration of oneself. Nevertheless, time allows for progress and concrete achievement. Self-realisation often occurs around thirty years of age when all is done to realise important life projects. The karmic mission is to brighten the inner image of the self.

In House II

This position indicates a conservative approach to the material aspect of life. Attention should be given to the food intake to avoid eventual physiological consequences of an inappropriate diet. A tendency to self-restriction may alter spontaneous enjoyment of the good things of life. The karmic mission is to be more open and spontaneous in dealing with matter, food, and money.

In House III

This position indicates difficulties in studies due to adverse circumstances or lack of motivation that repress the desire to learn and communicate. The influence of the elderly on the development and evolution of the literary interests and capacity. The karmic mission is to be more open and spontaneous in communication.

In House IV

This position indicates chronic home disturbance and a fatalistic approach to family responsibilities. It may also indicate a proletarian background that could temper the ability to climb up the social ladder. The influence of an older relative is often observed. The karmic mission is to ease up pressure to make family affairs less a burden than an enjoyable area of life.

In House V

This position indicates sentimental frustration due to lack of companionship. It may also hinder procreation and creativity. Time is a major factor in the development of romantic pursuits. Realisation is more likely around 30 years of age or much later, at about 60. The karmic mission is to restore personal faith in oneself to enjoy a more fulfilling love life and creativity.

In House VI

This position indicates that work and health may have karmic origins with a strong influence on the choice of a career. Periods of unemployment are possible, sometimes due to a difficulty to put oneself forward once the goals are set. Health may hinder employment. The karmic mission is to find the right job to fulfil the innate need to be of service, competent and stable.

In House VII

This position has a strong influence on the ability to share and cooperate with other people, especially in private life. This may lead to prolonged periods of celibacy and solitude with detrimental effect on personal wellbeing and moral or emotional health. The karmic mission is to get involved in a stable relationship to build a future together with the right partner.

In House VIII

This position indicates a life path marked by significant economic setbacks. Hence, a parsimonious approach of finances and joint resources. Libido is reduced. Unfortunate events may have produced an apprehension about death and the mysteries of life. The karmic mission is to accept the idea of death as an opening onto a new life rather than as 'dead end'.

In House IX

This position indicates a life path marked by problems to solve and obstacles to surmount within the social sphere on administrative and legal plans. A pessimistic philosophy of life does not motivate higher studies. There may be a karmic tie with a foreign land. The karmic mission is to come to terms with laws and regulations of our society while keeping a philosophical eye on life's challenges.

In House X

Saturn is strong House X, where its position enhances the desire to succeed while creating serious obstacles to surmount before reaching the desired objectives. Time and patience increase determination and favour ultimate success with long-lasting effects. The karmic mission is to focus on the objectives rather than on the time it may take to reach the coveted summit.

In House XI

This position indicates a life path marked by setbacks in the human or geographical environment. Wanting to help others is a source of difficulties that hinder potential success. The condition of the elderly may become a professional and social motivation to help. The karmic mission is to become and remain an essential and stable part of the community on a human and social point of view.

In House XII

This position indicates a karmic tie with the past, especially where difficult events are concerned. The elderly may be a source of responsibilities due to their need of care and attention. Religious beliefs and spirituality are linked to hardship and burden rather than God. The karmic mission is to bring dreams and reality together to obtain concrete results, thanks to a fruitful imagination put to good use.

Lesson 7

Link to the video: https://youtu.be/51aY6yVAuqc

Uranus

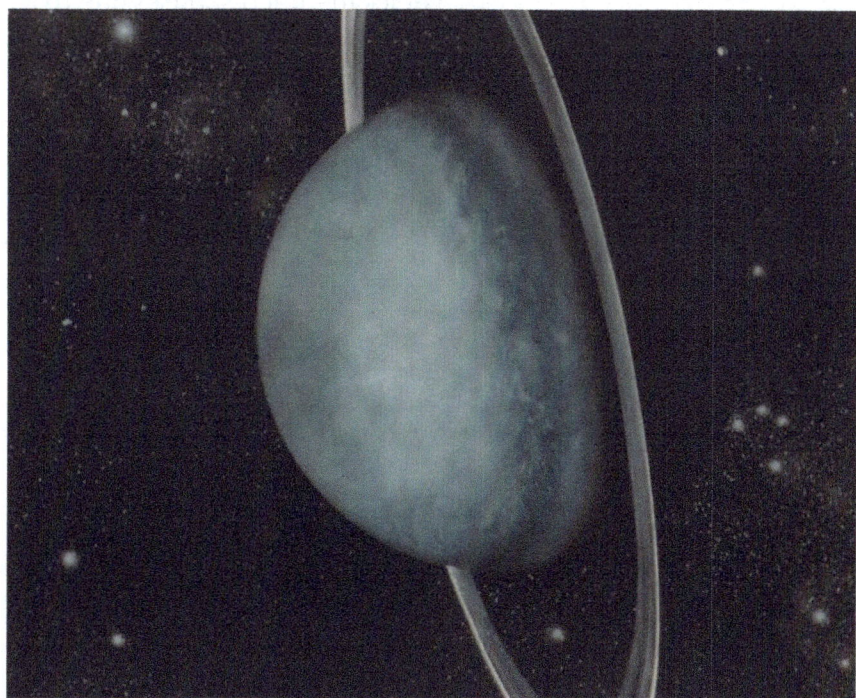

Uranus is the following planet from Saturn. Although between Saturn and Uranus is Chiron, but we have already studied the influence of Chiron in a previous lesson. Let's investigate the possible influence and the symbolic or symbolism of Uranus in a chart...

Uranus takes 84 years to revolve around the zodiac. It represents drastic and irreversible changes. It indicates a past life marked by unexpected turmoil. Uranus, ruler of Aquarius, the eleventh sign, is analogically associated with House XI. Therefore, Uranus is symbolically associated with people and populations.

84-year cycle

- Drastic and irreversible changes

- Past life marked by unexpected turmoil

- Uranus ruler of Aquarius, the eleventh sign = House XI

- Symbolically linked to people and populations

- Adaptability and inventiveness

- Quick reactions

- Neuronal activity (with Mercury)

Adaptability and inventiveness are also characterised by Uranus. Together with Mercury, it confers quick mental responses due to its action on brain function and neuronal activity. Mercury represents the 'grey matter', and Uranus the electrochemical stimulation that occurs in the brain to make it work and connect with the rest of the body and with the outside world.

Uranus remains about seven years in every sign of the zodiac where its energy is affected by the nature of the sign in which it is transiting. **In Aries** it indicates that the past life was exposed to sudden violence, to aggressiveness, or impulsiveness that triggered irrational conduct and excessive reactions.

In Aries	Past life exposed to sudden violence (war)
In Taurus	Past life exposed to sudden changes in feeding habits
In Gemini	Past life exposed to sudden communication changes
In Cancer	Past life exposed to sudden family and residence changes
In Leo	Past life exposed to sudden regime and sentimental changes
In Virgo	Past life exposed to sudden illness (pandemic)
In Libra	Past life exposed to sudden relational changes
In Scorpio	Past life exposed to sudden deadly threats (pandemic)
In Sagittarius	Past life exposed to sudden moral and social disorders
In Capricorn	Past life exposed to sudden leadership and status changes
In Aquarius	Past life exposed to sudden social, environmental changes
In Pisces	Past life exposed to sudden religious or ideological changes

(Excerpt from the video)

In Taurus it indicates that the past life was exposed to sudden changes in feeding habits, perhaps famine, and other changes that were necessary to adapt to a particular situation very quickly.

In Gemini it indicates that the past life was exposed to sudden communication changes such as the invention of the telephone, for example, or other means of connections that were very sudden and that were perhaps difficult for the person to adapt to.

In Cancer it indicates that the past life was exposed to sudden family and home changes due to what happened in the country, in the city, in the region, or in the place of residence.

In Leo it indicates that the past life was exposed to sudden regime and sentimental changes, artistic changes as well. But why regime? Because Leo is linked to monarchy and aristocracy. It means perhaps that the person went through a period affected by a drastic change from one regime to another, from one king or queen to another, and perhaps from monarchy to Republic.

In Virgo it indicates that the past life was exposed to sudden illness and to sudden changes in the way work had to be done. It may have had to do with a career, a profession as such, or with daily duties that were drastically affected because of a widespread health issue such as a pandemic, for example.

In Libra it indicates that the past life was exposed to sudden changes in relationships, partnerships, marriage facing great challenges that forced drastic modifications due to unexpected events.

In Scorpio it means that the past life was exposed to sudden deadly threats once again, perhaps a pandemic or something even worse because Scorpio is linked to Pluto which represents death. There was perhaps a period marked by a war or a situation that had a profound threatening effect.

In Sagittarius it indicates that the past life was exposed to sudden moral and social changes or disorders. What happened was very intense and could have had to do with a change of political regime, major legal changes, drastic changes in the country's administration.

In Capricorn it indicates that the past life was exposed to sudden leadership and status changes. Capricorn is the 10th sign of the zodiac. It is analogically linked to the 10th House representing personal, social, and professional status. It also represents the authority and power of certain leaders such as dictators and monarchs.

In Aquarius it represents a past life that was exposed to sudden social and environmental changes that affected the population in a widespread manner. It also represents changes to the geographical environment with perhaps a displacement of the place of residence with its profound impact on the notions of belonging to a social group.

In Pisces it represents a past life that was exposed to sudden religious and ideological changes. All those changes are somehow brought back in this present incarnation in terms of behaviour and inner needs and desires. It also represents how the person is going to adapt to sudden changes and situations in areas represented by the House concerned and the aspects involving Uranus in the chart.

The next step is to assess what Uranus indicates according to its House position in the chart where it transfers its energy to influence and produce major changes in the areas represented by the House concerned.

Uranus in the Houses

In House I Repercussions on personal behaviour and inner personality
In House II Repercussions in the material side of life
In House III Repercussions in communication, mobility and intellect
In House IV Repercussions in family affairs and place of residence
In House V Repercussions in love life and creativity
In House VI Repercussions in work area, health, and daily duties
In House VII Repercussions in marriage and other important partnerships
In House VIII Repercussions in finances, sexuality, and the ability to regenerate
In House IX Repercussions in legal matters, higher education, and morality
In House X Repercussions in social and professional status and personal realisation
In House XI Repercussions in social relationships, friendships, and environment
In House XII Repercussions on past events, traumas, and karma

In House 1 (I) the Ascendant or Rising Sign, it indicates that what the person is bringing back from the previous incarnation produces strong repercussions on personal behaviour and the development of the inner personality.

In House 2 (II) it indicates repercussions affecting the material aspect of life. This is showing in the way the person feeds, uses money and teats personal finances.

In House 3 (III) it indicates repercussions in communication, in mobility, intellect, and in exchanges with other people, it helps understand the way the person intellectually perceives the world around.

In House 4 (IV) Uranus indicates repercussions in family affairs and the place of residence. Uranus indicates a chronic need to change. A need to be original, different, and a need to adapt to various situations that may impose drastic changes in these areas.

In House 5 (V) it indicates repercussions in love life, creativity, and the arts. The person is probably quite original in romance and in areas where personal feelings and sentimental expression prevail.

In House 6 (VI) it indicates repercussions in the work area, health, and daily duties. What the person is bringing back from a past incarnation in terms of drastic changes is affecting their personal approach to professional activities and responsibilities.

In House 7 (VII) Uranus indicates repercussions in marriage and other important personal, social, or professional partnerships. They are subject to changes unconsciously linked to what the person went through during the previous incarnation.

In House 8 (VIII) it indicates repercussions in finances, sexuality, and on the ability to regenerate and withstand trials and other major challenges. Death may also be a source of financial returns (inheritance) and long-lasting grief.

In House 9 (IX) Uranus indicates repercussions in legal matters, higher education, and morality. The person may be quite unexpectedly changing opinion and position in these areas. Studies may also be marked by chronic complications due to an unorthodox approach to personal knowledge and experience.

In House 10 (X – MC) it indicates repercussions on the social and professional status with their effect on personal realisation and career choices. Authority and leadership are also subject to unexpected changes in direction.

In House 11 (XI) it indicates repercussions in social relationships, friendship, and human or geographical environment. Unexpected changes of situations may be triggered by a tendency to seek novelty and originality rather than routine and stability.

In House 12 (XII) Uranus indicates that the previous incarnation deeply influences the present life. The past may be filled with traumas, uncertainty, confusion, and karmic situations. Uranus intensifies the natural connection with the karmic load. In this House, the spiritual dimension of Uranus's influence in increased.

Let's take an example looking at the chart we have referred to since the beginning of this course on karmic astrology. In this chart we see that Uranus is in Taurus.

As seen earlier in this lesson, Uranus in Taurus indicates a past life marked by drastic changes as far as food feeding habits in relation to agriculture, the land and what the earth was able to provide agriculture also represented by Taurus, which also represents the approach to the need for food. Money is earned through work to buy food and other daily needs. Therefore, when Uranus is in Taurus it indicates drastic changes in the concept of earning one's bread. Such changes are forced by exterior circumstances such as family or social situations.

From 2018 until 2026, while Uranus is transiting in Taurus, drastic changes have become necessary in many people's lives who decided in favour of another type of work because of the situation created by the pandemic of Covid_19. They could not continue on working as they used to.

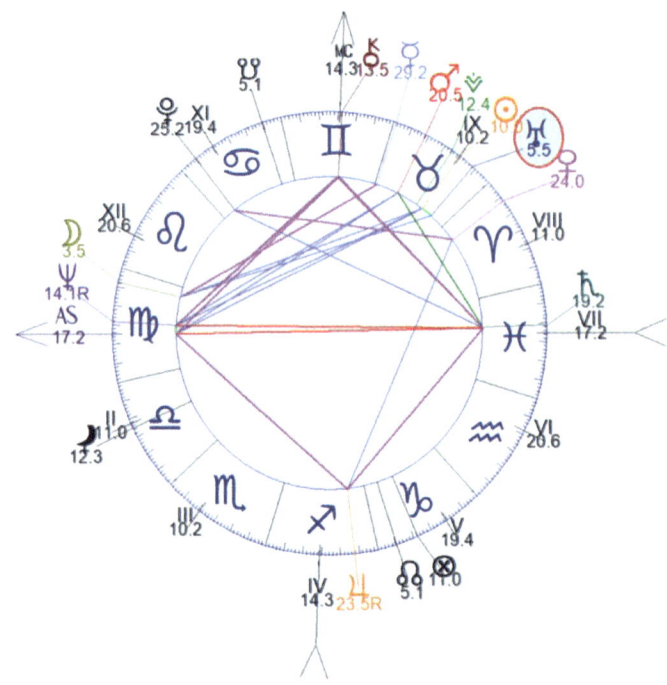

The consequences of this unexpected situation became a source of creativity because of the critical need to adapt to changing habits. What is represented by Taurus will continue on being revised and exploited until the end of the transit in this sign.

In this chart, we see that Uranus is in House 8 (VIII) which represents the consequences of what this person went through in a previous life and on the way this person deals with money in relation to the social environment. House VIII also represents the notion of death, regeneration, and the need to regenerate. It shows that money seen as a food provider is extremely important to this person. A reality emphasised by the zodiac sign, Taurus.

The Regent of Uranus

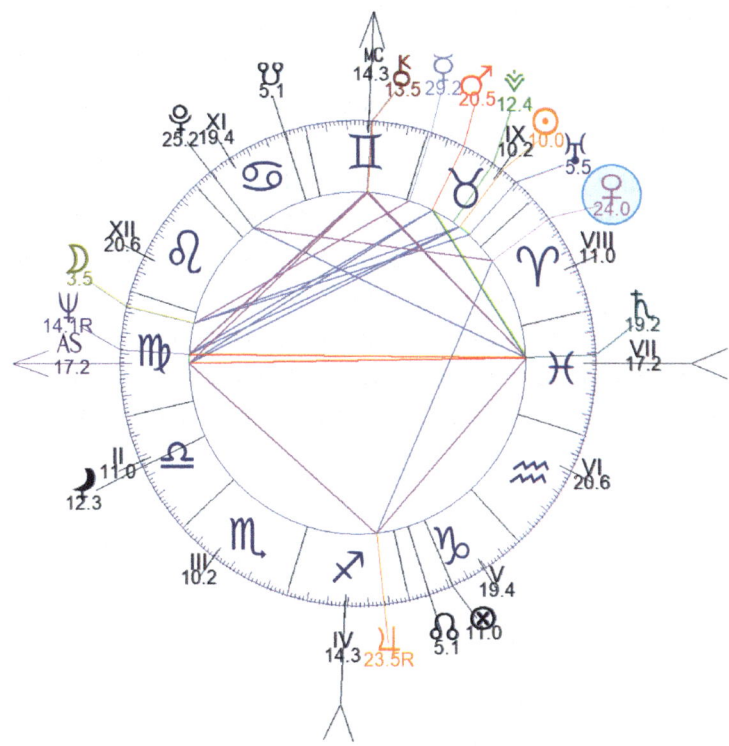

In the example chart once again, we can confirm that Uranus is in Taurus, a sign ruled by Venus, which is in Aries. Therefore, Venus becomes the *regent* of Uranus positioned in Taurus. Venus is, like Uranus, in House 8 (VIII) where it amplifies what we've just seen earlier about the position of Uranus in this House. In fact, when a planet is in a House and its regent is in the same House, it doubles the energy, making it a lot stronger. In this example chart, it makes it even stronger because Venus is in Aries, not in Taurus, in Mars's sign while Mars is in Taurus. This combination renders this person quite energetic, defensive, active, and reactive to protect and preserve, to defend personal material (House VIII) and sentimental (Venus) interests.

Exterior events represented by Uranus in connection with what this person went through in the previous incarnation have a very strong influence on the concept of money and the ability to make wise investments and get rewarding returns. Difficulties in this important area are emphasised by the presence of Mars in Taurus. As you can see in the chart on the previous page, Mars is in House 9 (IX) relating to the legal side of life, the administration, far-distant places, morality, and higher education. It is therefore quite difficult for this person to adapt to the various changes that tend to occur unexpectedly, the type of challenge that Uranus can trigger.

The aspects

We cannot do a reading of the influence of Uranus without taking the aspects into account.

—First, we see that there is a conjunction with the Sun

—A wider conjunction with Vesta in Taurus

—A sextile with the South Lunar Node

—A trine with the North Lunar Node

—A trine with the Moon in Virgo

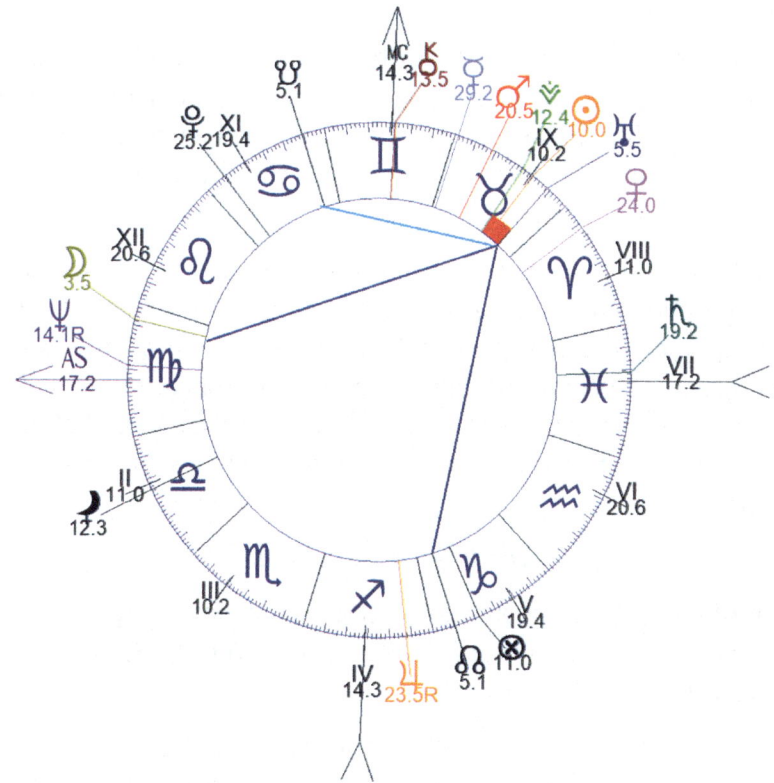

Those configurations are quite positive. They indicate a strong potential to change what needs to be changed to restore balance and harmony as much as possible (Vesta) and preserve a good social status (Sun).

The Sun represents the power that we all have to be someone in this world, to be seen and appreciated in various ways. The Sun represents what we show and share of ourselves with the world around. What others can see of us is represented by the Sun. It is the light that allows us to see and to be seen. It is the life force with its strong influence on our physical self because, without a body, we cannot be seen…

The link with the North and South Lunar Nodes indicate that this person seems to know where to go, what to do, and what not to do to preserve that balance, harmony, and wellbeing as much as possible despite unexpected events and the drastic changes they impose.

Then, there is a trine with the Moon that allows this person to use emotions and intuition to spontaneously know how to act and react, adapting quickly to change, thanks to the energy of Uranus, and to what this person went through in their previous incarnation. Indeed, the cosmic memory of what happened then is like a bagful of useful tools and tricks to tackle the unexpected realities of the present incarnation.

The Regent of Uranus

Then, of course, we must analyse the aspects involving the regent of Uranus. In the example chart, the regent is Venus because Uranus is in Taurus, Venus's sign.

There is a square with Pluto, a trine with Jupiter, a rather paradoxical combination because Pluto represents a threat, while Venus represents House 9 (IX in Taurus. It means that official and legal matters are likely to be more a source of problems than solutions. Pluto represents destruction, which means that this person may have a more destructive than constructive behaviour. Luckily, the trine from Jupiter in House 4 (IV) indicates that this person is somehow protected. Therefore, even though Pluto may represent a threat, when an important problem occurs, something happens to help find the right solution. It seems that Jupiter is looking after and protecting this person. The positive energy of the giant planet may come from the ability to love and to appreciate the good things of life. Venus is the goddess of love. It also has to do with the lessons that this person is able to learn from various mistakes that may have triggered destructive events or situations.

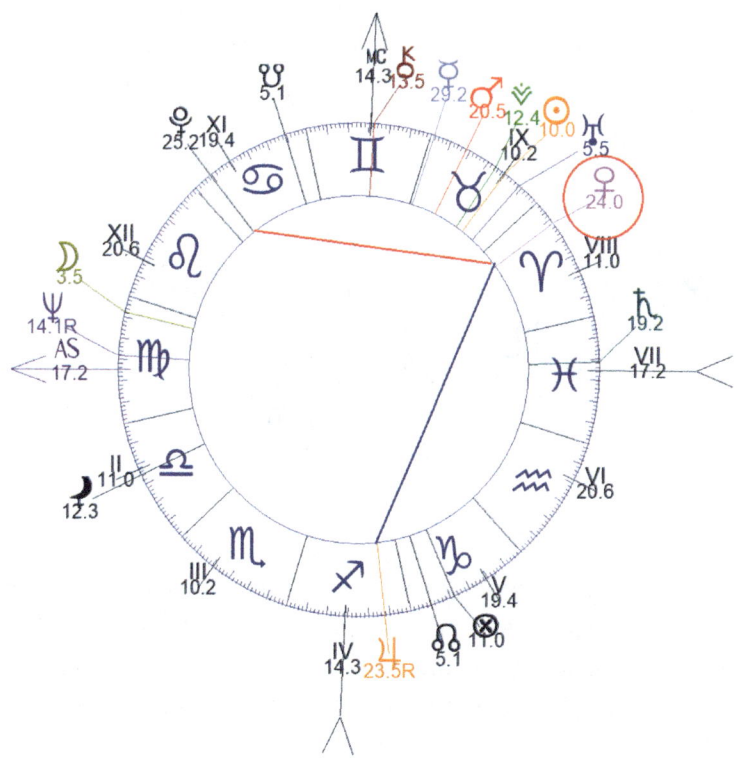

However, Jupiter shows that there is a protection coming from the family area represented by House 4 (IV). In a broader sense, House IV represents the town, the region, and the country of birth. Being in Sagittarius in Jupiter's sign positioned in this sign, the ruler of House IV is in House IV, enhancing the role and positive potential of Venus in Aries.

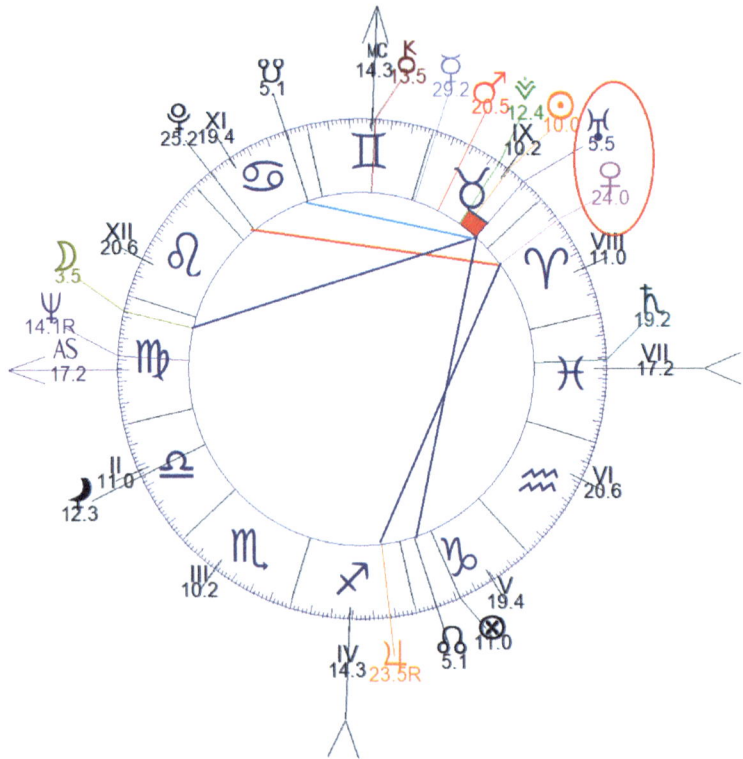

Looking at the chart showing the aspects involving Uranus and its regent, Venus is useful to synthesise the information derived from each aspect. Blending is an important step that should be considered as you progress through the reading of the chart.

As you can see in the example chart above, there are not many aspects involving Uranus and its regent, Venus. In many cases, there are a lot more, which makes the analysis more complicated. However, remember that when you and examine the position of a planet (like Venus is in Aries in the example chart) simultaneously assess that it is linked to Mars, the ruler of Aries which becomes the regent of Venus. In this chart again, Mars is in Taurus, Venus's sign. In this particular case, there is what we call an 'exchange of residence'. Venus is at Mars's place and Mars is at Venus's place. Such a situation amplifies greatly the link between both planets. From a karmic point of view, it confers to Uranus a double sided connotation. Venus is the goddess of love and Mars the god of war...

All planets and other elements must be dealt with in a similar manner. Immediately think of the regent or such planet or element and search the position of the regent. Doing so will help you analyse more precisely the influence of the element or planet in question.

Practise on this method because it will help you adapt quickly and effectively to any chart you will choose to analyse.

Blending is what you must do as you move through the chart's investigation. Blending should not be reserved to the end of the reading; it must be done systematically from the very first element you lay your eyes on. Blending enriches readings, making them more profound and more in adequacy with the person concerned.

Use the supplementary sections included in this lesson to help you understand and apply the influence of Uranus and of its regent in signs and in Houses. When you have done this, you can continue on to the next lesson in which I will explain the role of Neptune in karmic astrology.

Supplementary section

Uranus in signs

URANUS in ARIES

Drastic changes in social organisation have a strong influence on the ability to act and react. The first sign symbolises a new beginning, a new start. Initialising new projects is part of the behaviour of people born with Uranus in this sign. They are inventive and quick to respond. They always seem ready to rebel against the status quo. They fight to impose new concepts and ideas, but they also fight to combat reforms. Above all, they need to learn to slow down to avoid mistakes, accidents, conflicts, and painful breakups. Their vital energy may be subject to extreme highs and lows.

URANUS in TAURUS

There is a profound need to change the way nature and what it provides is considered. Food and feeding habits are subject to major innovations. The relationship between work and money is organised in an original manner. Using modernised or revolutionary tools of communication improves the ability to realise unprecedented social and material changes. There is a tendency to marginalisation due to a difficulty to accept laws and regulations. Instability may result and create a tortuous financial life path. Erratic eating inclinations may become a source of health concerns.

URANUS in GEMINI

Verbal and written interactions are essential to human life. Uranus here enhances originality, intellectual enthusiasm, adaptability, and the capacity to reach others and exchange thoughts and ideas spontaneously. Inventiveness and originality feed a strong need to reform communication by means of new concepts and the use of modern tools. Drastic changes in education and teaching methods are encouraged. They are a source of motivation to move forward with the times rather than stick to traditions. The nervous system and the lungs may become sources of health concerns.

URANUS in CANCER
The concepts of family, motherhood and patriotism motivate a strong need for major changes. Considered marginal by some and progressist by others, novelty is, however, essential to adapt to future necessities rather than keep on nurturing conventional models from the past. Bohemian tendencies are noticeable, although dependent on social, moral, and family situations. Single parenting is more attractive than the traditional home-life model. Frequent changes of residence are preferred to sedentary living. The stomach and the lymph may become sources of health concerns.

URANUS in LEO
Creativity is inherent to human nature, although it varies in intensity and value from one person to another. Originality calls for novelty and reforms of the meaning of creation. The expression of love is a source of sudden changes of direction. Instability may be considered a means to remain free and individualistically responsible. Unconventional forms of art are preferred to classic standards of the past. There is a need to change egotistic values to more universally useful forms of expression. The cardiovascular function may become a source of health concerns.

URANUS in VIRGO
Work and health are primary concerns that require constant re-evaluation to preserve social stability and progress. Uranus here expresses the need to change, to reform, and to transform conventional standards to innovate and allow more freedom in employment and innovations in health-related areas. There is a need to move away from routine work that generates boredom and

a loss of interest in the daily tasks. Original ideas about hygiene and duty may create unusual behaviour at home and socially. Digestion affects the nervous system and may become a source of health concerns.

URANUS in LIBRA

Humans are not solitary creatures. They need each other to share, to progress and to develop. Uranus here indicates a strong need to reform the basics of personal relationships. Freedom and independence in marriage are more important than the legal contract. Marginal or unusual partnerships may result. Unconventional means to communicate profoundly modify couples' connections. Laws and regulations in marriage and other forms of association or partnerships are revolutionised to accommodate new trends. The lower back, kidneys and urinary functions may become health concerns.

URANUS in SCORPIO

Sex is the most basic but essential way to procreate. It is the natural means that nature provides to transcend death by giving life. Uranus here indicates a need to reform sexuality to modernise it and express it more freely. Unusual practices are meant to provoke senses and satisfy profound needs to abide by the idea that whatever begins must invariably end. Attraction to the unknown and to the darker side of human nature, may create self-destructive tendencies viewed as essential to favour inner regeneration. The reproductive system and bowel function may become sources of health concerns.

URANUS in SAGITTARIUS

Some believe that God was 'invented' to create a monotheist religion intended to better control populations. Uranus here produces a strong need for freedom regarding philosophical thoughts and ideas. There is a tendency to reform and transform spiritual and ethical standards. Independence and originality characterise the revolutionaries who seek to renovate the moral and ethical landscape of society. Attraction to foreign cultures allows important gathering of information to serve the motto: 'Learning is growing.' Erratic hepatic function and blood pressure may become sources of health concerns.

URANUS in CAPRICORN
Tradition and hierarchy are essential to maintain social order. Uranus here creates a need to reform old-fashioned laws and change the way to deal with authority. Unusual projects and objectives develop from an attraction to new and unconventional tools and equipment. Climbing to the top requires determination and adaptability to the environment. Uranus here produces frequent modifications of direction that may lead to marginalisation. Inventiveness is a valuable asset to make the best out of the most unexpected and apparently unfavourable situations. Bones and joints may become sources of health concerns.

URANUS in AQUARIUS
The age of Aquarius is also the age of reality TV, mediatization of privacy and proliferation of the most complex and innovative devices to communicate with millions of people instantly. Dependence on electronic gadgets favours social predators who format youngsters to satisfy their mercantile purpose. Uranus here enhances the ability to quickly understand and show great ingenuity. There is also a tendency to voluntary marginal behaviour intended to drastically change and reform society. The nervous system, the peripheral blood circulation and the lower limbs may become sources of health concerns.

URANUS in PISCES
The need to believe is deeply rooted in societal archetypes. Religion

plays a major role for thousands of years to control populations to ensure social order and stability. Uranus in this sign indicates a strong need to reform, transform and innovate. Philosophically inclined to new ideas and concepts, the adventurous spirit proposes nonconformist and marginal methods to tackle blind faith and irrational beliefs. An innate interest in holistic medicine is a vector for profound changes in social opinion and tradition. The respiratory system and hormonal function may become sources of health concerns.

Supplementary section

Uranus in the Houses

In House I
This position enhances originality, and the way inner personality is expressed and put forward. It also increases the activity of the nervous system, conferring good reflexes and imagination, as well as a tendency to act and react in an unpredictable manner. Position comparable to Uranus in Aries.

In House II
This position enhances the ability to adapt and to make good use of imagination and originality in finance and other down-to-earth areas. It can also indicate sudden changes that drastically affect the source of income. Food may be a source of interest and innovations. Position comparable to Uranus in Taurus.

In House III
This position enhances intellectual performance and originality. It confers imagination and the faculty to quickly adapt to situations and people. It may, however, create too much mental energy and a state of nervousness that alters the ability to focus and concentrate. Position comparable to Uranus in Gemini.

In House IV
This position indicates an original or unusual family background or home environment. It confers mental creativity to adapt to sudden changes in family life. The mother may be perceived as someone quite exceptional although quite nervous or unstable in some way. Position comparable to Uranus in Cancer.

In House V
This position shows that imagination feeds creativity in arts or in dealing with loved ones. It can, however, indicate sudden turns of

fate and the necessity to adapt to them quickly. Unexpected or lucky surprises may suddenly contribute to radically change the way of life. Position comparable to Uranus in Leo.

In House VI

This position enhances imagination and originality at work or while pursuing a career objective. Sudden changes at work may be frequent but quickly dealt with. Success could be favoured in areas such as the audio-visual, aeronautics, or electronics. Health is erratic. Position comparable to Uranus in Virgo.

In House VII

This position indicates originality in marriage or other important relationships. Divorce is not unusual due to a need for variety rather than stability. Adaptability helps preserve harmony. The choice of partners depends on the situation more than the person concerned. Position comparable to Uranus in Libra.

In House VIII

This position enhances natural attraction to occult sciences, finance, and sex. Sudden changes may occur due to unexpected deaths or painful circumstances. There is an ability and possible desire to succeed in astrology, psychology, medicine, or criminology. Position comparable to Uranus in Scorpio.

In House IX

This position confers the ability to adapt to drastic changes with a philosophical approach that enables quick reactions and understanding of the situations. Higher education, foreign countries and cultures, and politics may be a lifelong source of motivation. Position comparable to Uranus in Sagittarius.

In House X

This position indicates potential career success in the media, show business, television, film industry, aeronautics, electronics, or computers. Uranus here also indicates frequent changes of professional position or situation, and places of residence accordingly. Position comparable to Uranus in Capricorn.

In House XI

This is the natural rulership House of Uranus. It enhances adaptability, essentially on the social plan. Spontaneous attraction to people contributes to popularity as much as scandals. Sudden changes may temper the social life, humanely and geographically. Position comparable to Uranus in Aquarius.

In House XII

This position indicates an unstable life path, marked by drastic changes with spiritual and physical consequences. The nervous system can also be a source of concern. Unusual spiritual needs may lead to involvement in sectarian or religious movements. Position comparable to Uranus in Pisces.

Lesson 8

Link to the video: https://youtu.be/5DCahzXsmpk

Neptune

Welcome to lesson 8 in which we're going to debate about Neptune.

165-year cycle

- Spirituality
- Dreams
- Hopes
- Intuition
- Inspiration
- Connexion with astral plan
- Connexion with spiritual dimension

Neptune is a slow planet, a very slow planet. It takes 165 years to revolve around the zodiac. In this lesson, I explain what Neptune means from a karmic point of view

Neptune represents, spirituality, dreams, hopes, intuition, inspiration, the connection with the astral plan, and the connection with the spiritual dimension of life. All that, of course, in the present existence.

Neptune has an interesting relation with the previous incarnation in which it represents a degree of confusion, what has not really been clear enough to be dealt with in a concrete and rational manner.

The sign where Neptune is found in a birth chart indicates how that degree of confusion expressed itself in the previous life. It represents what has been brought back in terms of acting and reacting on intuition and inspiration rather than on rational terms. Rational understanding and rational thinking are not produced by Neptune. It rather represents irrational thinking and that special impression before Mercury (the intellect) takes over.

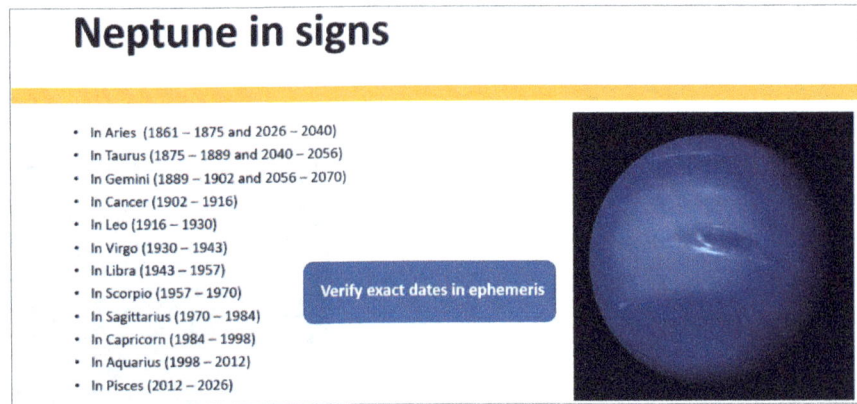

Neptune in signs

- In Aries (1861 – 1875 and 2026 – 2040)
- In Taurus (1875 – 1889 and 2040 – 2056)
- In Gemini (1889 – 1902 and 2056 – 2070)
- In Cancer (1902 – 1916)
- In Leo (1916 – 1930)
- In Virgo (1930 – 1943)
- In Libra (1943 – 1957)
- In Scorpio (1957 – 1970)
- In Sagittarius (1970 – 1984)
- In Capricorn (1984 – 1998)
- In Aquarius (1998 – 2012)
- In Pisces (2012 – 2026)

Verify exact dates in ephemeris

Let's see now what Neptune can tell us about our previous incarnation from its position in a sign. Take note of the periods of transit in each zodiac sign according to your year of birth.[4]

Neptune represents a degree of confusion. It represents what we feel and what we fear without the ability to rationalise such fear. It indicates doubt and uncertainty revealed by its position in sign.

---

[4] *If you are unsure, have your birth chart erected for free on this website:*
https://www.astrotheme.com/horoscope_chart_sign_ascendant.php

Neptune in sign (past life confusion)

In Aries	Past life confusion due to war, accidents, or major conflicts
In Taurus	Past life confusion due to food (famine) or laxist behavior
In Gemini	Past life confusion due to communication impairment
In Cancer	Past life confusion due to emotional or family distress
In Leo	Past life confusion due to sentimental or artistic uncertainty
In Virgo	Past life confusion due to health issues and medical uncertainty
In Libra	Past life confusion due to instability in human relationships
In Scorpio	Past life confusion due to pandemic, contamination, sex, death
In Sagittarius	Past life confusion due to political, social, and moral uncertainty
In Capricorn	Past life confusion due to domination by autocratic rulership
In Aquarius	Past life confusion due to social destabilization, riots, revolution
In Pisces	Past life confusion due to excessive influence of unrealistic beliefs

Neptune in Aries indicates that past-life confusion was due to war, accidents, or major conflicts.

In Taurus it indicates confusion due to food shortage or famine. It also suggests a kind of laxist behaviour as far as material values were concerned.

In Gemini it reveals past-life confusion due to communication due to speech impairment, intellectual, or mental impediment.

In Cancer it implies past-life confusion due to emotional or family distress.

In Leo, confusion was due to sentimental or artistic uncertainty.

In Virgo that confusion was due to health issues and medical uncertainty.

In Libra, Neptune represents past-life confusion due to instability in human relationships, partnerships, collaborations. Dealing with others was unclear and misleading.

In Scorpio, past-life confusion was perhaps due to a pandemic, to contamination, and to sexual practices.

In Sagittarius, past-life confusion was probably due to political, social, and moral uncertainty and instability.

In Capricorn, confusion was due to a kind of domination, perhaps by an autocratic rulership.

In Aquarius, confusion was due to social destabilisation, riots, or even a revolution.

In Pisces, where it transits between 2012 and 2026, Neptune indicates that past-life confusion was due to the excessive influence of unrealistic beliefs. What appeared to be, was not the reflection of reality...

Neptune in Houses

In your birth chart, Neptune is in a sign and in a House. Let's make a quick description of the twelve possible positions.

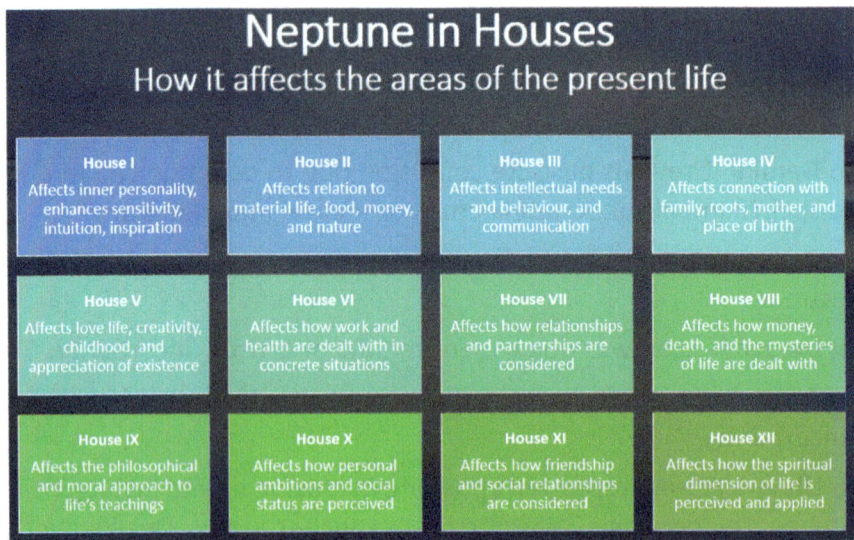

Neptune in Houses
How it affects the areas of the present life

House I	House II	House III	House IV
Affects inner personality, enhances sensitivity, intuition, inspiration	Affects relation to material life, food, money, and nature	Affects intellectual needs and behaviour, and communication	Affects connection with family, roots, mother, and place of birth
House V	**House VI**	**House VII**	**House VIII**
Affects love life, creativity, childhood, and appreciation of existence	Affects how work and health are dealt with in concrete situations	Affects how relationships and partnerships are considered	Affects how money, death, and the mysteries of life are dealt with
House IX	**House X**	**House XI**	**House XII**
Affects the philosophical and moral approach to life's teachings	Affects how personal ambitions and social status are perceived	Affects how friendship and social relationships are considered	Affects how the spiritual dimension of life is perceived and applied

Neptune in House I (Ascendant). It affects the inner personality, enhances sensitivity, intuition, and inspiration.

In House II, it affects relation to material life, food, money, and nature.

In House III, it affects intellectual needs and ability, and the behaviour in terms of communication. What a person went through in a previous life, represented by Neptune in a sign, has strong repercussions in the areas represented by the House concerned, the House where Neptune is found in the birth chart.

In House IV, it affects connection with family, the roots, the mother, and the place of residence.

In House V, it affects love life, creativity, childhood, and the appreciation of existence itself, because House V represents the joys and pleasures of life.

In House VI, it affects work and health, as well as one's daily routine, tasks, and responsibilities. It can either provide a innate sense of duty with good intuition to deal with life's realities, or it may produce a aura of confusion and uncertainty to operate in a rational and successful way.

In House VII, it affects relationships and partnerships, or marriage. There is a subtle spiritual connection with the partner. Keep in mind that Neptune does not represent what is concrete and rational. In

House VIII, it affects how money, death or the idea of death, and the mysteries of life are dealt with. It may give a spontaneous insight or a feeling, an innate and unexplainable knowledge of what life and death are exactly.

In House IX, it affects the philosophical and moral approach to life's teachings. We all have a lot to learn during our present existence. Learning becomes a spiritual need that generates a desire to understand, as well as to connect with faraway places, foreign places, and people.

In House X (MC or Midheaven) Neptune affects how personal ambitions and social status are perceived by producing some confusion or uncertainty on which direction to take. Neptune at the top of a chart has a strong influence on the rest of the chart. It can overcome other influences from other elements in that chart.

In House XI, it affects how friendship and social relationships are considered. It usually indicates spiritual, spiritualised, or spiritually oriented relationships. There is a spiritual connotation to friendship which may also become a source of disappointment. Social life is based on personal feelings stemming from forgotten motivations from a past existence.

In House XII, the last House of the chart, Neptune affects how the spiritual dimension of life is perceived and applied. As we all need to believe in something, ourselves to begin with, and perhaps in other people, or even in God, to believe is primordial to human existence. However, it is not enough to rationally assert that a belief is the reflection of reality.

Intuitions, inspirations, or beliefs need to be backed by concrete answers to rationalise and put perceptions and ideas to good use in various ways. Let's take an example.

In the example chart on the following page, Neptune is in Virgo, in House XII. However, it is very near the cusp of House I or Ascendant. Therefore, we can assume that if the time of birth was not precise, Neptune could be in House I, even though it is shown in this chart as being in House XII. In similar circumstances, take both Houses into consideration, to understand what this person may derive in the areas represented by both Houses.

In this particular case, it means that this person has a strong intuition (House XII) which enhances the connection with the spiritual dimension of life nourished by non-rational beliefs.

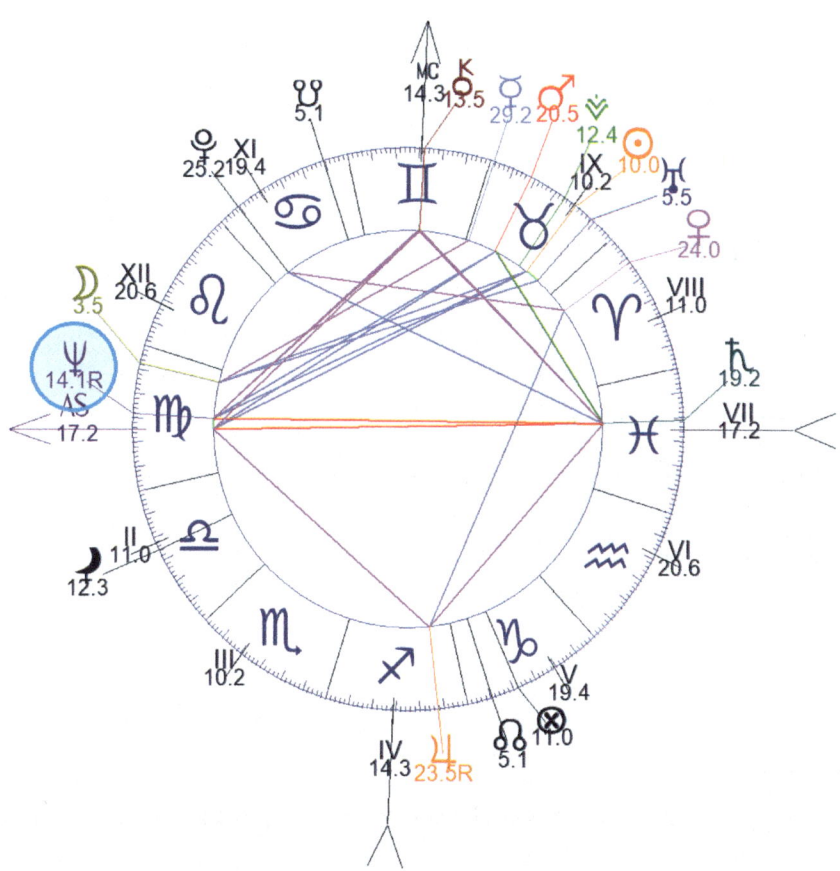

House I represents the inner personality, which is strongly influenced by Neptune, so much more because Neptune represents what this person needs to believe, but believing is never enough. However, it shows strong motivation emerging from the energy of Neptune. We will see why and how later in this lesson.

Neptune's regent in signs

Let's see now what the positions of Neptune's regent in sign may mean to help analyse your own chart and any other chart.

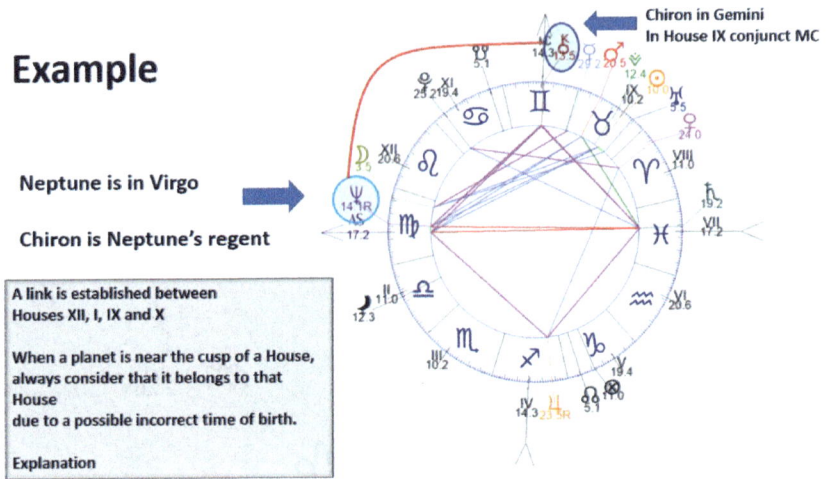

Example

Chiron in Gemini
In House IX conjunct MC

Neptune is in Virgo

Chiron is Neptune's regent

A link is established between Houses XII, I, IX and X

When a planet is near the cusp of a House, always consider that it belongs to that House due to a possible incorrect time of birth.

Explanation

In Aries, Neptune's regent means that there is a strong will to defend and impose personal beliefs.

In Taurus, there is a natural attraction to the good things of life and to nature.

In Gemini, it indicates an intuitive intellect and an ability to connect and to communicate spontaneously.

In Cancer, it means that there is a strong emotional response to beliefs and to spirituality in accordance with family background.

In Leo, spirituality oriented inspiration promotes creativity and artistic talent.

In Virgo, an interest in health-related subjects is indicated with hypochondriac tendencies.

In Libra, there is a search for balance and harmony in human relationships. It accentuates diplomacy except if another element or planet interferes with the influence of the regent of Neptune in this sign.

In Scorpio, there is a spiritual approach to death, sex, and to the mysteries of life.

In Sagittarius, there is a philosophical approach to spirituality with an urge to learn and progress. However, learning may not be precisely linked to spirituality, but from a strong need to promote a more spiritually oriented life.

In Capricorn, the rational approach to spirituality and beliefs promotes and motivate personal ambitions with a rational approach to spirituality. More concrete results are derived from personal feelings and inspiration, or intuition.

In Aquarius, it indicates that the interest in community and social activities has a strong spiritual connotation. Interacting with people is necessary to feel useful in some way with a strong spiritual undertone.

In Pisces, the regent of Neptune is in a strong position. It increases the connection with the spiritual dimension of life because it enhances the ability to understand and to connect with the invisible plan, with the astral plan, a quality that can be relied upon to understand life's lofty meaning in a subtle way.

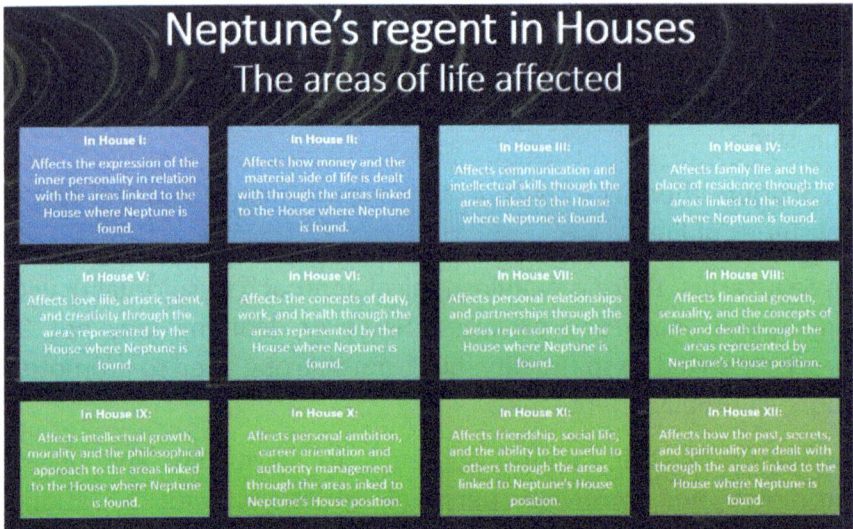

As usual, we must now consider the position of Neptune's regent in the Houses to complement the reading of the birth chart from a karmic point of view.

In House I:
Affects the expression of the inner personality in relation with the areas linked to the House where Neptune is found.

In House II:
Affects how money and the material side of life are dealt with through the areas linked to the House where Neptune is found.

In House III:
Affects communication and intellectual skills through the areas linked to the House where Neptune is found.

In House IV:
Affects family life and the place of residence through the areas linked to the House where Neptune is found.

In House V:
Affects love life, artistic talent, and creativity through the areas represented by the House where Neptune is found.

In House VI:
Affects the concepts of duty, work, and health through the areas represented by the House where Neptune is found.

In House VII:
Affects personal relationships and partnerships through the areas represented by the House where Neptune is found.

In House VIII:
Affects financial growth, sexuality, and the concepts of life and death through the areas represented by Neptune's House position.

In House IX:
Affects intellectual growth, morality and the philosophical approach to the areas linked to the House where Neptune is found.

In House X:
Affects personal ambition, career orientation and authority management through the areas inked to Neptune's House position.

In House XI:
Affects friendship, social life, and the ability to be useful to others through the areas linked to Neptune's House position.

In House XII:
Affects how the past, secrets, and spirituality are dealt with through the areas linked to the House where Neptune is found.

Aspects involving Neptune

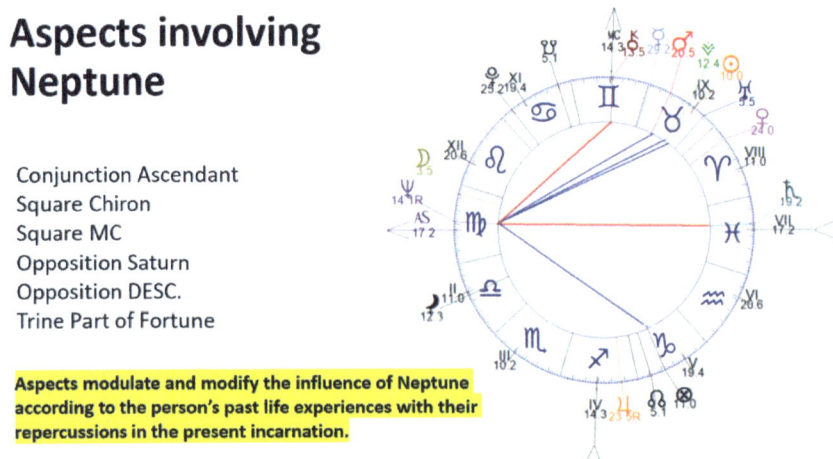

Conjunction Ascendant
Square Chiron
Square MC
Opposition Saturn
Opposition DESC.
Trine Part of Fortune

Aspects modulate and modify the influence of Neptune according to the person's past life experiences with their repercussions in the present incarnation.

Next, we must take into consideration the aspects involving Neptune and then the aspects involving the regent of Neptune. In the example chart above, you can see that Neptune creates a square with Chiron and the Midheaven or MC. There are trines with Mars, Vesta, the Sun, and more slightly with Uranus, and there is one with the Part of Fortune. There is an opposition with Saturn standing near the cusp of House VII or Descendant (DESC).

Aspects modulate and modify the influence of Neptune according to the person's past life experiences with their repercussions in the present incarnation. Use the supplementary sections included in my 'Astrology for a better life' book to help you analyse the influence of the aspects that I've just mentioned in this example chart, of course, but more especially in your chart and other charts you may want to analyse.

The same principle applies to the aspects involving the regent of Neptune, Chiron in the example chart. As you can see in the chart shown on the following page, there are a number of aspects involving Chiron. They have already been dealt with in the lesson about Chiron. But in this lesson, Chiron is the regent of Neptune. It therefore has a slightly different meaning that modifies the interpretation in accordance with Neptune's original influence.

Aspects involving Neptune's regent

Conjunct MC
Square Ascendant
Square Neptune
Square Saturn
Trine Lilith
Inconjunct Part of Fortune
Opposition NADIR

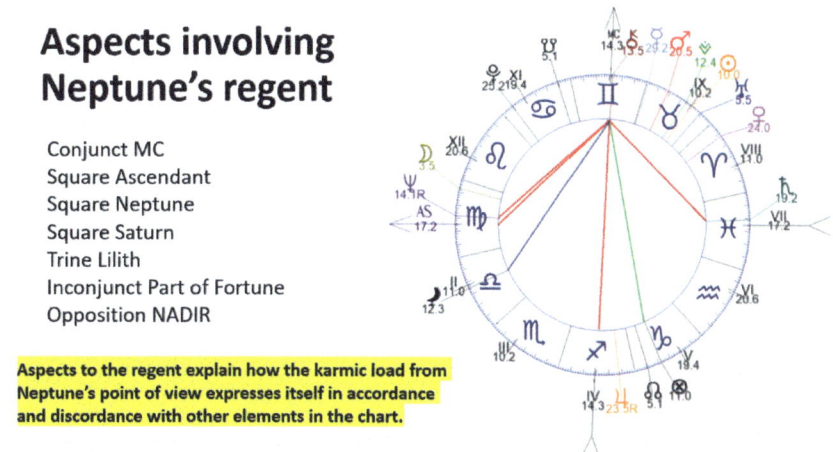

Aspects to the regent explain how the karmic load from Neptune's point of view expresses itself in accordance and discordance with other elements in the chart.

There is a conjunction with the Midheaven and a square with the Ascendant. There is a square with Neptune and Saturn. There is a trine with Lilith already discussed in a previous lesson. There is an inconjunct with the Part of Fortune and an opposition with the NADIR, which is the cusp of House IV.

All the above-mentioned aspects need to be analysed because they explain how the karmic load from Neptune's point of view expresses itself in accordance and discordance with other elements in the chart.

Next, we must analyse the aspects together, those involving Neptune and those involving its regent. There is a conjunction with the Ascendant for Neptune, a square with Chiron, a square with the MC, an opposition with Saturn, an opposition with the Descendant or House VII, a trine with the Part of Fortune.

Together

Neptune
Conjunction Ascendant
Square Chiron
Square MC
Opposition Saturn
Opposition DESC.
Trine Part of Fortune

Chiron
Conjunct MC
Square Ascendant
Square Neptune
Square Saturn
Trine Lilith
Inconjunct Part of Fortune
Opposition NADIR

About Chiron, Neptune's regent, there is a conjunction with the MC or Midheaven, a square with the Ascendant, a square with Neptune, a square with Saturn, a trine with Lilith, an inconjunct with the Part of Fortune, and an opposition with the NADIR.

All the aspects mentioned need to be analysed separately, but they will also need to be blended together. Don't forget that the House ruled by Neptune represents areas marked by a karmic load in relation with the influence of this planet in a sign and in a House, not forgetting the aspects for which the same rule applies to Neptune's regent.

Blending

The next step is blending. However, blending should not be kept for last. On the contrary, it should be done as you progress. While you analyse a position of Neptune, or any other planet or element acknowledge the position in sign which automatically means a position in a House. Blend those two elements and then continue on to the regent of the planet you are analysing. It is in a sign and in a House. Such simple exercise repeated every time you analyse a planet in a chart leads to an ability to blend and synthesise your reading of a birth chart to make it not only rich and interesting, but useful to the person concerned.

Don't forget

The House ruled by Neptune represents areas marked by a karmic load in relation with the influence of this planet in sign, in House and in aspect.

The same rule applies to Neptune's regent.

Example

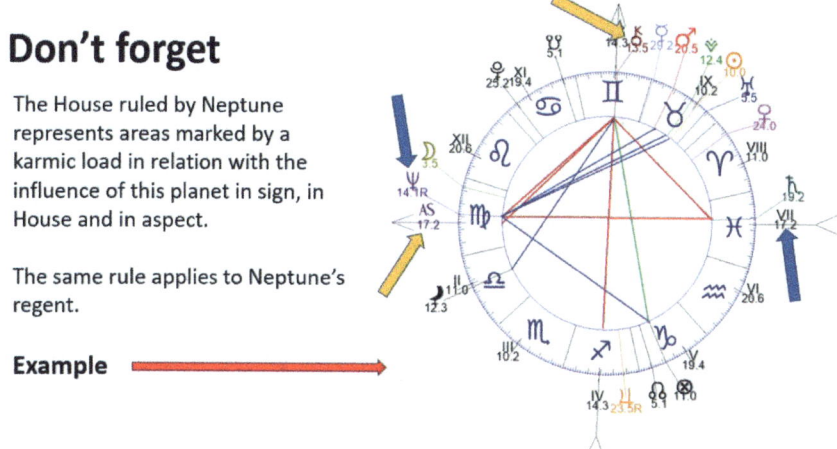

Aspects must also be blended. A square is known as a rather difficult configuration, but it may be made easier to deal with by a trine, which is an excellent source of positive energy.

There may also be somewhere else in the chart, represented by another planet or element in aspect, a disrupting effect that could contradict the positive influence of the trine...

That's why blending is so important. Do it from the start, don't keep it for last. Remember that because if you practise that way you will quickly be able to achieve quite precise and interesting readings.

This is the end of lesson 8. Thank you for your attention and for your interest in this course. In lesson 9 we will discuss the influence of Pluto.

Supplementary section

Neptune in signs

The following descriptions are meant to help you understand the basic influence of Neptune in the present life. The karmic meaning of Neptune has been discussed in this lesson.

ARIES

Neptune was in Aries, between 1861 and 1875, influencing a new generation of researchers and astronomers who tuned their head (Aries) to the sky. Many discoveries were made; some of which came out of the minds of enlightened, intuitive scientists. Occultists like Helena Blavatsky emerged and changed the spiritual concepts of the Western world. Neptune will return to transit in Aries from 2026 until 2040. Space manned missions to Mars (ruler of Aries) will become a reality and initiate a new era of discoveries for humanity. The less positive aspect of Neptune in fiery Aries influences some to act and react strongly and aggressively on presumptions rather than on fact and reality. Religious fundamentalism will also become more aggressive and irrationally determined.

TAURUS

It indicates a period from 1875 until 1889 during which a kind of idealism developed regarding the use of money and material resources. It marked the beginning of both Capitalism and Communism. The period was marked by major incidents involving water on the earth (Neptune rules the water sign, Pisces) similar to the great floods of 1856. Crops were destroyed creating food shortages which meant that many people missed out on the most elementary need to daily meals.

GEMINI

Between 1889 and 1902, Neptune marked a generation of people who did a lot to develop the intuitive and creative faculties of the mind that gave birth to the cinema at the end of the 19th century. There were major advances in communication since the invention of the telephone by Graham Bell in 1876.

CANCER

The transit lasted between 1902 and 1916, inspiring stronger psychic ties with the concepts of home and family. Religion had an emotional rather than intellectual significance. This position created excessive patriotism and ideological attachment to the home and country.

LEO

Neptune here conferred certain artistic talents to many people born between 1916 and 1929. This position enhances romantic tendencies and idealism in love, friendship, and other close relationships. Neptune in Leo illustrates the roaring twenties when unwise speculation and extravagant spending in pursuit of pleasure and lust led to financial ruin and to the great world depression of the thirties.

VIRGO

From 1928 until 1943 Neptune influenced a generation whose creative and imaginative faculties were thwarted by adverse material circumstances. The transit lasted through the period of the Great Depression and a part of World War II. Neptune here indicates a tendency to develop psychosomatic illnesses because of an over-sensitive approach to health and hygiene. Surges of anxiety derived from the influence of Virgo can lead to impractical methods and projects. Calculations based on unrealistic data produced incorrect results. This generation of people was deeply marked by uncertainty and disillusion when rebuilding the world from its own ashes was not a dream come true, but a painful reality.

LIBRA

From 1943 until 1957 Neptune here represents the post-war generation, people who brought about new concepts in the areas of marriage and partnership in general. The relationship itself became more important than the legal paperwork or contract. This led to an increasing divorce rate. The resulting broken homes produced uncertainty in the younger generation. The real value of relationship obligations became a source of error and disappointment. Inspired and sensitive, the artistic tendencies of this generation are enhanced by Neptune in Libra. It favours comedians, actors, musicians, and writers. These people found inspiration by connecting with the spiritual, some of them taking drugs or other substances to produce altered states of perception.

SCORPIO

Between 1957 and 1970, Neptune in Scorpio touched a generation led by basic natural desires. Sex, drugs, and alcohol became a formidable commercial exploitation with a harmful influence on morality and ethics. Drug addiction and alcoholism became an easy means to escape the 'sad reality of life'. A few people found true spiritual regeneration, but the greater number was marked by the negative effect of such destructive behaviour. However, clairvoyant abilities are also conferred by Neptune in Scorpio, together with profound sensitivity. The birth of the hippie movement in the sixties brought about a more sensible approach to nature's richness which led to the development of modern holistic medicine.

SAGITTARIUS

This position concerns people born between 1970 and 1984. They have a yearning for higher ethical and spiritual values in human customs. They dream of 'spiritualising' society. Their inspired perception is found in music and art. Interactions with foreign lands for cultural exchanges is also important to their moral and intellectual growth. They have a mystical and metaphysical approach to the meaning of life. Spiritual healers, brilliant lecturers and philosophers are other products of the positive influence of Neptune in this sign. However, they are descendants of the hippie generation, of fake prophets and gurus who preached a better world for their own personal gain. With Neptune in Sagittarius in their chart, some may be tempted to replicate a similar behaviour.

CAPRICORN

People born between 1984 and 1998 have Neptune in Capricorn. They display an innate sense of authority. Their intuition is down-to-earth. They want to keep their feet firmly on the ground, but their head is in the clouds. They want to succeed, and they have a good intuition when it comes to choosing the best way to get to the top of the mountain they want to climb. Some are too irrational, making grandiose plans that cannot be realised. Some understand that time is an unavoidable factor to include in their schemes. They are the most successful ones. To them, the soul is more a concept than a reality. Until they are proven wrong, they keep firm on their positions and beliefs.

AQUARIUS

This position concerns people born between 1998 and 2012. They have a genuine humanitarian philosophy and a spiritual approach to the meaning of life. They need to interact with others using modern tools of communication. They are intuitive and genuinely interested in the wellbeing of their entourage. They may get involved in charitable organisations to help the underprivileged. They are spontaneously connected, reaching out to the world in the hope of changing the essence of life threatened by the selfish behaviour of the older generations. The downside of Neptune's influence is a lack of objectivity and bohemian behaviour due to a certain confusion to adapt and accept laws and regulations.

PISCES

This position concerns people born between 2012 and 2026. Mystical, sensitive, and insightful, they are spontaneously connected to the spiritual dimension, where they may seek refuge when the realities of earthly life become too harsh. They tend to absorb the environmental energy like water in a sponge. Their extreme sensibility makes them vulnerable to negative and positive influences alike. Some are unable to distinguish between good and evil, between right or wrong. Some, with a higher IQ may become charismatic spiritual leaders. They will be teachers to those lost souls who will benefit from such lofty education. The downside of this position of Neptune is a tendency to lustfulness and an attraction to narcotics or alcohol, as well as fundamentalist religious practices.

Supplementary section

Neptune in Houses

In House I

Neptune here enhances imagination, sensibility, and artistic qualities. It also confers a degree of confusion in the expression of the inner personality due to a natural ability to perceive life on subtle plans. Sensitivity to the environment may trigger mysterious medical afflictions. Position comparable to Neptune in Aries.

In House II

This position enhances imagination to improve finances, but it can also indicate confusion and uncertainty wherever material values are concerned. A rational diet is a must to preserve physiological balance. Allergic reactions to some foods are occasionally observed. Position similar to Neptune in Taurus.

In House III

This position usually enhances imagination, sixth sense, and the ability to learn by osmosis. An interest in spiritual healing is present. In some cases, extreme sensitivity may induce mental confusion and a tendency to develop psychosomatic disorders. Position comparable to Neptune in Gemini.

In House IV

This position creates a subtle link with the mother and family members. The need to be living near the sea or to convert the home into an artist studio is not uncommon. Health concerns may be of genetic origin, mostly from the mother's side of the family. Position comparable to Neptune in Cancer.

In House V

This position enhances creativity and imagination in art and the expression of love. Success in music, dancing, painting, or writing is favoured. Neptune here may also indicate confusion and uncertainty in sentimental relationships or in dealing with children and loved ones. Position comparable to Neptune in Leo.

In House VI
This position indicates uncertainty in the choice of a profession. Any area requiring intuition, creativity, and sensitivity are potential avenues of success. Health and medicine or spiritual healing interests may also contribute to the choice of a career. Psychosomatic tendencies are observed. Position comparable to Neptune in Virgo.

In House VII
This position indicates a natural attraction to spiritually oriented partners. However, confusion and uncertainty prevail until the right person is met. There is an innate need to help others with a tendency to consider it a mission and a karmic earthly duty. Position comparable to Neptune in Libra.

In House VIII
This position often shows an innate ability to communicate with invisible or parallel plans. There is an intuitive approach to spirituality through a profound interest for the mysteries of life and death. Neptune may, however, create confusion in finances and other down-to-earth areas. Position comparable to Neptune in Scorpio.

In House IX
This position enhances the need for a spiritual and philosophical life path. Dealing with administrative or legal matters may, however, be a source of confusion. Morality and knowledge are major aspects of life to ensure personal wellbeing and success. Position comparable to Neptune in Sagittarius.

In House X
This position indicates potential to succeed in a wide range of professional activities including but not limited to religion, philosophy, teaching, politics, welfare, medicine, spiritual healing, chemistry, or ecology. However, there may be confusion in making the right choice. Position comparable to Neptune in Capricorn.

In House XI
This position enhances the ability to perceive humanity spiritually. There is a lofty approach to social issues. Friendships with people of similar philosophical trends are favoured. However, excess receptivity may affect both social and geographical environments. Position comparable to Neptune in Aquarius.

In House XII
Neptune here indicates extreme sensitivity to, and awareness of the spiritual aspect of earthly life. Intuition borders on clairvoyance, together with the ability to subtle perception. This position may also induce a need to withdraw due to both moral and physical vulnerability. Position comparable to Neptune in Scorpio.

Lesson 9

Link to the video: https://youtu.be/e-q2WublWec

Pluto

Lesson 9

Pluto

We now begin lesson number 9 in which we discuss the karmic influence of Pluto, the farthest planet from the sun. Pluto is a very interesting element as you will find out in this lesson.

In mythology Pluto is the god of death. It represents the darkest side of life. It also represents our regeneration capacity, the ability to regenerate on a physical, mental, and spiritual point of view. It also represents what death teaches us about life. Self-destruction and reconstruction are also represented by Pluto. Pluto is our connection to the underworld...

Take note of the dates when Pluto was passing through every sign of the zodiac. Because of the slow motion of this planet, it remains a long time in every sign, and in some signs much longer than others. That's because Pluto's orbit is not circular, it is elliptic. If you want to find out more about Pluto on an astronomical point of view, refer to my 'Astrology for a better life' book where everything is explained.

Pluto in signs

Pluto was in Aries from 1823 until 1853-54

Pluto was in Taurus from 1853-54 until 1882-83

Pluto was in Gemini from 1882-83 until 1912–1913

Pluto was in Cancer from 1912-13 until 1939–1940

Pluto was in Leo from 1939-40 until 1957-58

Pluto was in Virgo from 1957-58 until 1971-72

Pluto was in Libra from 1971-72 until 1983-84

Pluto was in Scorpio from 1983-84 until 1995-96

Pluto was in Sagittarius from 1995-96 until 2008–2009

Pluto was in Capricorn from 2008-09 until 2023-25

Pluto will be in Aquarius from 2023-24 until 2043-44

Pluto will be in Pisces from 2043-44 until 2068.

Pluto in a chart reveals how we died in the previous incarnation. Therefore, the sign in which it is found tells a lot about how we dealt with that passing away to this present life.

—In Aries, Pluto indicates a sudden and violent death through war, aggression, a fight, or a cerebral vascular accident.

—In Taurus, Pluto suggests that death was probably due to lack of food or food poisoning perhaps.

—In Gemini, Pluto shows that death was due to loss of or destruction of mental capacity.

—In Cancer, Pluto reveals that death was probably due to drowning in a river or lake.

—In Leo, Pluto tells us that death was probably due to heart failure or to a cardiovascular accident.

—In Virgo, Pluto indicates that death was probably due to the intestine or digestive system failure, or to a work accident.

—In Libra, Pluto suggests that death was perhaps due to the partner's aggression or criminal court judgement. It could also have been due to kidney failure.

—In Scorpio, Pluto shows that death was probably due to contamination, a pandemic, poison, or failure of the regenerative functions.

—In Sagittarius, Pluto indicates that death probably occurred far from the place of birth, while travelling for example, and in a foreign land or country.

—In Capricorn, Pluto evokes the possibility that death happened from a mountain-climbing accident, political destitution such as may happen to monarchs or dictators.

—In Aquarius, Pluto indicates that death was perhaps due to electrification, or during a revolution, a riot, or perhaps to a nervous system failure or seizure.

— In Pisces, Pluto shows that death was probably due to drowning at sea, or from pulmonary failure suffocation, gas inhalation, or chemical ingestion.

Pluto in Houses

Pluto in signs is one thing. Pluto in Houses is another. Pluto in signs, as we've just seen, represents the manner in which we died in our previous incarnation. Pluto in Houses refers to the present life where it represents the unconscious repercussions of the way we dealt with our passing away in our previous incarnation. Such consequence or repercussion operates in the present incarnation in the areas represented by the House concerned.

Here is a quick list of the potential effect of Pluto in each of the twelve Houses.

—Pluto in House I or Ascendant, shows that death and the mysteries of life influence the development and the expression of the inner self.

—Pluto in House II shows that the idea of death influences material life, earnings, and feeding habits.

—Pluto in House III suggests a deep intellectual interest in death and the mysteries of life linked to the meaning of Pluto in sign.

—Pluto in House IV indicates an unconscious need to regenerate family and residence marked by hardship and perhaps death.

—Pluto in House V suggests that creation and procreation, love, and romance are confronted to karmic difficulties linked to the influence of Pluto in sign.

—Pluto in House VI indicates that work and health are a source of difficulties due to an unconscious karmic need to reform the status quo.

—Pluto in House VII reveals that marriage and other important relationships are marked by karmic difficulties and suffering.

—Pluto in House VIII implies that death, sex, and money are major interests linked to unconscious reminiscences from the previous incarnation.

—Pluto in House IX shows a strong need to reform and transform the social system in reaction to past life situations.

—Pluto in House X (MC or Mid Heaven) demonstrates that personal ambitions, career choice, and social status are marked by the karmic influence of Pluto in sign.

—Pluto in House XI indicates that social life and friendship are marked by karmic difficulties, profound changes, and questionings linked to past-life unhappy experiences.

—Pluto in House XII shows that faith, spirituality, and personal dreams are a source of inner doubt and confusing feelings.

Of course, these short indications must be linked to the position of Pluto in sign which tells how fatality and hardship were managed and accepted or refused when passing away in a previous incarnation. Although that forgotten event has been forgotten, it has a profound influence on the way we live our life today. We all know that we are eventually going to die, but we don't want to die in the same way we did in our previous incarnation. However, the reminiscence is there, unconsciously, and it acts on the way we deal with the areas of life represented by the House of the chart where Pluto is found.

Example

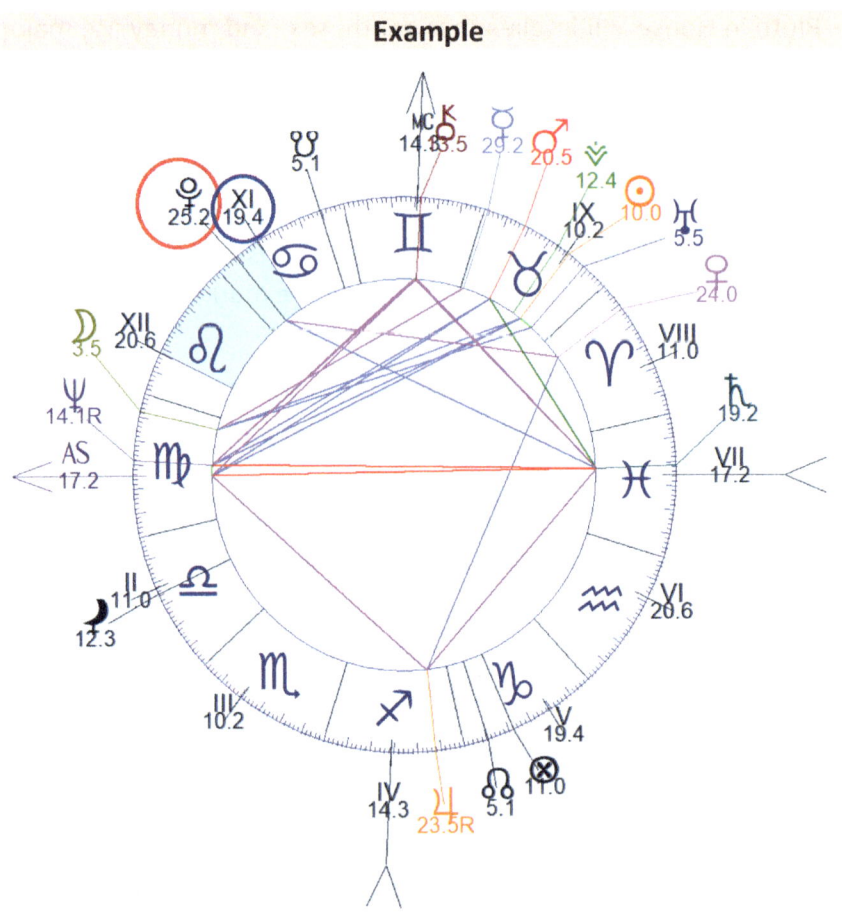

Now let's take an example. It is the same chart used since the beginning of this course. In it, we see that Pluto is in Cancer and in House XI. Therefore, we have two sources of information. Pluto in Cancer indicates that death may have occurred because of drowning in the river or lake. It also indicates possible loss of family, of the place of residence, or a situation that destroyed the life of the person and the life of the people around. Considering Pluto in House XI shows that what this person went through in the previous incarnation has a strong influence on the way this person deals with friendship and social life. Those areas are marked by karmic difficulties. It seems that this person is influenced by what happened socially or in the family environment, or perhaps in the country where this person was living at the time. It means that Pluto has a latent destructive influence with an effect in House XI which deals with friendship, social relationships, and the social environment, both human and geographical. That explains why this person moved so many times from one place to another right across Australia, north and south, east and west, for so many years...

As you know by now, a planet in a sign has a regent. The regent is the ruler of the sign in which the planet is found. Except when the planet is the ruler of the sign in which it is found, of course. Let us direct our reading to the regent of Pluto to find out what happens when it is in one of the twelve zodiac signs.

—The regent in Aries indicates that Pluto's karmic meaning is a source of chronic tension and various incidents linked to the previous life.

—The regent in Taurus means that Pluto's karmic meaning is expressed in the approach to materiality, food, and the good things of life.

—The regent in Gemini shows that Pluto's karmic meaning has a derived influence on communication and intellectual pursuits.

—The regent in Cancer indicates that Pluto's karmic meaning has an indirect influence on the expression and control of emotions.

—The regent in Leo suggests that Pluto's karmic meaning is expressed intensely with a strong influence of one's image and creativity.

—The regent in Virgo indicates that Pluto's karmic meaning is a source of questioning about health, hygiene, work, and daily routine.

—The regent in Libra reveals that Pluto's karmic meaning produces a need to preserve and restore balance and harmony in human relationships.

—The regent in Scorpio shows that Pluto's karmic meaning affects sexuality, physical and psychological regeneration, and mental determination.

—The regent in Sagittarius indicates that Pluto's karmic meaning is a source of motivation to progress on a moral and philosophical point of view.

—The regent in Capricorn suggests that Pluto's karmic meaning suggests a stronger motivation to reach the top with endurance and tenacity.

—The regent in Aquarius indicates that Pluto's karmic meaning affects social life and friendship where sudden fluctuations and changes are observed.

—The regent in Pisces shows that Pluto's karmic meaning is a source of inspiration and spiritual questioning to deal with life's confusing situations.

Pluto's regent can be in any House in the chart where it has an indirect effect in the areas represented by the House concerned. Simultaneously refer to the meaning of Pluto's position in sign to better understand how its regent in a House can affect the areas of life represented.

—The regent is in House I or Ascendant transfers Pluto's meaning to the development and expression of the inner personality.

—The regent in House II dealing with the material side of life is indirectly influenced by Pluto in sign's karmic meaning.

—The regent in House III shows that communication and intellectual interests are indirectly linked to the role of Pluto in the previous life according to its position in sign.

—The regent in House IV indicates that family life and the place of residence are indirectly influenced by the karmic meaning of Pluto in sign.

—The regent in House V shows that creativity, love, the pleasures of life, and romance are influenced by the karmic meaning of Pluto in sign.

—The regent in House VI suggests that the way work, health, and daily routine and duties are perceived stems from the karmic influence of Pluto in sign.

—The regent in House VII shows that important personal relationships and partnerships are subject to the indirect influence of Pluto in sign.

—The regent in House VIII tells us that sexuality and the concept of life and death unconsciously stem from the karmic influence of Pluto in sign.

—The regent in House IX indicates that moral and philosophical values stem from an unconscious connection with the karmic influence of Pluto in sign.

—The regent in House X or Midheaven shows that personal ambitions, career, and social objectives are influenced by the karmic role of Pluto in sign.

—The regent in House XI suggests that friendship and socialising are motivated by an unconscious influence of Pluto's role in the previous life from its position in sign.

—The regent in House XII indicates that the spiritual dimension of life is deeply motivated by the indirect influence of Pluto in sign.

Remember that the energy and nature of the planet regent of Pluto must be considered to better understand its meaning in the chart. If the regent is Mars instead of Mercury, for example, the inference is very different and needs to be considered. Your reading of the chart will only benefit from such an approach.

Looking at the example chart once again, we see that Pluto is in Cancer, creating a link with the Moon because it is the regent of Pluto. Being the ruler of Cancer, we see that the Moon is in Virgo and in House XII. It is interesting because the Moon in Virgo indicates that Pluto's karmic meaning is a source of questioning about health, hygiene, work, and daily routine. In House XII it indicates that the spiritual dimension of life is deeply motivated by the indirect influence of Pluto in sign. Being in House XI and in Cancer, Pluto indicates that this person went through very difficult times family-wise, maybe in the country where this person was living then, and because of the manner in which death occurred (drowning).

Reading the above, we agree that it is very important to bear in mind the basic influence of Pluto in sign to better understand what this planet means through its House position, and through the position of its regent in sign and in House.

Then, we need to analyse the aspects involving Pluto. We cannot do without the aspects. They are the back bones of the astrological reading. In the example chart, Pluto in Cancer forms a sextile with Mercury and another with Mars. They are rather wide aspects, but sufficiently strong to be considered as such. There is a square with Venus, a trine with Saturn and the cusp of House VII or Descendant (DESC) and an inconjunct with Jupiter.

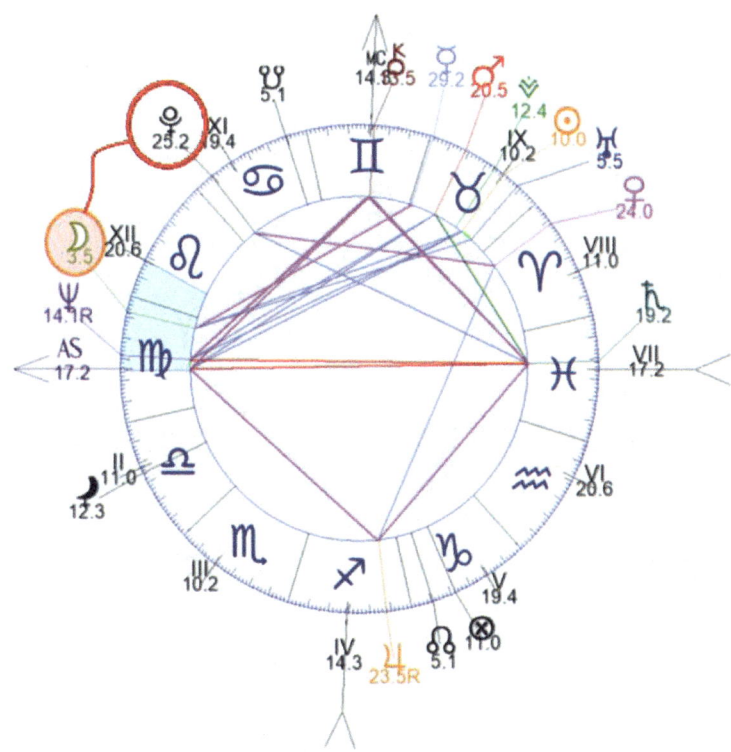

Taking note of all the aspects and analysing them help us understand how this person, influenced by what happened in the previous incarnation, deals with the present life through the other planets involved in the aspect. Mercury is communication, Mars is action, Venus is love, Saturn is resilience and determination, and Jupiter represents generosity and the need to expand and to improve in many ways.

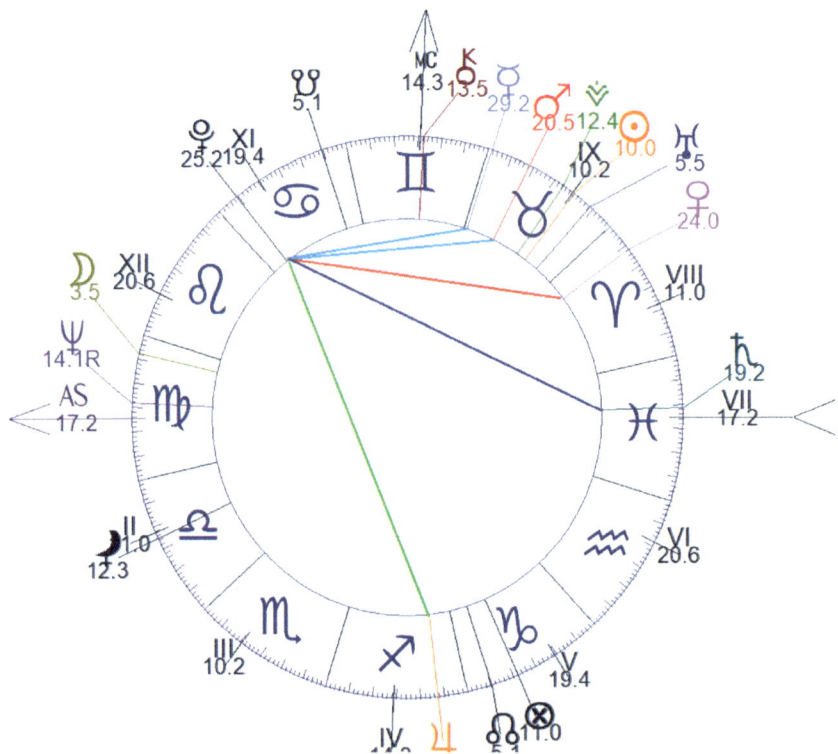

Once the aspects involving Pluto are analysed, we have to turn to the aspects involving the regent of Pluto.

There are quite a number of aspects involving the Moon in this chart. There is a sextile with the South Lunar Node, which means that there is a trine with the North Node, there is also a trine with the Part of Fortune, a square with Mercury. This one is interesting because we have seen that there is a sextile between Pluto and Mercury but, there is a square between the regent of Pluto and Mercury.

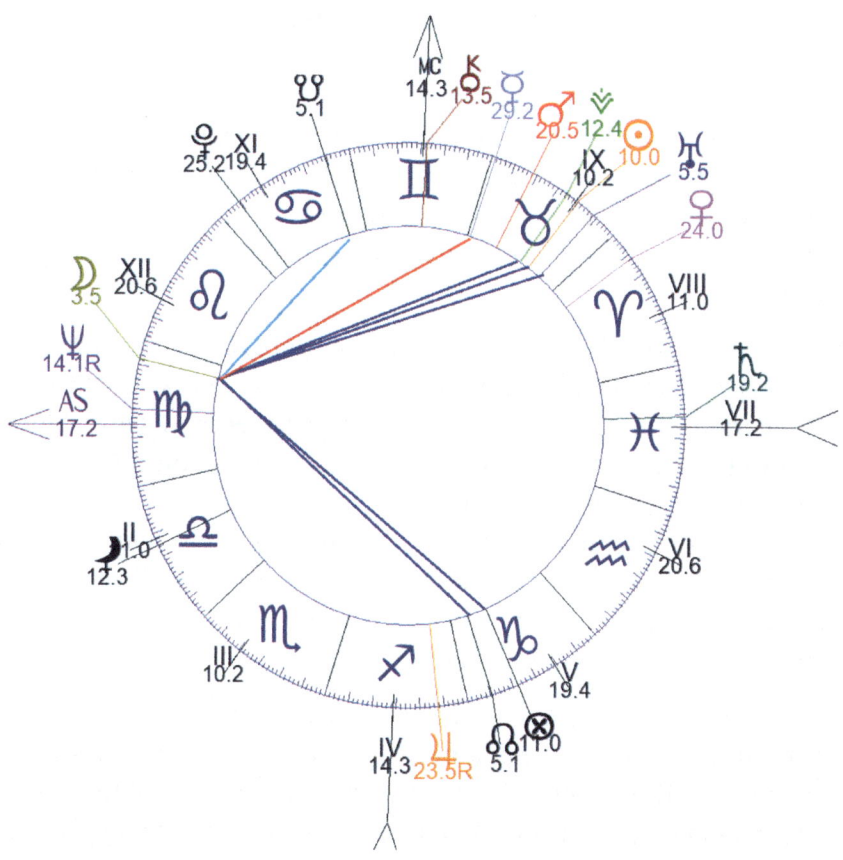

Contradicting aspects tend to balance out the energy that they produce. It indicates when there is a situation where the emotions are really triggered hard strong and when this person doesn't feel able to control the situation then there is a loss of the ability capacity to communicate and to express what needs to be expressed, explained, or defended. Therefore, when a conversation turns sour and becomes an argument this person turns to Mars because Mars is not far from Mercury indicating that this person can be mentally and intellectually very reactive and perhaps aggressive, and impulsive, or prone to get quite angry when contradicted. The aspects involving the Moon show emotional vulnerability justifying defensive reactions for protection and assertion. And, of course, that is all because of what this person went through in the previous life shown by the karmic position of Pluto in Cancer. Unconscious memories of those difficult times trigger chain reactions as soon as the present life situation resembles what happened in the previous existence...

However, there are three trines that counterbalance the troubling influences of the discordant aspects. There is one with Vesta, a second one with the Sun, and a third one with Uranus. Don't hesitate to analyse this chart as a practical exercise on the aspects. You may find out some very interesting facts about this person...

The next step is to analyse the aspects involving both Pluto and its regent. There are quite numerous and if you add all the other aspects between planets and other elements in the chart that makes it even more intense to read and analyse.

Doing so, don't forget that Pluto in sign gives us a first basic information about its influence and its role in the previous incarnation. Then, Pluto in House gives us another information about the influence of this planet in the areas represented by that House. Then, of course, we consider the regent (the Moon in this example). It is in a sign which gives us a further information about the way Pluto acts in this person's life.

And the regent (the Moon in this example) is in a certain House. In the example chart in House XII. Therefore, the areas represented by House XII are also influenced by Pluto, but indirectly because it is influenced by Pluto *through the energy of the Moon.*

The aspects are essential to analyse because they involve other planets and elements. In the example chart, there are a number of planets in Taurus, a sign ruled or represented by Venus which is found in Aries, a sign ruled by Mars which is found in Taurus... That's what we call an 'exchange of residence'. It means that Mars is very important in this chart, which makes the aspects involving Mars more important too. Let's see what they are.

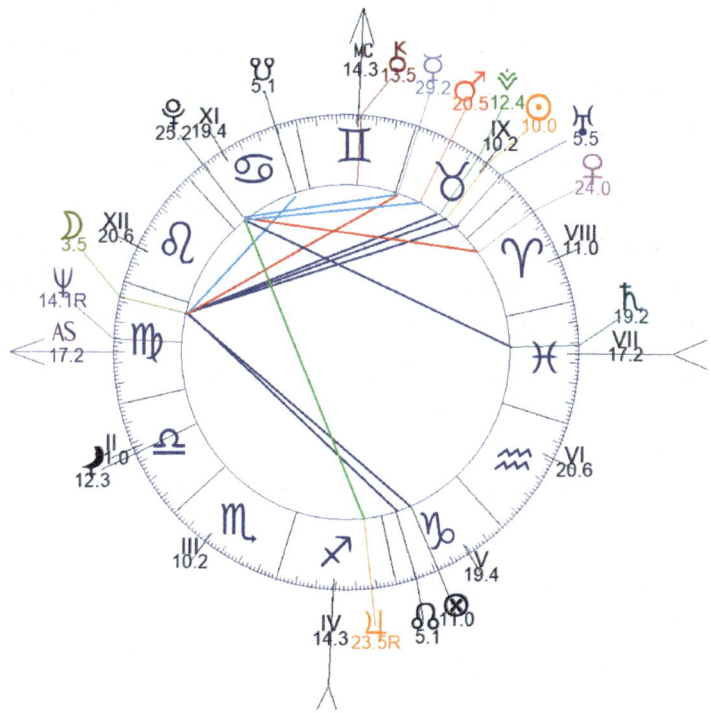

There is sextile between Mars and Pluto indicating that this person has a very strong will and physical as well as mental ability to obtain what this person wants with determination and authority, a character trait represented by Mars.

We also see in this chart that Saturn is in Neptune's sign (Pisces) making Neptune the regent of Saturn. This was explained in lesson 6 about Saturn. You may need to study the lessons again and again until you really understand how to analyse a chart from a karmic point of view, as well as from this present life's point of view. Therefore, when you analyse a chart for someone remember that it is very important to obtain an in-depth reading rather than a superficial one.

Last but not least, we need to blend the gathered pieces of information together. As I have explained earlier, blending should be done as you go along. From the position of Pluto in sign to its position in House, you can start blending to synthesise the influence of Pluto. Then, apply this technique to the regent in sign and in House before turning to the aspects which are treated in the same manner. I understand that it is a difficult exercise, but it is as necessary as playing repeatedly the scales on a musical instrument to master the art and become a virtuoso…

This is the end of lesson 9. Thank you for your attention. Use the supplementary sections in the following pages to guide your personal readings of the influence of Pluto in your chart and anyone else. Lesson 10 deals with the retrograde planets.

Supplementary section

Pluto in signs

ARIES

Pluto is quite fierce and can be very destructive in Aries, the combative and competitive sign. Pluto here generates a good amount of energy to launch new projects. The need to destroy old traditions to impose new concepts was obvious during the period between 1823 and 1852. It was a time of extensive colonisation when force seemed the only way to defeat and conquer territories and countries alike. The next transit of Pluto in Aries will begin in 2066...

TAURUS

In Taurus, Pluto indicates a tendency to question and revolutionise the economy and its materialistically profitable connotation. Pluto transited here between 1852 and 1882. Because Taurus represents food, agriculture and the good and beautiful things of life, there was an overwhelming need to radically transform and modernise. The Industrial Revolution that led to the establishment of numerous factories throughout the world and to the first problems of unemployment and desolation. The era of the 'Machine' had begun.

GEMINI

Pluto was in Gemini between 1882 and 1913. It coincided with a period of complete regeneration in communication at all levels and in all areas of life. A new way of thinking emerged, and the transport industry was revolutionised by the invention of the automobile and the aeroplane. Edison, Tesla, Bell, and others discovered the uses of electricity for modem technology and communications. Individually, Pluto encouraged a tendency to question and destroy the old ways of thinking to comply with the exigence of the extraordinary progress that took over the world in the twentieth century. Healthwise, this position may trigger various brains and neurologic disorders.

PLUTO in CANCER

Pluto began its long transit in Cancer in July 1913. World War I began in July 1914. World War II followed in 1939 when Pluto was nearing the end of its transit in this sign. In Cancer, Pluto marked an era of great patriotic concerns. The death of millions of people and children of all ages brought fear and destruction to many parts of the earth. The individual influence of this position is seen in a tendency to question and transform family ties and values. To rebuild on the ashes of the old world became an upmost necessity, but the task had to be led in a totally different manner, with the idea that deadly conflicts and global destruction would never again be a menace. Healthwise, Pluton in Cancer seems to trigger various pathologies affecting the digestive system and the lymph.

PLUTO in LEO

This position marked a generation of people whose education and growth were deeply influenced and strongly motivated by the events of World War II. Pluto transited in Leo between 1939 and 1957. Its effect is seen in the direct suffering caused by family losses, and in the psychological and affective impact of such disastrous times in world history. Pluto generates a need to question and transform with great courage and a sense of responsibility to help the weak and vulnerable. It confers a definite ability to express deeper feelings and emotions in new forms of art and in human relationships. Healthwise, when involved in discordant configurations in the chart, Pluto in Leo may produce cardiovascular pathologies, as well as eye and spine ailments.

PLUTO in VIRGO

Pluto was in Virgo between 1957 and 1972. People born then tend to question, reform, and transform their work environment. They need to destroy the 'old school' to build a totally new concept. The role of the syndicates and other leadership-contesting movements emerged and eventually led to situations such as riots and demonstrations in various parts of the world. They are good examples of the influence of Pluto in this sign. Excessive worry about working conditions and health issues produce various pathologies affecting the digestive system.

PLUTO in LIBRA

People born between 1972 and 1984 with this position tend to question and seek reforms and regeneration in the areas of personal, social, and professional partnerships. There is a profound need for fairness and equity that may lead to revolts and other revendication movements. Artists challenge the old school to rejuvenate the status quo and impose a different approach of their work in literature, theatre, cinema, and music. Pluto in Libra also indicates a strong desire to reform the justice system to restore its neutrality and clarity. The kidneys, bladder, and the lumbar region may become sources of health concerns.

PLUTO in SCORPIO

This is Pluto's sign of rulership where its influence is strong and profound. The transit lasted between 1984 and 1996. It indicates an attraction and an interest in the occult, the mysteries of life and death. People born with Pluto in Scorpio are usually determined and cold-blooded. They are not afraid to die. Some may even show masochist leanings due to their unusual resistance to pain. Plutonian types of professions are preferred to more conventional careers. The army, the police force, the funeral industry, perilous or hazardous activities, and any profession that can satisfy their physical need for adrenaline. The reproductive system and the colonic function may become sources of health concerns.

PLUTO in SAGITTARIUS

Pluto in Sagittarius affects people born between 1996 and 2009. They belong to a generation seeking to regenerate the administration and justice system of their country with worldwide consequences. Some may develop a rather nihilist philosophical approach to life and lack positive drive to more constructive achievements. Regeneration seems necessary to obtain a more insightful meaning and purpose to higher studies, academic knowledge, and communication. Relations with foreign countries and cultures may deeply change due to fateful events, such as pollution, pandemics, and other calamities. These people grow up in difficult times. They need to be strong and remain optimistic, however negative the events may be. Blood pressure and liver function may become sources of health concerns.

PLUTO in CAPRICORN

This position concerns people born between 2009 and 2024. They will be motivated by a much-needed reorganisation of the world's banking system. They will strive to get rid of the common perception of money and profit. They will find it necessary to avoid increasingly frequent frauds, and dysfunctions at the highest levels of society. They will create a more equitable evaluation of people's incomes. They will strive to eliminate all kinds of dictatorship and other authoritarian behaviour. To avoid a global war or revolution, it will seem urgent to these people to revise and transform the notions of power and social status. Bones, skin, and joints may become sources of health concerns.

PLUTO in AQUARIUS

From 2024 onwards, we can expect a global phenomenon of total social regeneration. Aquarius represents social and geographical environments, peoples, and populations. Those born between 2024 and 2043 will live to destroy society in view of building a new world. The previous transit of Pluto in this sign began in 1779, when the monarchy in France and America was nearing the end of its reign. Chaos ensued, but revolution eventually led to Republic and democracy. In 2024, the Internet may crash and be replaced by a more suitable system of communication. Control of the population will become so tight that it will create remarkably fierce reactions. The victims of these dark times will become sources of inspiration for the strongest and most determined ones to fight for a better world even at the cost of their life. The central nervous system and the peripheral blood circulation may become sources of health concerns.

PLUTO in PISCES

Pluto will transit this spiritual, mystical, and religious sign between 2043 and 2068. It may produce a total regeneration in these areas and the destruction of the old churches to the benefit of new laws and new mystical and religious approaches. At the same time, our planet will be almost completely drained from its natural fossil resources. Other consumable forms of energy will have already appeared. Wars for oil will not be possible any more. Energy will be derived from the Sun and other natural sources. Disasters related to gas, water pollution, seismic activity, and floods will be common during this transit. People born with this position of Pluto may deplore a weakness of the respiratory system and of the lower limbs, especially the ankles and feet. Psychosomatic illnesses will also be more frequent.

Supplementary section

Pluto in Houses

PLUTO in House I
Pluto here indicates a greater ability to regenerate from illnesses and other setbacks, together with sustained concentration, determination, and strength. An interest in the mysteries of life and death is observed. A nihilist tendency may, however, deter the joy of being alive. Position comparable to Pluto in Aries.

PLUTO in House II
Pluto here indicates a life path marked by great upheavals and misfortune that may seriously threaten finances and material life. Food may be considered poisonous or health threatening. However, spontaneous regeneration helps solve the harsher upheavals. Position comparable to Pluto in Taurus.

PLUTO in House III
This position indicates an innate interest in psychology, the mysteries of life, occultism, and sexuality. Mental focus and endurance enable long-lasting studies and most intellectual endeavours. Communication may be sarcastic, caustic, or morbid. Position comparable to Pluto in Gemini.

PLUTO in House IV
This position indicates a life path marked with family upheavals. Leaving home early to settle away from the 'troubled nest' is often observed. However, Pluto enhances the natural ability to regenerate and recover from the worse suffering and hardship that may be endured. Position comparable to Pluto in Cancer.

PLUTO in House V

This position indicates sentimental difficulties due to a strong and profound, but often dark approach to love and romance. There may be deep moral traumas from hardship endured during childhood. Relationships with loved ones have a deep karmic connotation. Position comparable to Pluto in Leo.

PLUTO in House VI

This position indicates a tendency to strong actions, reactions, and decisions to deal with professional responsibilities. The need to question and transform work conditions is a source of chronic tension. Health may be affected by infections, poisoning, or contamination. Position comparable to Pluto in Virgo.

PLUTO in House VII

This position strongly affects private partnerships and marriage. Pluto confers authenticity and determination to deal with important relations efficiently. It is also responsible for destructive tendencies. Relationship difficulties leave deep scars that may deter personal reconstruction indefinitely. Position comparable to Pluto in Libra.

PLUTO in House VIII

Pluto's influence is strong in this House and essentially linked to the regeneration principle. It confers willpower, determination, and physical endurance. There is a strong sex drive playing a major role in personal relationships. Finances may be a source of chronic disturbance. Position comparable to Pluto in Scorpio.

PLUTO in House IX

This position confers a strong need to contest and revoke the social, religious, educational, political, or legal system. Revolutionary philosophical values may lead to radical decisions with socially detrimental repercussions. Death may occur in a strange or foreign place. Position comparable to Pluto in Sagittarius.

PLUTO in House X

This position confers a 'do-or-die' approach to important goals. When ambitions are too far-fetched, they create family disruptions. There is a tendency to question authority to the point of alienation. Determination and regeneration foster great realisation when applied sensibly. Position comparable to Pluto in Capricorn.

PLUTO in House XI

This position confers an overwhelming need to reform or transform the social environment. It enhances the ability to deal with others to change and regenerate their life in various ways and areas. Radicalised positions may become a source of disruption and separation from the conventional. Positions comparable to Pluto in Aquarius.

PLUTO in House XII

This position indicates a life path deeply scarred by unfortunate events that may have taken place as far back as the intrauterine period. It can produce an unrealistic tendency to feel threatened that may lead to paranoid reactions. However, karmic disruptions are a means for spiritual progression. Position comparable to Pluto in Pisces.

Lesson 10

Link to the video: https://youtu.be/PMYHV83LJz8

Retrograde planets

First, a bit of astronomy. Many astrology enthusiasts talk about retrograde planets without knowing precisely what they are. Some people imagine that the planets are driven back and forth on their orbits and literally go into reverse motion from time to time on their way around the zodiac. Much is also said about these 'poor' retrograde planets generally considered quite negative. This is what gives them a highly valued character in karmic astrology.

For my part, I admit to giving them only a limited importance, both in so-called judicial astrology (personality analysis) and in karmic astrology. However, this book would be incomplete if I did not cover those mysterious retrograde movements. Let's see what it is all about.

All the planets of the solar system revolve around the Sun. Only two of them never retrograde. Do you know which ones? The Sun, obviously, since it is fixed and does not revolve around the Earth, unlike the way the 'geocentric' chart whose centre is the Earth is represented. The second is the Moon. It revolves around the Earth, which revolves around the Sun.

The other planets take different periods to complete a full circle around the Sun. As you probably know, synodic revolutions (revolving around the Sun) differ greatly from one planet to another. Mercury is the fastest because it is the closest to the Sun. Its orbit is therefore much shorter than that of Venus, of the Earth, and of all the other planets up to Pluto, the farthest one.

Mercury takes about 88 days to circle the Sun. The Earth takes 365 1/4 days. It orbits at an average 150 million kilometres from the Sun.

These differences give rise to periods of apparent retrogradation that occur when a planet aligns with ours from our point of view on Earth and is then eventually overtaken. The result is the impression that it is reversing. A similar impression occurs when you travel by train or car and the vehicle where you are, overtakes another that seems to be reversing while yours is moving away from it. The table below details the distances of the planets to the sun and the periods of synodic revolutions.

Planet	Distance to the Sun	Synodic period
Moon	~ 370,000 km from Earth	~ 27 days ¼
Mercury	~ 58 million km from Sun	~ 88 days
Venus:	~ 108 million km from Sun	~ 225 days
Mars:	~ 228 million km from Sun	~ 2 years
Vesta:	~ 350 million km from Sun	~ 3 years ½
Jupiter:	~ 778 million km from Sun	~ 12 years
Saturn:	~ 1.427 billion km from Sun	~ 29 years ½
Chiron:	~ 1.3 à 2.8 billion km from Sun	~ 50 years ½
Uranus:	~ 2.87 billion km from Sun	~ 84 years
Neptune:	~ 4.496 billion km from Sun	~ 165 years
Pluto:	~ 6 billion km from Sun	~ 248 years

The above data is approximate (~), but sufficient to understand how much the revolution periods differ according to the distance of each planet from the central celestial body, the Sun.

Pluto rotates on average six billion kilometres from the Sun in about

248 years. Mars, meanwhile, orbits at 'only' 228 million kilometres from the Sun. Its revolution period is a much shorter journey than Pluto's. It therefore goes faster around the Sun since it only needs a little less than two years to do so. As a result, from our point of view on Earth, these differences of speed of the planets give rise to the phenomenon called 'Retrogradation' when the Earth on its orbit aligns with the celestial body concerned.

The retrograde situation of a planet is noticeable in the drawing of a chart by an 'R' added to its position indicated in degrees. *Mars at 28°R in Aries means that Mars is retrograde*.

The art of forecasting with astrology

The transits

Roland Legrand

From an astronomical point of view, the phenomenon of retrogradation would therefore be an optical illusion. Retrogradation seems to drag a planet back on its orbit around the Sun. It is interesting from an astrological point of view when analysing transits. As you will find out by reading my book '*The Art of Forecasting With Astrology*' published by *Create Space* and sold by *Amazon*. Note that the speed of a planet in retrograding motion is slower than in direct motion. Here's an example.

On 2 September 2007, Saturn entered in Virgo. It took seventy-nine days to travel to 8° 34' in this sign. On 20 December, it went into retrograde motion until 4 May 2008, when it was back at 1° 41' in Virgo. Therefore, Saturn travelled only 6°53' in four and a half months or 136 days while retrograding, which is around half its direct motion speed.

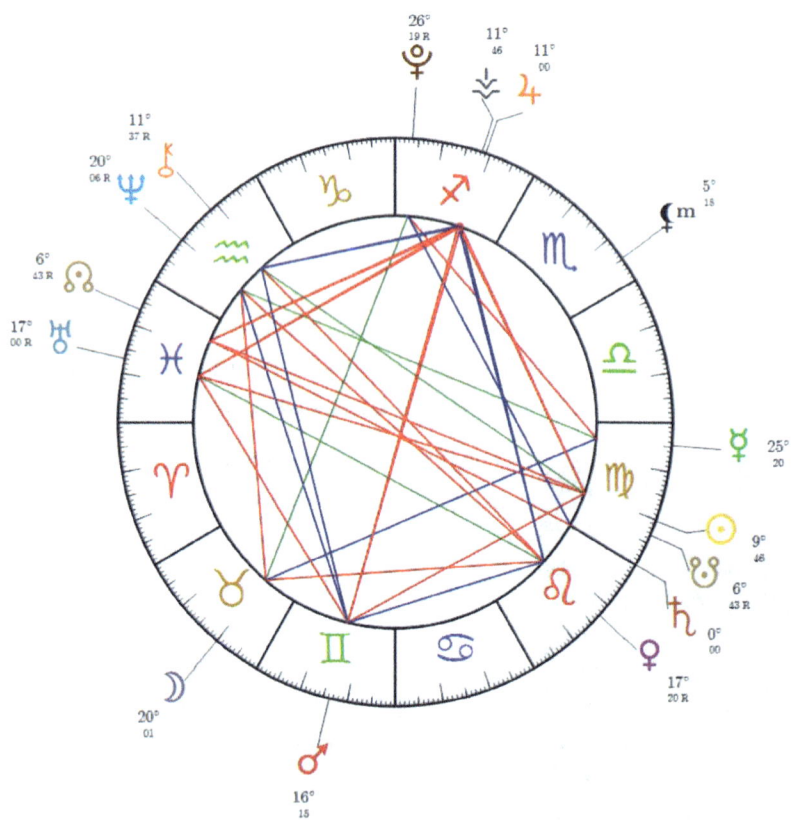

Saturn's retrograding speed went from 0° 06' 30" to 0° 03' 02" per day, a slowdown of nearly 50% compared to direct motion. This difference is due to the speed of the Earth on its orbit compared to Saturn's. In fact, during the retrogradation phase, a planet goes through two 'stationary' phases; one before the retrogradation begins and the other when it ends. This is called 'loop input' and 'loop output' periods. The two-dimension representations of retrogradation form loops similar to what is reproduced on the following page.

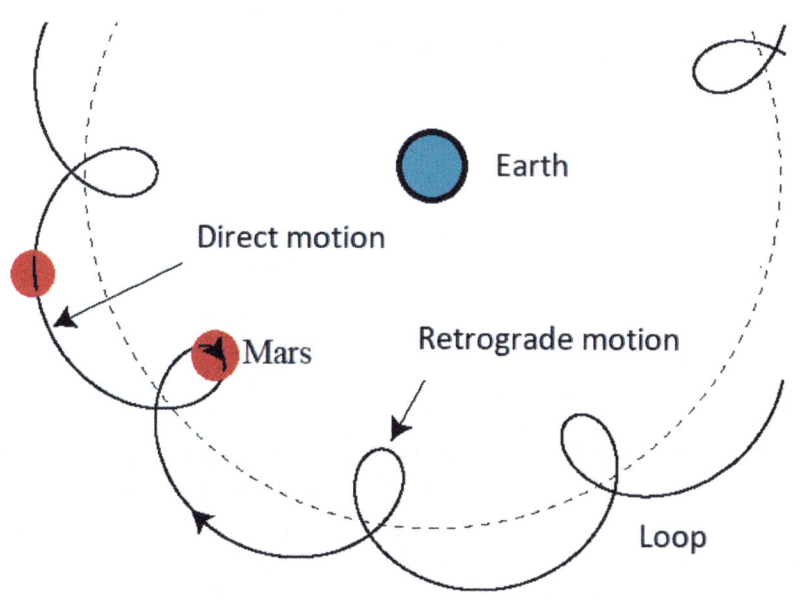

Earth

Direct motion

Mars

Retrograde motion

Loop

Retrograde Planets and Karma

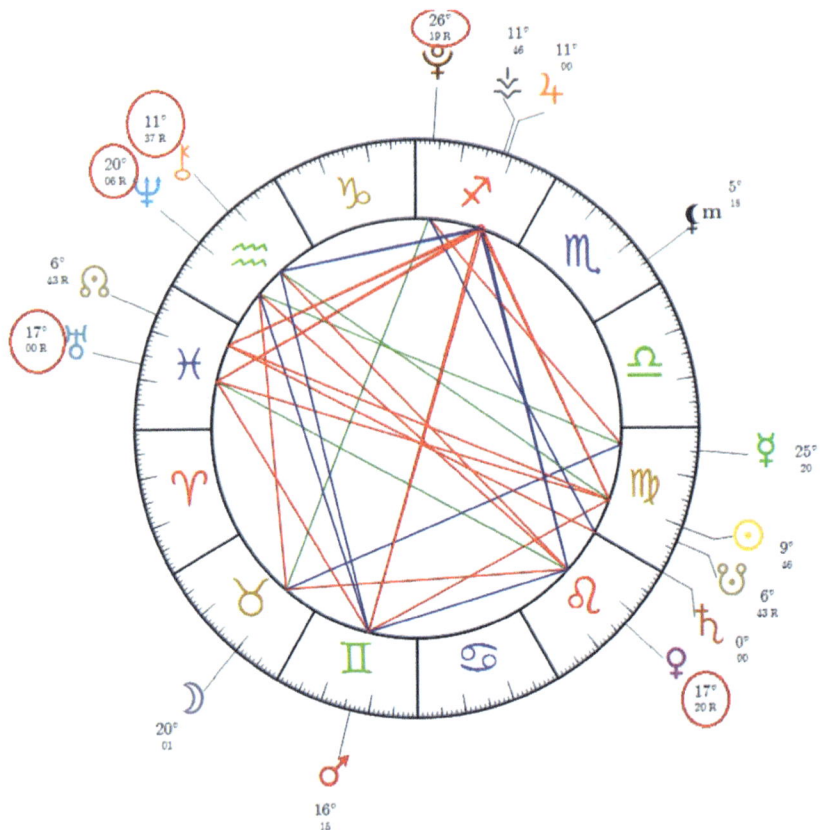

I remain cautious about putting into practice the theories that are circulating about what retrograde planets supposedly represent from a karmic point of view. I have two main reasons for such carefulness. One is the too often negative approach that a retrograde planet suggests to many astrologers, and the second one is the lack of flexibility too often found in both conventional and karmic readings about retrograde planets. However, I readily admit that a retrograde planet can represent an additional effort needed to benefit from its influence in a more constructive than restrictive manner. The analysis of a retrograde planet must therefore be a 'practical guide' and a warning against the tendency to stagnation of a latent quality, talent, or potential inherited or brought back from a previous existence to exploit it more happily in the present life.

Retrograde Planets' Karmic Meanings

Here is a list of what retrograde planets indicate in a chart from a karmic point of view. The Sun and the Moon are not included in this list because they never retrograde.

Mercury

Would indicate in the previous life a lack of determination needed to make good use of intellectual faculties and communication ability. This trend didn't lead to convincing and satisfactory achievements.

In the present life, an effort is necessary to boost the latent potentialities to use them in the areas represented by Mercury in the chart (House in Gemini). Retrograde Mercury can also indicate a family karma more particularly concerning male siblings. Mercury = a brother, a brother-in-law, a cousin, or a close friend.

Venus

Indicates emotional setbacks due to low self-confidence, perhaps due to a physical malformation or from a lack of morality. Romantic relationships have been a source of setbacks and suffering. Artistic creativity has not been exploited. An inner frustration ensued.

In this life, lack of self-confidence is still present. It could slow down the evolution of intimate life and delay romantic realisations. Spontaneity in human relations would greatly help to take advantage of latent potentialities in love or artistic pursuits, according to the disposition of Venus in the chart. Familial karma related to female siblings is indicated.

Mars

Indicates outbursts of reactivity in the past life, excessive authority, significant risk taking, and tensions or fights in human relationships. War or other conflict situations may have caused injuries, unexpected aggression, and treachery.

In this life, reminiscences of tensions, incidents or accidents induce a tendency to hesitate when it comes to making quick and important decisions. A lack of self-confidence or fear of consequences can delay concrete achievements of various projects. Anxiety generates impatience, errors, and setbacks.

Vesta

Indicates balance impairment and a lack of harmony in human relationships. External events may have been a source of inner questioning and a need to keep standing no matter what. Troubling social situations or legal clashes had unfortunate consequences.

In this life, diplomacy is at the centre of human relations at the expense of more personal wellbeing. There is a tendency to act as if we had to pay the consequences of past mistakes. Creativity, art, and love are major values. Yet, they are subject to unexpected events that produce more setbacks than concrete satisfaction.

Jupiter

Represents moral errors, spiritual confusion or excessive opportunism in a previous life marked by material limitations and major social disruptions. Projects were very ambitious and impossible to achieve. A feeling of being the victim of injustice gradually developed.

In this life, the emphasis must be on generosity, sharing, and human interactions to unlock innate abilities and favour social, professional, and sentimental achievements. It is not enough to hope for success if nothing is done to deserve it. Obstacles tend to produce a latent dissatisfaction often hidden behind an over-optimistic appearance.

Saturn

Indicates the extent to which the time factor may have worked against achievements in the previous life. An element of 'fatality' resulting from an older karma may have accentuated a feeling of incapacity. Loneliness and lack of self-confidence had their pernicious role and put a heavy weight on an existential vehicle that was already struggling moving forward to reach its goals.

In this life, the feeling of not being up to the task promotes failure rather than success. By becoming aware that limitations are mostly self-induced, it becomes easier to overcome them and release the constructive energy that Saturn represents with patience, serenity, and endurance. Focusing more on the goal than on the time needed to achieve it lightens the pressures of responsibilities stemming from existential realities personal ambitions.

Chiron

Suggests health disorders that were not treated effectively in the previous life. Hygiene criteria at that time had a large part of responsibility in the evolution of chronic disorders. The existential journey was disturbed by sudden fluctuations affecting more particularly the organs and functions represented by the sign where Chiron is found in the birth chart.

In this life, a pathological terrain represented by Chiron and its regent in signs must be taken into consideration to avoid the development of pathologies from a previous life during which little or no concrete care was possible. The karmic load weighs on the power of realisation and wellbeing in the areas represented by Chiron in House. Rigour and proper hygiene at all levels must be privileged to better fight adversity.

Uranus

Indicates unexpected changes and their adverse effects on daily needs and habits. Events beyond personal control such as revolts, manifestations of discontent, social unrest, and demonstrations, or revolutions could have been the causes for such drastic changes. The irreversible effects that events imposed were at the origin of profound discontent and resignation.

In this life, the slightest suggestion of change can become a source of exaggerated anxiety or anguish. A strong need to cling to one's acquisitions and to indulge in an often-uncomfortable 'comfort zone' offers a form of maintained safety to compensate for the lack of adventure and originality. A conscious effort is needed to free oneself from the grip of habits and routine and make the most of life's unexpected opportunities spontaneously.

Neptune

Indicates the influence of religion in the previous life and the effect of spirituality on the potential for concrete realisation of dreams. Intuition and inspiration were sources of disillusions due to lack of rationality and combativeness. Beliefs became both a refuge and a prison for the soul, from which it seemed almost impossible to escape.

In this life, there is often a reluctance to any form of so-called spirituality. Inspiration, although strong, remains dependent on principles imposed by education. Imagination is a refuge in which one can prepare and organise the future without guaranteeing the realisation of personal projects. An effort is necessary to believe; in oneself, in one's plans, and in God if necessary. Believing is both the engine and the fuel to get going and realise the greatest projects and the wildest dreams.

Pluto

Suggests a previous life deeply marked by death, misery, suffering and various calamities. The result is a sense of powerlessness in the face of fate and its relentless power of destruction. Epidemics, cataclysms, deadly wars have destroyed hope for a better life. Black was worn as a sign of resignation and respect for the dead and the unfortunate.

In this life, an effort is necessary to accept the might of the great cycles and move forward despite the sacrifices and sufferings that may occur. Fear of error is often irrational and mostly derived from the fear of death. Accepting this deadline positively opens up to life and to all the good things it provides. We must not forget that the present life serves to prepare the next one...

Note that the above aphorisms explain the phenomenon of retrogradation by deduction rather than from concrete verification. The aspects play a major role in accentuating or reducing the blockages represented by the retrograde planets. A trine from Saturn to Jupiter retrograde, for example, greatly reduces the Jovian effect to make it a tool for concrete realisations rather than errors of judgement.

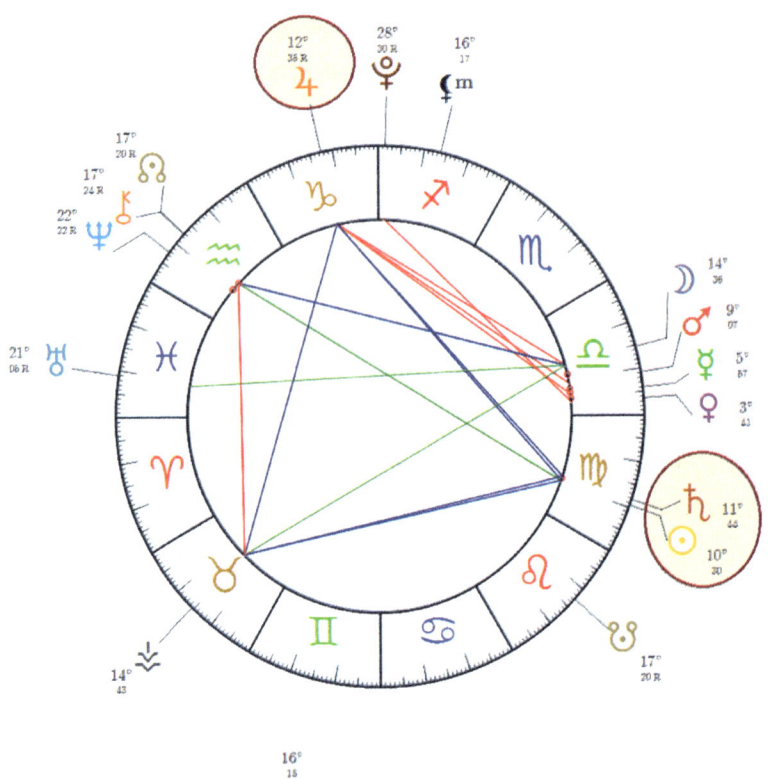

Make it a habit to always analyse an element in its relationship with
the rest of the chart. A planet or other object alone remains itself as
long as it does not enter the logic of the group and doesn't form
aspects with other elements around the chart. In the same way that
an individual's behaviour can radically change when interacting
with other people, the basic personality of a planet can undergo
radical changes when it is involved in harmonic or dissonant aspects
in the chart, let alone its position in sign which can also affect its
primary expression.

Let's look once more at the example chart to explain further what
retrograde planets mean for this person.

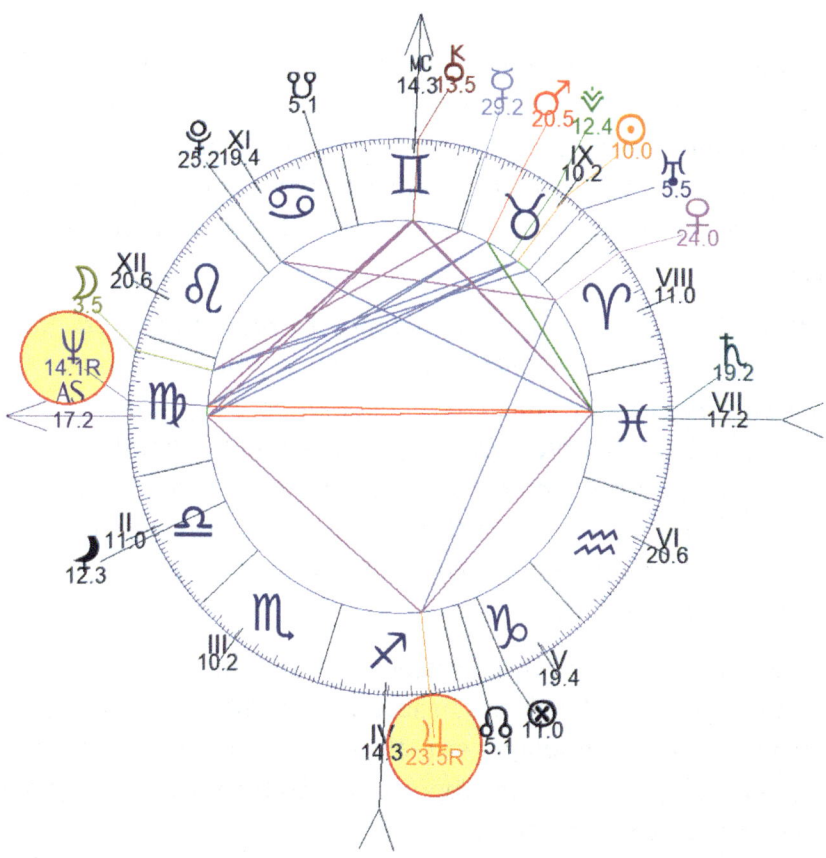

Only two out of ten planets are retrograde, Jupiter and Neptune. They are located near two angular houses' cusps (Houses I and IV) and they form aspects with the other two cusps (Houses VII and X). In addition, Saturn and Chiron are involved to form a large square in the centre of which this person adapts as well as possible to life's various troubling circumstances.

From the short interpretations provided in previous pages, the following information is noted.

Neptune

Indicates the influence of religion in the previous life and the effect of spirituality on the potential for concrete realisation of dreams. Intuition and inspiration were sources of disillusions due to lack of rationality and combativeness. Beliefs became both a refuge and a prison for the soul, from which it seemed almost impossible to escape.

In this life, there is often a reluctance to any form of so-called spirituality. Inspiration, although strong, remains dependent on principles imposed by education. Imagination is a refuge in which one can prepare and organise the future without guaranteeing the realisation of personal projects. An effort is necessary to believe; in oneself, in one's plans, and in God if necessary. Believing is both the engine and the fuel to get going and realise the greatest projects and the wildest dreams.

This description is entirely consistent with that person's existential journey. However, she always believed in herself enough to impose herself on others, although her realisation of life is not in line with her dreams of greatness well represented by the second retrograde planet, as you can read below.

Jupiter

Represents moral errors, spiritual confusion or excessive opportunism in a previous life marked by material limitations and major social disruptions. Projects were very ambitious and impossible to achieve. A feeling of being the victim of injustice gradually developed.

In this life, the emphasis must be on generosity, sharing, and human interactions to unlock innate abilities and favour social, professional, and sentimental achievements. It is not enough to hope for success if nothing is done to deserve it. Obstacles tend to produce a latent dissatisfaction often hidden behind an over-optimistic appearance.

Here again, this description is very much in line with what this person has experienced. Her expectations, projects and hopes were disappointed, but she retained a natural dynamism, a need for sharing, a generous nature. Achievements were multiple and often unexpected. The positions of Jupiter and Neptune are relevant to this person's facts of life.

Jupiter in House IV is in Sagittarius, its own sign, where it is strong. It encourages ambitious projects and indicates a need for a successful family environment. The retrogradation suggests disappointment rather than accomplishment. There were many obstacles and setbacks that prevented this lady friend from reaching her far-fetched goals.

Neptune in House XII conjunct the cusp of the Ascendant confirms the role played by dreams, hopes and illusions. Neptune is the ruler of House VII of important partnerships such as marriage. In this area too, disappointments were deplored. Although involved since 1980 in a karmic and fusional relationship, this person regularly remembers the 'error of choice' she made when deciding in favour of the relationship with that man despite the fact that she also recognises that her life would not be conceivable without him.

The large square implies the angular Houses of the chart. Saturn is conjunct the cusp of House VII. This person was 46 when she gave up everything she had in favour of a relationship with the 'love of her life', her soul mate. However, Saturn in House VII (the Descendant) rules House V in Capricorn (love, art, creation, and procreation), where positive personal achievements together with major setbacks and hardship occurred.

Chiron up in the Midheaven dominates the chart. It is there to indicate this person's ability to manage discordances between Jupiter, Saturn, and Neptune. It is interesting to note that this person enjoys giving 'medical' advice and pseudo treatments, or grandmother's remedies. In the chapter about Chiron, his position in House X is described as follows:

This position is common in the charts of doctors and other medical practitioners or therapists. It also indicates health problems related to paternal heredity, a karmic debt or important events concerning the father.

However, we see that Chiron is actually in House IX, suggesting this:

Indicates an interest in medical education, but not necessarily success in this area. A foreign person or country can play an important role in solving or aggravating health problems of karmic nature.

Indeed, this person migrated to Australia at the age of 30 (first Saturn's return) and did not do medical studies. She only graduated as a beautician at a time when it involved a paramedical section according to what this person explained. Her rather robust health does not prevent her from intestinal disorders (Ascendant in Virgo = Chiron) of nervous origin (Chiron in Gemini).

Nevertheless, retrograde Neptune is well supported by a number of trines from Mars, Uranus, and Vesta near the Sun, and Mercury in Taurus, this person's zodiac sign.

These powerful aspects are representative of the physical, mental, and moral strength that always allowed this person to remain faithful to her convictions despite life's vicissitudes and setbacks.

To conclude on this example, while knowing that the explanations provided in this lesson are only a small part of what can be obtained by pushing the analysis further, **do not neglect the aspects**. Indeed, if the trines were squares or oppositions in the previous life, they confirm a positive karma inherited from the efforts made to manage difficult situations. The powerful positive energy of harmonic aspects is extremely useful, if not to totally counter the blockages represented by retrograde planets, at least to hold on and take advantage of the good things in life that we know how fond the natives of Taurus are...

Practical exercise

Retrograde planets in your chart

Which ones are they?

Where are they (signs and Houses)?

Do they form aspects with other elements in the chart?

If so, what aspects?

Use the texts provided in my '*Astrology for a Better Life*' book (sold by Amazon) to improve your analysis of retrograde planets. You will also find the aphorisms included in the present book useful to guide your first readings of retrograde planets.

Use a chart format similar to the one below to list and analyse retrograde planets. It will help you to quickly visualise the links between them and the rest of the chart. It will be useful until you can do this spotting at a glance with no other support than your own eyes and brains!

Retrograde planet/s	In sign	In House	Ruler in sign and House	Aspects

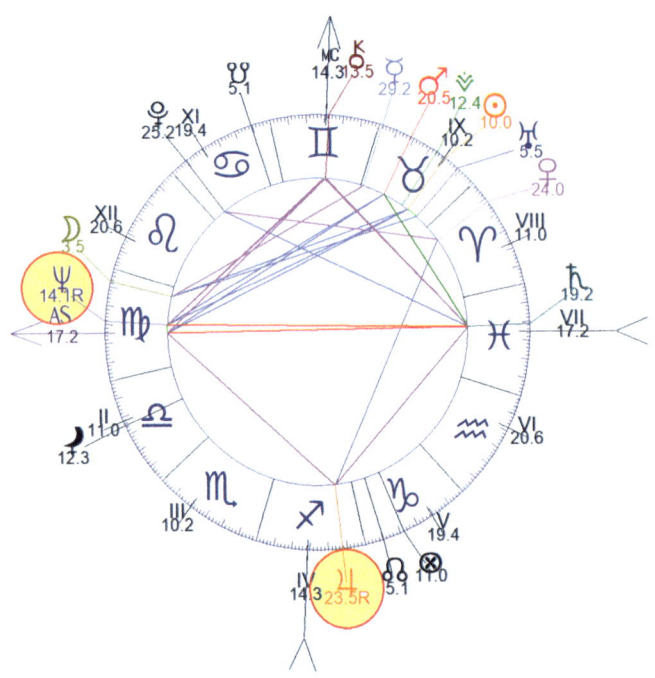

Retrograde planets	In sign	In House	Ruler of	Aspects
Jupiter	Sagittarius	IV	IV	**Square** Saturn Neptune Ascendant **Trine** Venus
Neptune	Virgo	XII	VII	**Conjunction** Ascendant **Square** Uranus **Opposition** Saturn Trine Sun, Mars, Vesta, Uranus

As mentioned earlier, turn to the supplementary sections included in this book and in my '***Astrology for a Better Life***' book to gather relevant information about the retrograde planets' positions in signs and House, not forgetting their regents' positions in signs and Houses, and of course, the aspects.

This is the end of lesson 10. The next one deals with the faster objects.

Lesson 11

Link to the video: https://youtu.be/2N_ybNlYotg

The faster objects

The information collected from the positions of the faster objects (Sun, Moon, and planets) is a valuable add-on to support or bring interesting elements to the karmic reading of a birth chart. They are not essential, perhaps, nor are they paramount, but they have their say which often reveals what the slower planets don't. Fast planets play a more important role when they are regents of slower ones or fictitious points. It is the case in the example chart, where Uranus in Taurus has Venus for regent, while Pluto is under the regency of the Moon.

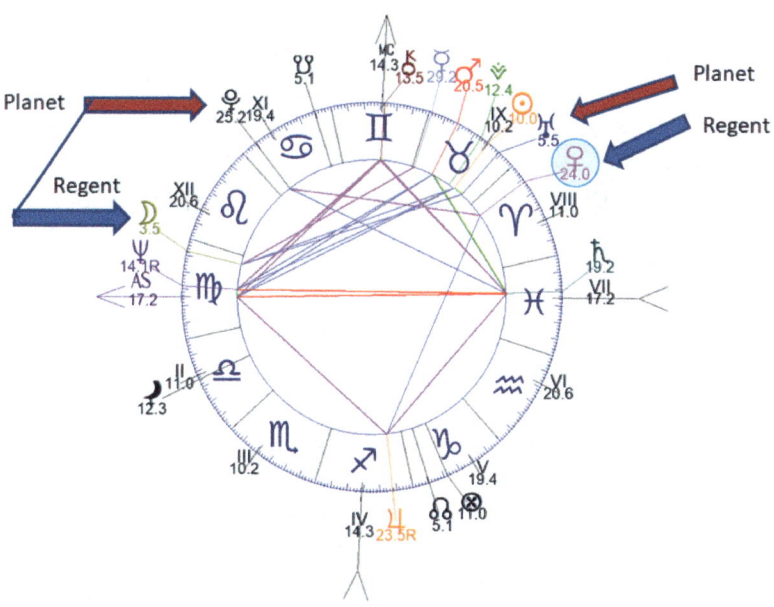

Here is a list of what you can expect from the faster objects with some indications to get you going while leaving open the range of possibilities you decide upon according to the chart you analyse.

The sun

It represents the power you sought in the previous life, the rank you aimed at and the position you reached. It also represents the authority you showed and the authority you had to obey. The Sun is also paternity, fatherhood, or patriarchy, the leader you have been or wished to become. It is also the role of the karmic charge on your vital force in the areas represented by the House ruled by the Sun and the House where it is found in the chart.

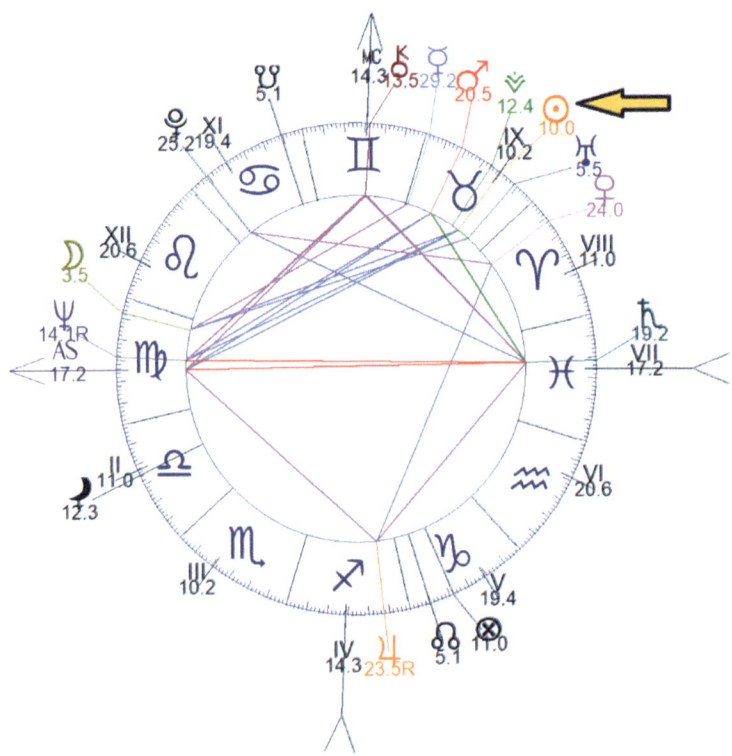

Have a look at the example chart. The Sun is in Taurus in House VIII. But it is almost in House IX. Therefore, we must consider both Houses. House VIII informs on the karmic load that this person is bringing back from a previous incarnation. House VIII represents money, death, the interest in the mysteries of life, and the great questions we have about what life really is, what afterlife is, what was before this life, what will be after, etc. The mysteries of life are represented by House VIII. Sex is also represented by this House.

House IX represents foreign countries and cultures. It also represents the administration, the legal side of social life, what is official, as well as religion, because religion is the law of God transcribed by men in a book which they called 'Bible'. Therefore, House IX is also a very important area of this person's life from a karmic point of view. In this example chart, the Sun is next to Uranus, and it is in a very good configuration with Neptune, and with the Ascendant, which is, of course, something that this person can benefit from.

The Moon
It represents the home, the family, the tribe, the village, maternity, the mother, or matriarchy you depended on in the previous life. It is linked to fertility or sterility depending on the position of the Moon in sign and on the aspects. It shows the role of the emotional karmic charge in the areas represented by the House ruled by the Moon and the House where it is found in the chart.

Observe the example chart on the following page. The Moon is in Virgo. It is almost in harmony with the Sun. There is a harmonious link between these signs because they are both Earth signs. It reinforces the vital force, the vital energy. The Sun and the Moon represent the poles through which the vital energy passes. Just like two wires conduct the electricity to the apparatus or to the lamp. The light is really strong when there is a harmonious configuration between the Sun and the Moon. In this chart, it is a trine (120°).

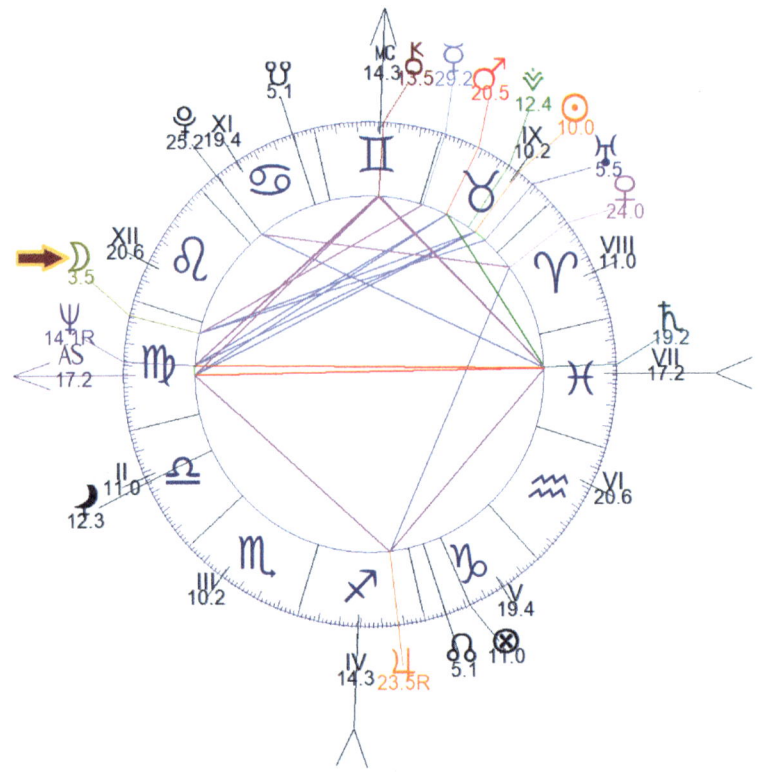

There is a discordance with Mercury that shows that perhaps this person finds it difficult to deal with siblings or people around the family or getting involved in a conversation as soon as the emotions take over her rational thinking. Then, it can become quite complicated. However, the Moon is in harmony with Uranus. This configuration confers adaptability and quickness to change, to adapt, to move, and to understand. That is quite interesting on a karmic point of view because the Moon represents the family and I know for a fact, because I know this person, that family is very important to her. That is her home, home life, looking after her interior and being there always for members of her family. These are predominant values in this person's mind.

Mercury

It represents brothers, and other male siblings, close friends, or cousins. It shows the way the intellect and the need to communicate operated in the previous life to understand what was happening then. It is also linked to mobility, curiosity, and sharing acquired knowledge. It represents intellectual interests and their roles in the current life in the areas represented by the House ruled by Mercury and the House where it is found in the chart.

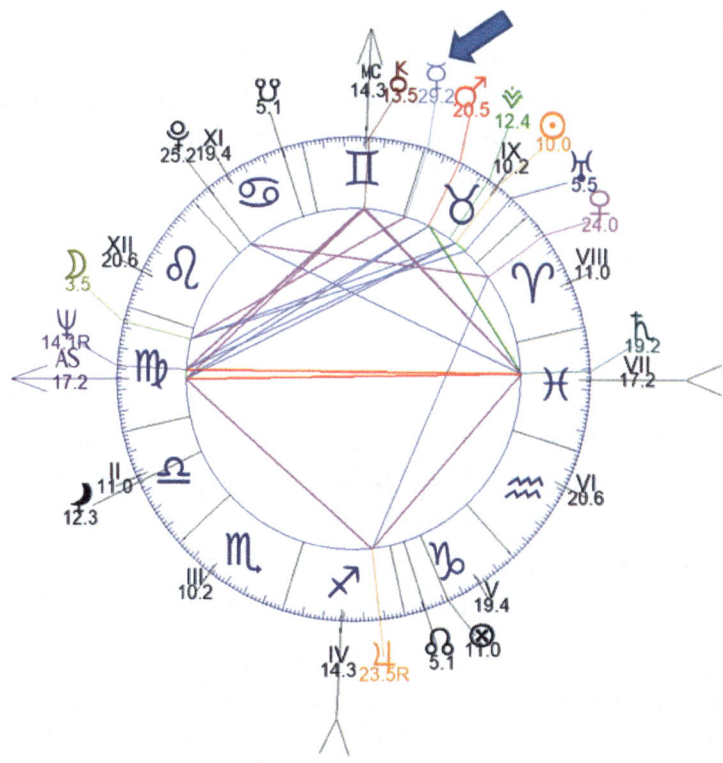

In the example chart, Mercury is at the very end, at 29° in Taurus. There is a square aspect with the Moon, but it is what we call a hidden or false aspect. I've explained that earlier on. It means that

there is a potential difficulty to deal with brothers, sisters, siblings, and with anybody in fact, as soon as the family is concerned, or the place of residence, the home, the city, the country, and it also indicates the interference of emotional stress. When it does become strong, this person finds it difficult to keep on analysing, discussing, and communicating in a rational way. In this chart, you can see that Mercury is not far from Mars. It's not a strong conjunction, but Mars is a strong element. This wide conjunction indicates that this person can be quite reactive, even aggressive, when there is a potential danger, or when the emotions take over. Then, this person becomes strongly excited, and she can have very intense reactions that lead to complicated consequences, rather than solve problems. Her behaviour would be motivated by unconscious reminiscences of a past life when she had a lot of difficulties to deal with, regarding or concerning friends, cousins, male siblings, or brothers…

Venus

It represents sisters, female siblings, close feminine friends, as well as artistic creativity and romantic needs. It shows to what extent love and affection influenced the previous life, and the degree of attraction to good food and beautiful things. It also represents intimate desires and cravings for physical and material satisfactions with their present repercussions in the areas represented by the House ruled by Venus and the House where it is found in the chart.

Let's have a look at the example chart once more. It is reproduced on the following page. Venus is in Aries. That is an intense position. It means that this person has a very strong sense of affection. When she feels for someone, it is expressed in a very intense manner. It works both ways, of course. If she dislikes someone, the person concerned is going to understand it very quickly. The same applies if she appreciates someone; it is expressed very spontaneously, impulsively.

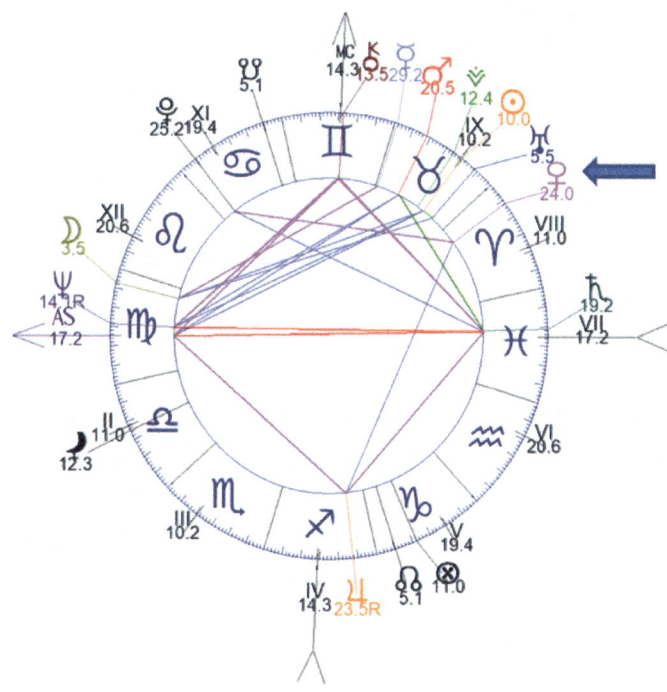

There is a square, therefore a discordance, with Pluto. Pluto represents what may have affected this person in a previous incarnation on a sentimental point of view, in her sentimental life, in her romantic life. Death is represented by Pluto, and I know for a fact that death has had a very strong influence in this person's life. Indeed, she went through very difficult periods caused by the death of a close parent... There is also a very nice link with Jupiter. That is a very positive configuration. Whereas Pluto represents the darker side of life, Jupiter represents the brighter side. It shows that this person has that very positive approach to life as soon as she feels in tune with something or someone, a situation, or something she appreciates. She goes shopping for example, and she may fall in love with something that she will want to buy immediately, and she will

buy it, even though this buy may create financial strife. There is a biased type of influence stemming from the darker energy of Pluto confronted to the brighter energy of Jupiter. If this person only had the square Venus/Pluto in her chart, her approach to life in general would be a lot darker than it is, thanks to Jupiter.

Mars

It represents in the previous life the degree of combativeness, aggressiveness, and defensiveness expressed to impose oneself with force and authority. It also represents the use of physical strength or weapons to dominate others or to be feared and respected. In the present incarnation, Mars is the 'karmic enemy' returning to cause problems with no apparent reason. Settling karmic debts with such person is essential to free oneself from their unconscious need for revenge which may affect the areas linked to the House Mars rules and the House where it is found in the chart.

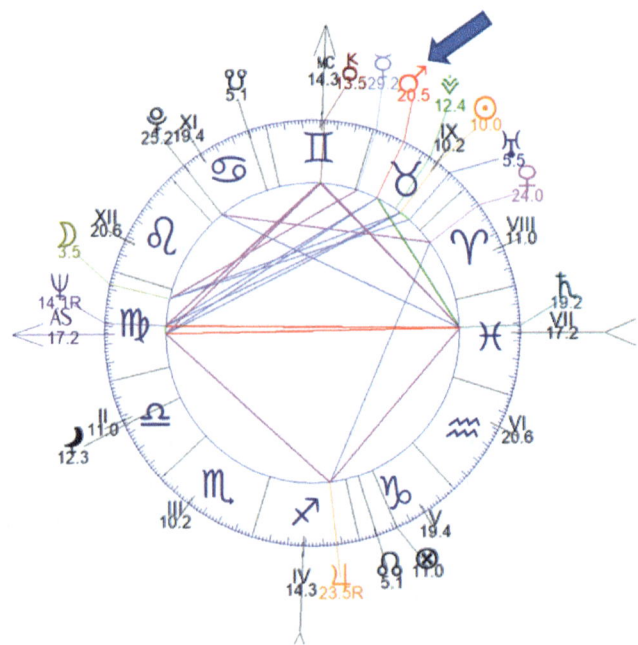

In the example chart, Mars is in Taurus, it rules House VIII of money and, as I said earlier, anything to do with sex and death. And it is in Taurus, in House IX. It means that there is a link, a karmic link, indicating that perhaps this person had to fight to impose what she wanted in life, and what she could achieve financially and officially or legally. However, Mars is in harmony with the Ascendant, with Neptune, and with Saturn in House VII. That gives a lot of positive energy that suggests that this person has never actually met any karmic enemy during her lifetime, but rather, people who are willing to help her, to protect her, and perhaps to fight her potential karmic enemies. These people may have a karmic debt to repay…

Vesta

It represents justice in the moral rather than the legal sense of the term. It shows how the need for harmony and wellbeing was perceived and exercised. It also represents a feminine influence such as a friend, a counsellor, or a mediator playing an important role in the previous incarnation. That person may return to this life to pursue a similar trend of generosity and helpful friendship. The influence of such positive relationship is transferred into the areas represented by the House ruled by Vesta and the House where it is found in the chart.

Let's have a look again at the example chart. Vesta is in Taurus. It is in House IX, together with Mercury, Mars, and the Sun perhaps, if this person was born a couple of minutes or even less than that before the time recorded on her birth certificate. Then, the Sun would be in House IX, which would be in tune with this person's decision to migrate from France to Australia, a move well represented by the Sun in House IX. Because the Sun represents the vital force and this person's life, it shows that it was meant to be led through or in a foreign land or foreign country…

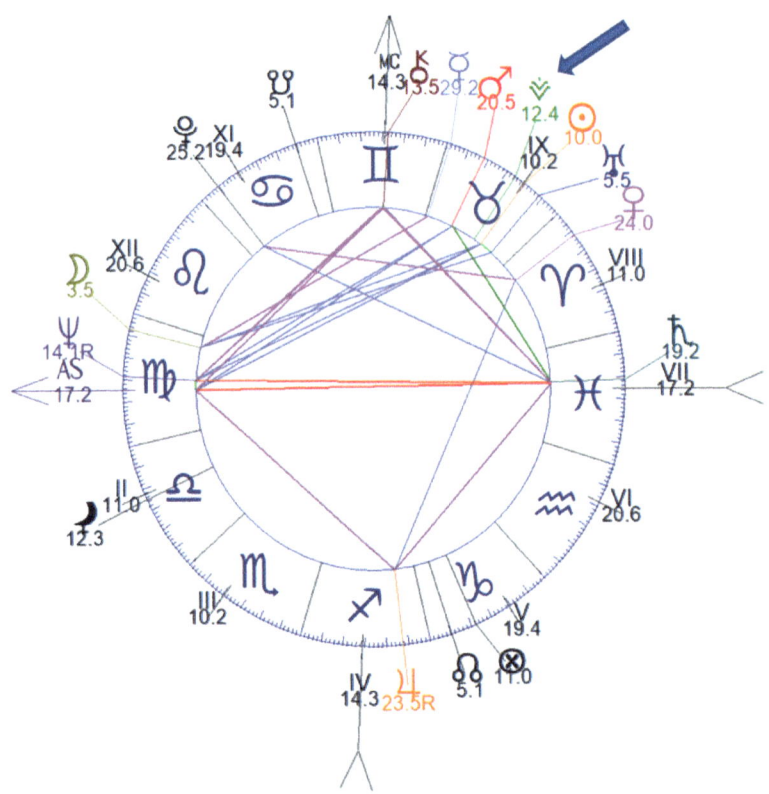

Vesta is in Taurus, a sign represented by Venus, which becomes the regent of Vesta. Vesta rules House II of money earned, and it is a fact that this person, when going through periods of financial difficulties, always found, or met someone who could help her solve the problems. It is an interesting configuration also because, as you can see, Vesta is in harmony with the Ascendant, with Neptune, and with Saturn. These configurations show how much help on a spiritual point of view, thanks to Neptune, this person could benefit from, thanks to her friends and social relationships with various people she met throughout her life.

Practical Exercise

Now, just like you've done with the slower planets, determine the regents of the faster objects to provide more information on the influence of their position in the chart. In the example chart, as seen earlier, the Sun is in Taurus, a sign rule by Venus, which becomes the *regent* of the Sun. And then, Mercury is in Taurus too, therefore also under the regency of Venus. Mars is in Taurus, under the regency of Venus, **but *Venus is in Aries***, which is Mars's sign. I've mentioned that earlier on as well, there is what we call ***an exchange of residence*** for both planets. Vesta is also in Taurus, therefore also regented by Venus. It's interesting to note that most faster objects, except the Moon, are in Taurus and regented by Venus, making this planet a dominant element of this birth chart...

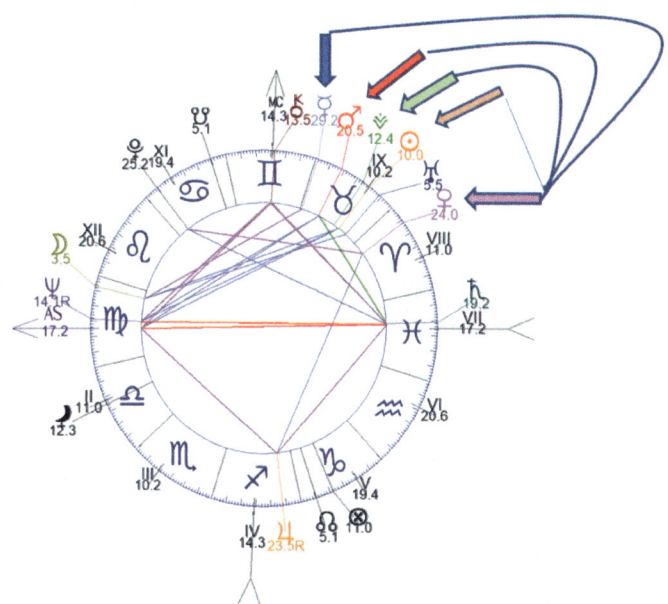

Use the supplementary sections included in this lesson to guide your first interpretations of a birth chart from a karmic point of view, in relation with the faster objects. Do that as well for the slowest ones, of course. I believe there are enough supplementary sections in this book to help you understand and analyse a birth chart from a karmic point of view. Don't forget that you can also use my '**Astrology for a better life**' book to complement what you need to know about the positions of the planets, the aspects between planets, and many more parameters and elements. I hope they will help you realise an accurate reading of a birth chart from a karmic point of view.

Supplementary section

The faster objects in signs

Take note of the basic influences of the faster planets (objects) in signs and in Houses to guide your personal approach to their role from a karmic point of view. Ask yourself what may have produced such an influence in the person's life whose chart you analyse. Then, apply your acquired knowledge to explain the karmic value of the planet considered in the chart. Do this for each one of the faster objects described in this lesson. Use the supplementary sections freely, but keep in mind that they are not a finished product. They are only a tool to improve your personal reading of a chart from a karmic point of view. Last, but not least, don't forget to analyse the roles of the regents and of the aspects.

THE SUN IN SIGNS

In ARIES

There is a tendency to act and react promptly and impulsively. Various incidents are predictable due to a certain lack of patience and diplomacy. Authority was of upmost importance in the previous life and created a tendency to reproduce similar behaviour patterns in the present incarnation.

In TAURUS

There is an unconscious need for the good things of life and the immediate pleasures they produce. Nature is a source of important beneficial influence if it is perceived and exploited as such. Excesses may be issued from a latent fear of lack of affection stemming from a previous life marked by sentimental setbacks.

In GEMINI

There is an innate need for movement and personal expression. Be them spoken or written, words have a special resonance that can be both a source of intimate positive motivation and painful dismay. Being fidgety is contrary to long-term realisations which are perceived as a burden while short-term prospects give more sense to existential progression. Lack of discipline is derived from too many restrictions during the previous incarnation.

In CANCER

Emotions are a constant source of motivation or discouragement. Fluctuations stem from the influence of the close environment (family and place of residence). Proximity with water is essential to wellbeing. It is a vital element, a carrier of various messages that must be recognised and exploited. Such leanings come from past-life damages caused by water and emotional traumas.

In LEO

The Sun is strong in its own sign, as is the ego. There is a latent need to be seen and appreciated. A father-like approach to human relationships is linked to a previous life marked by a domineering father image, or authoritarian aristocratic social standing that used force to impose rules and regulations. Self-image is strengthened or weakened depending on aspects involving the Sun to suggest past-life achievements or failures.

In VIRGO

There is a tendency to focus on petty details rather than look at the broader picture. It may become a source of excessive worrying with its consequence on the digestive system and general state of health. A past life marked by imposed restrictions due to lack of work, hygiene and environmental circumstances promoted poor health and an unconscious need for perfection in the present incarnation.

In LIBRA

There is an innate need to preserve balance and harmony with tact and diplomacy rather than force and authority. This tendency comes from a previous life when it was essential to remain calm and pondering in conflict situations such as riots, revolutions, wars, and other social disorders. The ability to behave like a comedian to both convince and appease is derived from a previous life when difficult human relationships had to be handled prudently.

In SCORPION

There is a strong unconscious innate need to go deep into whatever seems important or essential. The tendency to self-punishment is also a characteristic of this position of Sun. From a karmic point of view, it indicates a past incarnation marked by profound sufferings and questionings that may have led to a nihilistic perception of life. In the present one, an effort is necessary to avoid carrying the world upon one's shoulders.

In SAGITTARIUS

There is a latent influence of a past life marked by political unrest that motivated much thinking and concerting to impose new laws to improve and progress the social and philosophical perspective. In the present life, the interest in higher education and foreign subjects or cultures is a source of positive energy and attraction to long-distance travel, both physical and intellectual. Justice and fair play are major values that may or may not be put to good use, depending on the position of the Sun in House and the aspects in the chart.

In CAPRICORN

There is a latent need to climb slowly but surely to the top of a mountain. It comes from a past life when hard work and patience were essential to deal with major difficulties. A tendency to save, rather than spend, is linked to periods of sheer misery in the previous incarnation. Prudence was a chief requirement for survival. In the present life, time must be considered as an ally to allow long-lasting results from far-fetched projects.

In AQUARIUS

Socialising is a means of attracting attention and to feel useful to others in various and often surprising ways. This is motivated by a past life marked by radical public unrest that required quick adaptability to survive social chaos or such major uncontrollable events as natural catastrophes and disasters. In a present life marked by unexpected changes, using one's personal image and freewill may prove efficient if well directed to avoid reproducing a kind of bipolar tendency.

In PISCES

This position reveals the impact of religion and spirituality to which people were confronted in a previous life. It also shows the importance of water, especially the sea or the ocean. It indicates a possibility to have been a victim of floods or other natural catastrophes. Health may also have been affected seriously by a tendency to body fluid retention. These are perhaps reflecting in the present life, with various effects in the areas represented by the House ruled by the Sun and the House where the Sun if found in the chart.

The following aphorisms are taken from my 'Astrology for a Better Life' book of lessons.

THE MOON IN THE SIGNS

In the present incarnation

In ARIES

The emotions are of an 'aggressive' nature. The feminine principle becomes almost masculine here because Aries is a sign ruled by Mars, dealing more with action than emotion. The natural response to stimuli is spontaneous, fiery, and subject to sudden surges of strong energy.

In TAURUS

The Moon here is in a strong position. It enhances the emotional tie with matter, nature, art, and the good and beautiful things of life. Wellbeing is expressed in a sensual rather than intellectual or spiritual manner.

In GEMINI

The emotions are subject to various fluctuations and changes. Communication is an asset, but a tendency to fantasise or even to lie is present, especially during childhood. Brotherhood and friendship are important sources of motivation.

In CANCER

Family ties and emotional security through harmonious relationships are most important for the native's wellbeing. Emotions can be overwhelming and a source of excessive sensitivity. The Moon here also indicates a more emotional than rational approach in human relationships.

In LEO

This position of the Moon confers pride and a sense for leadership. The need to be admired or appreciated is strong. It can lead to an unconscious need to be the centre of attraction. The feminine tendency of the Moon is masculinised in this Sun-ruled sign. Pride may interfere with one's true emotions.

In VIRGO

The analytic characteristic of this sign seems to reduce the spontaneity of the emotions. Sensitivity is voluntarily limited to avoid over exposition to discords and disappointments. Artistic tastes and creativity centres on elaborate and intricately detailed works of art.

In LIBRA.

Emotions are subject to variations due to a tendency to strive for balance and harmony in human relationships to the detriment of emotional stability. The spontaneous link between mind and feelings enhances the appreciation of intellectual and artistic creativity.

In SCORPIO

The emotions are triggered by a natural attraction to the mysteries of life, sex, and death. Strong independent tendencies and inner energy enhance natural charisma and magnetism. At times, socialising is awkward because of blunt and somehow distasteful manners.

In SAGITTARIUS

Gives the emotional pattern a philosophical and spiritual sense. It also confers a natural interest in foreign languages and cultures, philosophy, religion, and higher education. A good sense of humour, loyalty and self-confidence are also indicated.

In CAPRICORN

This position favours patience and the ability to sustain long-lasting efforts. Spontaneously aiming at earthly targets and motivated by materialistic pursuits, the native is shy and reserved, but shows good self-control of personal emotions.

In AQUARIUS

The emotions are subject to sudden and unexpected changes. Laughter and tears, joy and sadness, sociability and withdrawal cohabit closely with this intriguing position of the Moon. Originality, humour, and spontaneous attraction to others favour success and reputation.

In PISCES

Intuition and sensitivity to human and physical environments confer a natural ability to connect with the invisible and metaphysical sides of life. Emotions become a source of inspiration that can border on daydreaming, with a lack of common sense and realism.

MERCURY IN SIGNS
In the present incarnation

In ARIES

The intellect is overactive and at times rather aggressive and impulsive, with abrupt and sudden flows of unrestrained energy. The intellectual interests appear and disappear quickly. Communication is tensed and arguments are commonplace. Although it depends on the rest of the chart, this position of Mercury is less remarkable a male's chart. That is perhaps because Aries is a masculine sign. Short distance travels are decided in an instant. Headaches are also frequent with this position.

In TAURUS

Mercury here confers a rather practical mind and an interest in material comfort manifesting in relationships often motivated by the pleasure derived from sharing the same food, the same ideas, and the same tastes. Music, painting, cooking, and the many good and beautiful things of life are a source of intellectual satisfaction. The manner of speech is usually rather pleasant. The learning process is slow, but the memory is usually good.

In GEMINI

Mercury here is the impersonation of its mythological role of *messenger of the gods*. Quick-witted and intelligent, a person with Mercury in Gemini is always 'on the go', but not quite persistent enough to reach the finish line. The Mercurian person easily adapts to new currents of thoughts and ideas, and to changing social patterns. Communication comes easy, especially when the subject is light or superficial. Short distance travels are preferred. The nervous system and neuronal activity may become a source of concern.

In CANCER

The intellect and communication process are subject to variations due to the emotional connotation of this sign. Family life is important and personal interests often include history or the family tree. Mental activity is enhanced by a correlation between sensitivity and objectivity. Mercury being under the rulership of the Moon, moodiness is likely to hinder one's natural ability to deal with important subjects objectively and rationally. Variations of the state of mind may have a disruptive influence on the primary digestive function (the stomach).

In LEO

This position indicates an intellectual interest in arts, together with a creative mind. Pride and a tendency to have a strong image of oneself may interfere with the wellbeing of close human relationships. However, generosity, enthusiasm, honesty and stability of thoughts and ideas are usually conferred by this position of Mercury in the Sun-ruled sign of the lion. There is a tendency to be either excessively humble and shy, yet quite domineering and paternalistic.

In VIRGO

This position confers a pragmatic and down-to-earth intellectual approach of life. A practical analysing mind favours success in business or retail work. However, a tendency to focus on details may temper the broader picture. This position is excellent for commercial, scientific, medical or office work, because it bestows a methodical approach and a good sense of order and classification. Mercury in Virgo is also found in the charts of hypochondriacs.

In LIBRA

Mercury here confers diplomacy, good taste, and a genuine interest in balance and harmony. This position is found in the charts of musicians, writers, and poets. It is also favourable to mathematicians and people involved in justice, architecture, and politics. Intellectual behaviour is rather pleasant and positive, honest, and sensitive. It usually goes with a sympathetic approach to human relationship, which tends to increase popularity and the potential to succeed.

In SCORPIO

The intellect and manner of speech are direct and insightful, but often sharp or caustic. An independent mind makes it complicated to keep relationships harmonious. There is a strong intellectual attraction to the unknown, an interest in scientific or human research, and a fascination for life's mysteries. In some cases, moral values need to be occasionally reasserted to avoid various clashes, misunderstandings, and a tendency to use charisma and authority to influence others incorrectly.

In SAGITTARIUS

The intellect is attracted to religion and philosophy as well as to foreign countries and cultures. However, it may remain on a mental level rather than involving deeper feelings. Mercury here also indicates a spontaneous interest in long-distance travels, and foreign languages favoured by an ability to learn and acquire a high level of knowledge in many areas. A respectful approach of the notions of heavenly justice and wisdom is also indicated.

In CAPRICORN

Mercury confers a down-to-earth intellect with long-term and long-lasting interests. The preference goes to conservative learning patterns and efforts to climb the social and professional ladder. Patience, reflection, and seriousness favour success and far-fetched objectives and ambitions. In some cases, lack of optimism and shyness come from a tendency to intellectual underestimation. Nevertheless, Mercury in Capricorn goes with a persistent and determined mindset.

In AQUARIUS

Intellectual originality and virtuosity are indicated. The mind is connected to the universe around, interested in human nature and in the modern tools of communication. The downside of this position of Mercury is mental eccentricity that can lead to marginality. There is a degree of difficulty to focus on any one subject due to impatience. However, sociability with a charitable approach to human relationships enhances the potential to succeed.

In PISCES

Logic and understanding processes rely on intuition and sensibility rather than rational reasoning to obtain better results. Imagination and inspiration are valuable assets to the art-oriented person. The mind is easily influenced by environmental ambience and vibrations. Connection to the invisible confers clairvoyant tendencies. An interest in religions and mystical subjects is also indicated.

VENUS IN SIGNS

In the present incarnation

In ARIES

Venus here confers ardent and fiery feelings in personal and intimate relationships. It also indicates sudden changes in the expression of love and friendship, and a degree of aggressiveness and competitiveness in seeking affection. Venus is not at ease in this sign because Aries is ruled by Mars, the god of war, turning the goddess of love into a warrior lover. A tendency to demand too much attention and to dominate loved ones may have spoiling effects on relationships because of such intense needs and desires.

In TAURUS

In its sign of rulership, Venus confers fixed and constant feelings and affections. Emotional security and stability are important to ensure and preserve wellbeing. Sensuality is well developed, and physical contacts are essential in intimate personal relationships. Artistic tastes centre on the beautiful in all earthly manifestations. Decoration, clothing, food, and music are some typical interests conferred by Venus in Taurus. This position also tends to preserve good health, thanks to one's spontaneous interest in the positive role of earthly matter.

In GEMINI

The love principle is certainly adaptable and versatile, but sometimes superficial. The need for variety, movement, and excitement can make it difficult to keep a steady relationship for long. A mentalised expression of love creates an attraction to more intellectual than carnal partners. This position favours social success, thanks to an innate ability to use words and imagination in a pleasant and charming manner. Like a butterfly going from flower to flower, this lover likes to discover and experiment before settling down durably.

In CANCER

Venus here shows how the love of family and home can make life agreeable for close ones. There is a tendency to be oversensitive and romantic, moody, and fluctuating in one's demonstration of love and affection. Emotional attachment to the home and family environment makes for a usually pleasant atmosphere and agreeable personal relationships. This position indicates a strong mother instinct and a keen interest in cooking, decorating, and creative activities. A compassionate and usually gentle nature favour popularity.

In LEO

This position confers ardent, passionate, and stable feelings in sentimental relationships. Personal pride, however, can interfere with emotions in romantic situations. Artistic taste and creativity are enhanced, together with an outgoing, sunny, and affectionate nature. Venus in Leo goes with a loyal and sincere approach to love and romance. It also indicates a tendency to take things too much at heart and to be easily hurt. Venus in Leo also seems to favour physical beauty. Charisma and positive personal magnetism are also present.

In VIRGO

Venus here confers an over-analysing approach to love and affection. The intellect interferes with direct and spontaneous reactions triggered by personal feelings and can inhibit and restrict the evolution of the intimate life. This position of Venus in Virgo is frequently found in the charts of unmarried people. Virgo confers highly critical standards of appreciation of the other person and of the self, together with a tendency to worry too much about loved ones. Artistic tendencies are present and can contribute to social and professional success.

In LIBRA

Venus here makes marriage, associations, and social relationships true affairs of the heart. They are a major factor of wellbeing. Hence, the 'love potential' of Venus is spontaneously and often 'theatrically' expressed. Venus here confers physical beauty, personal charm, and charisma. This position is especially favourable to artists, comedians, musicians, and writers. A constant search for harmony makes discord and arguments upsetting and unpleasant. Diplomacy and concessions are therefore usually preferred to painful arguments.

In SCORPIO

Love is mixed with strong sexual desires together with a deep and passionate approach to romance. Feelings are expressed with pride and possessiveness. Jealous and secretive, the person is moved by a sense of self-sacrifice to sublimate love. Profound resentment becomes a source of inner grudge when romantically deceived. This position often goes with love/hate types of intimate relationships. Artistic tastes lean toward strong, dramatic styles, with a touch of mystery, erotism and occult fantasy.

In SAGITTARIUS

In Jupiter's sign, Venus gives idealistic and spiritually oriented feelings and emotions. Friendliness and sociability go with this position. Close human relationships are based on ethics, morals, philosophy, religion, and other socially recognised values. Traditions are encouraged to preserve emotional wellbeing. Artistic tastes are rather flamboyant and expensive. Love is coloured with religious or philosophic convictions. Extreme generosity is a source of disappointment in a world where personal profit is a primary motivation.

In CAPRICORN

The love principle is 'cooled down' by Venus in this sign. It may even confer a rather cold approach to intimate relationships. Introversion of personal feelings produces melancholy rather than 'joie de vivre'. Saying 'I love you' does not come easy. There is a tendency to self-denial. Believing not to be nice or handsome enough does not favour spontaneous romantic and sentimental accomplishment. Celibacy or late marriage is frequent. Nevertheless, quiet as they may be, affections are profound and extremely durable.

In AQUARIUS

Venus here gives a suave, light, gracious and pleasant attitude to express love and affections. High moral standards are usually present in the search for meaningful sentimental relationships. A tendency to love-friendship relations may be a source of ambiguity and misunderstandings in private life. Free love and independence in marriage are common. The need for variety and excitement may favour celibacy rather than long-lasting partnerships. Original and unusual artistic talents can lead to social or professional success and recognition.

In PISCES

Venus here indicates an over-sensitive nature, prone to ambiguous romantic adventures and relationships. Mystery colours one's love life with an inclination for mystically oriented partners. Universal love on a spiritual level is often preferred to individual relationships. Religion may deeply influence the expression of love and creativity. Compassion and altruism toward mankind are also present. Music and dance may become a source of creative expression and satisfaction.

MARS IN SIGNS

In the present incarnation

In ARIES

Mars here is in its sign of rulership where it confers a 'primal' and spontaneous expression of combativeness. Action is the keyword to success with this position of Mars in Aries. Authoritarian tendencies, however, can alienate friendship and harmonious relationships with co-workers, friends, or family members. A tendency to feel threatened may produce a need to develop self-defence skills. Dedicated martial artists or sports competitors are favoured from Mars in Aries in their chart.

In TAURUS

Mars here confers a combative behaviour wherever material possessions are concerned. Financial success is favoured, together with a tendency to spoil loved ones and to be over generous in romance or friendship. However, selfishness and greediness may also be present, bestowing an ambiguous approach to earthly matters. Food, beauty, and the arts may favour professional and social realisation. The eagerness to satisfy personal desires may, however, become a source of chronic tension with the entourage.

In GEMINI

Mars here confers an assertive and sharp manner of expression. Social life may be a source of chronic tension, due to impatience and a tendency to fervently impose personal opinions. Relationships with siblings are often tensed. Neuronal activity favours quick comprehension and quick learning skills. However, lack of endurance impairs long-term realisations. Self-discipline is needed to ensure concrete actions rather than theories.

In CANCER

Mars here centres the combative principle on home affairs and family life. Its influence in this water sign confers a kind of 'passive aggressiveness'. Tenacity and determination depend essentially on the emotional state. To defend and protect one's family and home environment is a must that may develop far beyond the immediate human and geographical limits. Hence, chauvinistic, or nationalist character traits are often conferred by Mars in Cancer. A keen interest in the cause of the environment is also present.

In LEO

This position is strong. Mars here confers creativity and good fighting ability. Pride motivates spontaneous commitment to deal with life's realities. Competitiveness, together with vibrant energy and inner strength help realise and achieve important goals. Fits of anger and bad temper are also present, with their disrupting incidence in social, professional, and personal relationships. The desire to fight for grand causes, sometimes at the cost of one's own life, is another characteristic of the influence of Mars in Leo.

In VIRGO

Mars here gives energy and skill wherever work and duties are concerned. Minute precision and patience make it possible to undertake extremely intricate tasks. This position would certainly favour watchmakers or surgeons. Fussiness and perfectionism, however, may discourage from achieving any major project. Focusing on small details increases the tendency to excessive worry with their disruptive repercussions on physical and psychological health. The digestive system is vulnerable and can become a source of chronic discomfort.

In LIBRA

This position shows that the combative principle is triggered by other people's requests rather than one's own needs. Always to be ready to help or defend close ones, Mars here favours family and social popularity. Mars in this Air sign tends to confer a jack-of-all-trades ability but not the means to concrete realisations. Diplomacy, counselling, and coaching are potential sources of professional success. The ability to control or dominate and direct others increase leadership abilities.

In SCORPIO

Mars in Scorpio confers strength and a more effective approach to life's realities and responsibilities. Courage and a cold-blooded attitude to deal with hardship and difficulties are useful to do well in challenging situations. However, Mars here can also create offensive qualities, such as aggressiveness, excessive authority, forcefulness, and stubbornness. Sexual appetite is usually strong and may motivate prejudicial tendencies, health-wise or socially.

In SAGITTARIUS

Mars here brings the combative principle to a more spiritual or philosophical level. Personal beliefs and moral ethics are a source of strong motivation. The ability to succeed is favoured by applying the social and legal rules. Excesses produced by Mars in this sign range from acts of heroism to radical religious tendencies that can alienate from pleasant social interaction. This position also increases the interest in sports and adventure with positive motivation and enthusiasm.

In CAPRICORN

Tenacity and determination are enhanced and favourable to the realisation of far-fetched goals. Ambition is a source of motivation. Time is a positive factor to fulfil personal ambitions. Leadership ability allows for more responsible professional positions. The Saturnian influence of Capricorn transferred to the energy of Mars increases spontaneous determination and endurance. But rigid authority prejudices social wellbeing.

In AQUARIUS

This position confers a tendency to act in an original and unconventional way. Battling to impose reforms and social changes, is a source of renewed stimulation. Inventiveness and spontaneous search for solutions to the most trivial problems of life does not deter from attending to much more important situations. However, excessive rebellion against the status quo may marginalise and deter the ability to remain in good terms with society. Human relationships become tensed and unpleasant.

In PISCES

In a water sign, Mars is not as virulent than in other elements. It does not make its influence weaker; it gives it a more subtle manner of expressing the combative principle of life. It confers a more intuitive reactivity based on higher principles, both philosophical and spiritual. Religious beliefs may stimulate the need to act to the point of losing touch with reality. Mars here enhances the ability to defend personal convictions derived from education or social trends, regardless of their realism and practicality.

VESTA IN SIGNS

In the present incarnation

In ARIES

Balance and harmony depend on the ability to act and decide. The energy put to the service of various life's objectives and goals is a source of inner tension. Impulsiveness causes multiple setbacks and various mistakes. To control personal impulses and other contradictory reactions is essential in maintaining a positive and constructive approach to life's events. When stability and efficiency become the main source of motivation, they prevent chronic destabilisation and promote success and wellbeing durably.

In TAURUS

Harmony and balance depend on the access to the good and beautiful things of life. Creativity favours wellbeing and success. Money is a means to please oneself and to benefit from what life has to offer to the astute buyer. Artistic talent can also play a role to promote social and professional achievements. Love and material security are essential to maintain harmony and wellbeing in various areas of life. However, the quest for pleasure may tend to go beyond reasonable limits and produce pernicious yearnings.

In GEMINI

Intellectual complicity and spontaneous communication are essential to preserve balance and harmony in personal and social relationships. Reading, writing, travelling, teaching, and communicating in many ways are sources of wellbeing and accomplishment. They can motivate a career and favour professional success. However, lack of perseverance is also present. A shallow approach to the realities of life produces disappointments and errors with damaging consequences. Self-discipline is a must to benefit from Vesta in Gemini.

In CANCER

Family relationships and home environment heighten the necessary motivation and effort to maintain balance and harmony at home. Venus in Cancer confers a fluctuating approach to the realities of life. Personal wellbeing depends largely on the emotional quality of the immediate surroundings. However, excessive sensitivity may become a source of chronic physiological and psychological disorder. Motherhood often has a remarkable influence on the emergence of the need to search for inner peace and contentment.

In LEO

Creativity, personal charisma, and the need for love and recognition are viewed as essential sources of intimate wellbeing. Natural attraction to the brighter side of life favours higher levels of social and personal realisations. Vesta confers a compassionate approach to the needs and conditions of the underprivileged that may motivate spontaneous involvement in humanitarian or charitable activities. However, if talent and empathy are driven by pride and self-centredness, authenticity and sincerity are impaired.

In VIRGO

Harmony and wellbeing depend on the quality of human relationships in the social or professional environment. The ability to restore or preserve balance confers diplomatic tendencies that can influence the choice of a career. Health care is viewed as essential in pursuing and attaining personal objectives. However, excessive worry may contribute to the aggravation of various physiological disorders. It is necessary to avoid focusing on petty details to the detriment of the broader approach needed to solve most problems.

In LIBRA

This is Vesta's strongest position. Inner balance and harmony are essential values to preserve and feed. They motivate and encourage creativity, kindness, open-mindedness, and wellbeing, both personally and socially. Diplomacy favours pleasant and productive social, professional, and personal relationships. However, the desire to be good to others, and appreciated as a person, may overcome one's own needs and necessities. Alas, generosity and compassion do not ensure durable inner peace and comfort.

In SCORPIO

This position shows that sexuality is a major factor to preserve or restore inner harmony, balance, and wellbeing. A profound approach to personal relationships enhances their significance and positive potential. A tendency to feed on hardship to find the strength to overcome difficulties helps maintain a cold-blooded approach to the most troubling circumstances. However, the need to get too deeply involved in hazardous situations may prove detrimental to peace of mind and existential and satisfaction.

In SAGITTARIUS

Personal enjoyment and inner harmony are derived from philosophical, moral, and ethical values. Long-distance travels and a spontaneous interest in foreign cultures and languages are recurring sources of positive motivation and wellbeing. The respect of rules, laws, and traditions favour social balance and success. However, over-optimistic tendencies may prove detrimental and deceiving. Vesta here can also confer excessive opportunism together with a more cunning than genuine interest in human relationships.

In CAPRICORN

Inner harmony and balance depend on the rigour with which responsibilities are tackled. To comply with the realities of life and to accept their role and importance are necessary for personal wellbeing and achievement. The top of the mountain is a source of motivation to the climber eager to reach it rather than remain in the valley. Patience and determination are the keywords to personal realisation. Rigidity and lack of enthusiasm, however, may temper one's self-image and delay reaching the finish line in a reasonable time.

In AQUARIUS

Imagination and adaptability help maintain balance and harmony despite the ups and downs and sudden and unexpected changes of circumstances. Inner wellbeing is maintained by the diversity of human contacts that stimulate the ability to communicate in an original and creative manner. Quick reactivity is conferred to preserve or restore inner balance. Effective solutions and answers to most questionable situations come easy with Vesta in this sign. Let loose, however, originality can border on marginality with detrimental consequences.

In PISCES

Enhanced intuition and spontaneous connection to the invisible favour inner harmony and wellbeing. Creativity is a source of excitement and positive motivation. Artistic tendencies are often remarkable with this position of Vesta. The ability to progress in the most dubious situations is derived from spontaneous intuition. Music, dance, and various natural talents contribute to preserving or restoring inner balance and peace. However, lack of concrete direction backed by rational action may interfere with the positive use of innate potential.

Supplementary section

The faster objects in the Houses

THE SUN IN THE HOUSES
In the present incarnation

IN HOUSE I
This position enhances the potential to express the inner self, especially if this House begins in the Sun sign. It confers an innate need to 'shine' and be noticed in a varying pressing manner depending on the sign involved (Fire signs are more intense than Earth signs).

IN HOUSE II
This position enhances the desire for material possessions and money. There is an affective need for material possessions that may produce a defensive behaviour and a tendency to focus on personal acquisitions. Food and nature are other sources of interest.

IN HOUSE III
This position enhances the desire to communicate and to be, 'on the move'. Interests are numerous and heteroclite. Mental energy is fuelled by intellectual projects, travels, and amusing human relationships. There may be a tendency to shallowness and gossiping.

IN HOUSE IV
This position enhances the importance of family relations and the need to live in a comfortable home. Interest in history and patriotism are observed. The father or father image may be linked to the role of the mother for various reasons.

IN HOUSE V

This House is 'naturally ruled' by the Sun and enhances creativity and romanticism. The need for love may be expressed artistically as well as in personal relationships. The ability to take advantage of opportunities is also conferred and enhanced by a strong ego.

IN HOUSE VI

This position enhances the need to work to be of service to others in various ways. There is a prevalent interest in health and medicine. It may lead to a career as much as to a tendency to excessive worry that to the point of developing a hypochondriac tendency.

IN HOUSE VII

This position enhances the need to get actively involved in a meaningful relationship such as marriage. There is a natural ability to be useful and appreciated by others. It also confers a tendency to be more efficient in the group rather than in personal realisations.

IN HOUSE VIII

There is a natural interest in the mysteries of life and death. An innate attraction to the hidden side of life can lead to lifelong involvement in research with sustained determination and passion. Sex drive, inner strength and regeneration potential are enhanced.

IN HOUSE IX

There is a spontaneous interest in long-distance travel, higher education, and philosophy. High moral principles help overcome many obstacles by being sincere and authentic. Life's circumstances are perceived as positive and useful to progress.

IN HOUSE X

This position enhances the desire to succeed and to reach a higher social status, no matter how long it takes. Ambition makes dealing with others at work and privately a source of tension. The father or father figure is a major influence in all important choices made.

IN HOUSE XI

This position indicates a friendly and sociable nature. There is a need to be a 'lighthouse' for friends as much as for the community with a strong desire to help in any possible way. Dislike of solitude confers a tendency to depend on others for company.

IN HOUSE XII

There is a need to hide and keep personal energy and talents within rather than share them with others. The connection with the spiritual dimension of life is enhanced. The past is a source of answers to many existential questions. The idea of karma prevails.

The MOON IN THE HOUSES
In the present incarnation

IN HOUSE I
This position enhances femininity and confers sensitivity and creativity. Emotions need to be controlled and channelled to harmonise private relationships and the energy of the inner self. The influence of the mother is strong and may be a source of emotional surges.

IN HOUSE II
This position renders emotionally attached to material possessions with various fluctuations due to dependence to the good things of life. Food has a strong influence on the ability to channel emotional outbreaks. Nature has a positive influence.

IN HOUSE III
This position enhances the need for intellectual stimulation to create emotional reactions and make life more interesting or exciting. Movement is the keyword to being alive. There is strong emotional need and ability to communicate and express feelings effectively.

IN HOUSE IV
This House is symbolically ruled by the Moon. This position therefore enhances the emotional nature of the family sphere. It also indicates the importance of the mother or confers a strong mother instinct. Creativity is expressed through children and art.

IN HOUSE V
This position enhances the ability to create and to express emotions through art and love. Children have a privileged position. They are a strong motivating factor. Emotional pride causes memorable fits of anger. The mother has an influence on the development of creativity.

IN HOUSE VI

This position enhances the emotional need to work and be of service to others, although this is subject to various fluctuations linked to the nature of our natural satellite. There is an interest in health and medicine. Hypochondriac tendencies are often observed.

IN HOUSE VII

This position enhances the emotional need for harmony and wellbeing in all kinds of partnerships, both private and social or professional. There is a tendency to spontaneously help others. Excessive personal involvement may leave a feeling of ingratitude.

IN HOUSE VIII

This position indicates an emotional attraction to the mysteries of life and death. Anything to do with the occult generates interest. Sexual needs are enhanced. Financial investments may be responsible for the accumulated wealth but also for ruin or bankruptcy.

IN HOUSE IX

There is an emotional interest in philosophy, spirituality, religions, and academic knowledge. Intellectual human relationships are favoured. Interests in ancient history and foreign cultures are often observed. The home may be chosen far from the place of birth.

IN HOUSE X

The mother or mother figure has a dominant position and may influence or motivate the choice of a career. Emotions are a source of motivation to accomplish personal or professional missions. Lack of emotional self-control is detrimental to social stability.

IN HOUSE XI

There is a motherly approach to human relationships, friendships, and socialising in general. The emotional interactions with others may motivate involvement in charity or charitable organisations. Impatience could deter long-term commitments.

IN HOUSE XII
There is a tendency to withdraw rather than openly express emotions. Emotional fluctuations are often derived from the intrauterine period or troubling family secrets. A strong karmic tie with the mother may be a source of spiritual motivation or moral depression.

MERCURY IN THE HOUSES
In the present incarnation

IN HOUSE I

This position enhances the ability to communicate and to express ideas and opinions in a spontaneous and sometimes impulsive manner. People born with Mercury here are intellectually interested in learning more about themselves to understand who they really are.

IN HOUSE II

Money is spent for intellectual purposes such as reading, travelling, and studying. There is an interest in food and nature, and a need for a privileged environment where thinking and reflecting are favoured. The intellect relies more on practice than theory.

IN HOUSE III

This is the natural rulership position of Mercury. Here its influence is greatly enhanced and favours intellectual activity. It also creates a natural ability to communicate and express one's own ideas, although they may remain trivial or superficial.

IN HOUSE IV

This position enhances the natural ability and desire to communicate with and about family members. A keen interest in past events relating to the family tree and various family members is also present but depends on the sign position of Mercury in the chart.

IN HOUSE V

This position usually goes with an artistic mind. The intellect strongly influences romantic life and creativity. Communication with children, teaching, and interaction with loved ones are favoured in accordance with the sign position of Mercury in the chart.

IN HOUSE VI

The intellect and need to communicate strongly intervenes in the work environment and the overall accomplishment within the professional arena. Excessive health concerns may lead to a medical career or to psychosomatic illnesses.

IN HOUSE VII

This position enhances the desire and ability to communicate with others, especially close ones such as partners, both in private and professional or social areas. Mercury can, however, tend to hinder the desire to communicate especially about oneself.

IN HOUSE VIII

This position enhances the intellectual interest in the mysteries of life and occult sciences. Money and the material side of life produce a taste for financial investments. Research, investigation, psychology, or psychiatry are some subjects that may motivate a career. Position comparable to Mercury in Scorpio.

IN HOUSE IX

This position enhances the desire to learn, to discover and to progress on the mental and intellectual plans. There is an attraction to foreign countries and cultures and a disposition for foreign languages. The need to learn is motivated by a desire to share.

IN HOUSE X

This position enhances the potential to use the intellect and the ability to communicate to succeed socially and professionally. Careers in teaching, public speaking, politics, journalism, or in the media are some of the areas of possible success and achievement.

IN HOUSE XI

There is an innate need to communicate with others freely. Friends and social acquaintances are a source of renewed motivation for the expression of thoughts and ideas. A sincere interest in humanity may become the basis to a community-oriented career.

IN HOUSE XII

This position indicates a mystical or spiritual way of thinking, an intuitive mind, and a preference for the imaginary rather than in the real world. A tendency to withdraw may be derived from past events or traumas. The need to connect with the soul is prevalent.

VENUS IN THE HOUSES
In the present incarnation

IN HOUSE I
This position enhances the natural need for love and romance and dependence on affection. It often confers a certain vulnerability in private relationships due to a strong need to be appreciated at all costs. Creativity and artistic tendencies are present.

IN HOUSE II
This position enhances the desire to possess, to earn money and to spend it for sentimental reasons. Sensibility to the beautiful surpasses the practical aspect. There is a strong need for approbation. Venus here is found in the charts of collectors, artists, or renown chefs.

IN HOUSE III
This position enhances the ability to communicate in a pleasant manner to convince in various ways. Sociability and friendliness are also conferred. The love principle is intellectualised producing talent in writing, public speaking and music making.

IN HOUSE IV
This position enhances family ties and interests in family affairs with a genuine appreciation for anything to do with the home and family environment. Venus here enhances procreation and the desire to have a family in a pleasant and natural environment.

IN HOUSE V
This position greatly enhances the natural ability and desire to love and be loved and appreciated. Pride and possessiveness in romantic relationship are observed. Having children and a loving family are a prime motivation. Artistic creativity is significantly increased.

IN HOUSE VI
This position indicates a sense of responsibility in love and romance

that may lead to a tendency to worry too much. There is dependence on wellbeing in the work arena. Professional choices are based on personal taste rather than exclusively financial conditions.

IN HOUSE VII

This strong position enhances the need to be loved and to love others, privately, socially, and professionally. Overdependence on affection is observed, with the possibility of moral disappointment and disillusion. The more you give, the more they take…

IN HOUSE VIII

This position indicates a tendency to consider love on the physical and metaphysical plans. Sexual Drive is strong and may influence personal feelings to the point of getting deeply involved for physical rather than spiritual reasons. Difficulties in romance are likely.

IN HOUSE IX

This position enhances the importance of love and affections in a philosophical or spiritual rather than emotional way. There is a need to express feelings in a profound and lofty way. Love is sometimes found in a far distant land. Spiritual creativity is enhanced.

IN HOUSE X

This position indicates that love is a top priority. It influences major choices and decisions in relation to the career and the realisation of important projects. Art may also be a source of motivation and an avenue to a successful career. Feelings are expressed assertively.

IN HOUSE XI

This position indicates a spontaneous empathy toward others issued from a need to be appreciated socially as much as privately. Creativity is motivated by an affectionate perception of humanity. Friendships are numerous and occasionally ambiguous. Position comparable to Venus in Aquarius.

IN HOUSE XII

This position confers a spiritual approach to love and affection. It may also indicate a tendency to secret or imaginary love affairs. A predisposition to hide personal feelings to protect privacy is also observed. The past may be a source of ambiguous creativity.

MARS IN THE HOUSES

In the present incarnation

IN HOUSE I

Mars is the natural ruler of House I where it enhances the ability to fight and to defend oneself in a rather aggressive way. Impulsiveness is responsible for various incidents and for extraordinary decisions that may save lives, thanks to heroic acts in perilous situations.

IN HOUSE II

This position enhances the natural ability to fight to defend and protect material possessions. A tendency to spend impulsively may create various problems and financial shortcomings. There is a need to exercise patience to avoid conflicts for materialistic reasons.

IN HOUSE III

This position enhances the natural desire to express ideas and to impose them in an assertive manner. There is a need to slow down and to be more careful when talking, writing, or driving. Difficulties at school, or with brothers or sisters are also observed. Position comparable to Mars in Gemini.

IN HOUSE IV

This position enhances the natural need to defend and protect one's family and home environment. It also indicates a tendency to argue and to generate conflicts within the family sphere. Excessive authority with loved ones may be responsible for domestic disorders.

IN HOUSE V

This position enhances the natural tendency to direct love affairs and romantic relationships. This may lead to various disruptions and breakups. Excessive authority or reactivity with children, and overprotection of loved ones may also become a source of tension.

IN HOUSE VI

This position indicates a strong desire to dominate and to show authority and leadership aspirations at work and in health or medically related matters. A natural liking of aggressive animals is also observed. This position may also motivate a career in surgery or the military.

IN HOUSE VII

This position indicates various tensions in private relationships to the point of becoming detrimental to wellbeing in marriage and other types of close partnerships, both private and social. The need to lead and to direct others is the cause for discord and breakups. Position comparable to Mars in Libra.

IN HOUSE VIII

This position indicates an intense sexual drive linked to a tendency to dominate partners. This may lead to conflicts which could profoundly threaten inner wellbeing. Hygiene is to be considered seriously to avoid health issues. Self-control of inner tension is necessary.

IN HOUSE IX

This position enhances the desire to defend moral principles and to fight injustice in a determined, spontaneous, and sometimes aggressive way. Various problems with the law or the administration would be due to mistakes made from impulsive reactions.

IN HOUSE X

This position enhances the desire to be first, to lead and to dominate one's own life, enforcing personal decisions to succeed. The father or father figure has a strong influence on the development of authority, ambitions, and choice of career. Action is the key to success.

IN HOUSE XI

This position enhances the need to be of service to others in an active and spontaneous, but rather impulsive way. Overactive involvement in collective activities lead to fatigue and loss of vigilance. Excessive authority can have disturbing social consequences.

IN HOUSE XII

This position tends to hinder natural combativeness, putting it on a spiritual rather than terrestrial level. There is a need to act in secret due to a feeling of being a potential victim of betrayals. Karmic enemies are occasionally met. Paranoiac tendencies are seldom observed.

VESTA IN THE HOUSES
In the present incarnation

In House I
It favours inner peace and harmony. Wellbeing depends on how the self is perceived. Vesta confers a positive vibration rate that enhances charisma and charm. Its soothing energy softens any "hostile" presence in the immediate surroundings.

In House II
Earthly foods, creativity, art, and the appreciation of the good and beautiful things of life are essential to inner wellbeing and harmony. A balanced budget means more enjoyment without the worry of being caught up by excessive spending.

In House III
The intellect functions on the notions of balance, harmony, and fairness. These essential values promote mental wellbeing, with happy repercussions in human relationships. Siblings and friends are essential to ensure inner joy and peace.

In House IV
This position promotes family harmony or reduces the intensity of any difficulties represented by adverse configurations in the chart. Diplomacy and fairness increase popularity and improve the quality of life in the home and close environment.

In House V
Vesta here promotes creativity and love in art and romantic relationships. There is a strong need for appreciation and approbation. Musical creativity is enhanced. Balance and harmony are prevalent values. Children are a source of inspiration.

In House VI
Vesta here protects health and promotes harmony at work or dealing with daily routine and responsibilities. There is a need to

restore or preserve balance that may motivate medically oriented careers. Success relies on subtlety and charm.

In House VII
Personal and social partnerships are fuelled by a positive approach meant to preserve harmony and balance in the relationship. Caring for others ensures inner satisfaction and wellbeing. A tendency to overdo it may trigger disappointment.

In House VIII
Innate understanding of the cycles of life and death is a source of positive energy that helps maintain inner peace and harmony. Finances are protected by a positive and honest approach to material responsibilities. Inheritance is likely.

In House IX
The notions of balance and harmony are a source of positive motivation to study, discover, travel, with a philosophical perception of life in all situations. The need to learn and to share favours teachers, writers, journalists, and politicians.

In House X
Ambitions are fuelled by a need to do well and to be appreciated and in harmonious relationship with the idea of success. The aspiration to reach the top while preserving inner peace and wellbeing is a major source of positive motivation.

In House XI
Preserving balance and harmony in social relationships makes it easier to deal with others, even in the most delicate situations. Friends are a source of enjoyment and positive motivation that promotes inner peace and wellbeing.

In House XII
Inner peace and harmony depend on the ability to get away from the madding crowd. In the quiet comfort of a special place, the soul

can rest and allow body and mind to recharge in positive energy. True spirituality needs no words. Position comparable to Vesta in Pisces.

Conclusion

I hope you have enjoyed this 'journey' into karmic astrology and that it has triggered in you the need to find out more about your own karma with its subliminal influence on your future. Knowing that an astral chart contains important information about our previous life, it also provides information about the next one. Everything is connected. What we are, what we have been and what we will be, are one; **our cosmic being**. It is therefore logically possible to obtain useful data from a birth chart about the next incarnation. In fact, if the present life derives from the previous one, the next incarnation must depend on the present one. It simply means that we are in this life to prepare for the next one.

Professor Dutheil's book, **L'Homme super lumineux** (The super luminous Man) published only in French as far as I know, is extremely interesting on this subject.

Time has imposed itself on Earth because we exist according to two crucial moments: our birth and our death. The aging of the body is a criterion to rationally evaluate the influence of time. This notion was somehow 'invented' by human intelligence. From what we know about animal intelligence, we understand that a dog, for example, reuniting with her master after an absence of five minutes or five hours triggers a similar degree of pleasure and joyful reactions. Reflect on this sentence by Henry Miller to understand how much human intelligence influences the value of life. *In the beginning, death did not exist; Man 'invented it' because he was afraid of life…* He also wrote: '*Of course you don't die. Nobody dies. Death doesn't exist. You only reach a new level of vision, a new realm of consciousness, a new unknown world.'*

Here is another quote from this enlightened mind: *In the attempt to defeat death man has been inevitably obliged to defeat life, for the two are inextricably related. Life moves on to death, and to deny one is to deny the other.*

The notion of time may be subject to the same rule. This would explain the early ageing of some people compared to others who remain indefinitely young…

In cosmic terms, time does not exist. Thinking is an example of how quickly it is possible to move from one thought or memory to another, or from one subject to another. These movements are instantaneous, immediate. The same applies to astral travel experiences. You just have to want to be somewhere to be there immediately. It is what we call *teleportation*…

From this point of view, we can deduce that present, past and future are on the same plane, on the same dimension (the fourth dimension). Depending on the mental state at a given moment, it is therefore possible to perceive images of the past (memory), the present (situations in progress) and the future (intuition or visions). If it is possible in this space and time (our current life), it must therefore also be possible about past lives and about future lives…

I'm working on the idea. When I obtain conclusive results, I will share them with you by writing a book on the subject.

For the time being, I thank you for your interest in astrology and in my work, and for the trust you have placed in me by reading this book while using it to conduct your own research regarding karma and past lives. Sharing my passion is for me a way to perdure far beyond the present life.

Roland Legrand – April 2022

Links to the online video lessons

Lesson 1 (The Lunar Nodes): https://youtu.be/823kKumiCSk

Lesson 2 (Lilith): https://youtu.be/w3tD3HlHw8U

Lesson 3 (The Part of Fortune): https://youtu.be/hV2d54w1C6Y

Lesson 4 (House XII): https://youtu.be/MU8ILnwi5OY

Lesson 5 (Chiron): https://youtu.be/8c1cRiA7tzo

Lesson 6 (The slow planets – Saturn): https://youtu.be/7BxCs0GQxQA

Lesson 7 (Uranus): https://youtu.be/51aY6yVAuqc

Lesson 8 (Neptune): https://youtu.be/5DCahzXsmpk

Lesson 9 (Pluto): https://youtu.be/e-q2WublWec

Lesson 10 (Retrograde planets): https://youtu.be/PMYHV83LJz8

Lesson 11 (The faster objects): https://youtu.be/2N_ybNlYotg

Table of content

Made in the USA
Coppell, TX
14 August 2024